Financial Reform in Central and Eastern Europe: Lessons from the West, Poland and Further East

Financial Reform in Central and Eastern Europe: Lessons from the West, Poland and Further East

Edited by

Andy Mullineux

NOVA SCIENCE PUBLISHERS, INC.

Art Director: Christopher Concannon
Graphics: Elenor Kallberg and Maria Ester Hawrys
Manuscript Coordinator: Roseann Pena
Book Production: Tammy Sauter, Benjamin Fung
and Michelle Lalo
Circulation: Irene Kwartiroff and Annette Hellinger

Library of Congress Cataloging–in–Publication Data
available upon request

ISBN 1-56072-233-9

6080 Jericho Turnpike, Suite 207
Commack, New York 11725
Tele. 516-499-3103 Fax 516-499-3146
E Mail Novasci1@aol.com

Printed in the United States of America

To Judith, Ruth and Joe

CONTENTS

Part II Lessons from Poland

Preface

This book contains papers arising out of a collaborative project for which funding was gratefully received from the Commission of the European Communities under the ACE programme of the PHARE initiative in 1991/2. The collaborators, who are listed separately, are associated with the Departments of Economics at the Universities of Birmingham (UK), Bordeaux (France) and Lodz (Poland) and the project (No: 90-999-040-001-013) was entitled: "Financial Reform in Poland and the Evolution of the Single EC Banking Market". In addition it contains a report (Chapter 7) which was produced by the editor with the assistance of a grant from the Anglo-German Foundation. This too is gratefully acknowledged along with the permission granted to reprint the report in this book.

A number of the other papers have also been published elsewhere and the editor would like to take this opportunity to thank the publishers for giving permission for their republication in this volume. These papers are re-published as Chapter 2 (originally published under the title "Hard Budget Constraints, Credit Crunches and Central Bank Independence" in the **University of Wales Business and Economics Review, No. 8, Jan/Feb 1992, pp 35-38**); Chapter 3 (originally published under the same title in the **Oxford Review of Economic Policy, 8(1), pp 27-43**); and Chapter 5 (which is a shortened version of a paper originally published in French as "Evaluation du Risque de Défaillance Bancaire en Europe", **Revue d'Economie Politique, 102(2), Mars-Avril, 1992)**; Chapter 6 (originally published in French in **Cahiers Economiques et Monétaires de la Banque de France, 41, 1993**; and Chapter 8 (originally published under the same title in the **University of Wales Business and Economics Review, Summer 1993**).

The thirteen papers fall naturally into two groups, with the introductory chapter, written by the editor, providing an overview. The first part of the book consists of seven chapters which draw lessons for the transforming economies from the experiences of EC member countries (including, Eastern Germany), the U.S., and South-East Asian 'Pacific Rim' countries. The second part of the book contains a further six papers which focus on the experiences of Poland in the early phase of its transition with regard to privatisation, the microeconomic impact of monetary policy and banking sector reform, and draws lessons for other transforming economies.

The book will be of interest to students, academic and professional economists, and policy makers working on issues relating to the transformation of formerly centrally planned economies. Its prime focus is on financial sector reform; which is crucial to the establishment of an alternative, to the central plan, means of allocating capital and to establishing a system of corporate governance. As a result, it highlights the need to develop an institutional structure, and particularly an efficient and stable banking system, to support the 'marketisation' process.

The collaborating institutions, along with the Institute of Economics (Czech National Bank, Prague) were awarded further funding in 1992/3 from the EC(ACE) programme for a project (No: ERB4012 PL910252) entitled: "Hard Budget Constraints, Privatisation and Financial Sector Reform with Particular Reference to Poland and Czechoslovakia". The resulting papers are to be presented at a conference in Prague on September 3rd/4th, 1993 and a companion volume is being published also by Nova Science reporting its findings.

Dr Andy Mullineux,
Director of Money,
Banking and Finance Programmes,
Department of Economics,
University of Birmingham, UK.

July 1993

CONTRIBUTORS

Jarek Bauc	Institute of Economics, University of Lodz, Poland.
Marek Belka	Professor of Economics, Institute of Economics, University of Lodz, Poland.
Christian Bordes	Professor of Economics, LARE (Laboratoire d'Analyse et de Rescherche Economiques), Department of Economics, University of Bordeaux 1, France.
David G. Dickinson	Department of Economics, University of Birmingham, UK.
Maxwell J. Fry	Tokai Bank Professor of International Finance and Director of the International Finance Group, University of Birmingham, UK.
Eric Girardin	Professor of Economics, LARE (Laboratoire d'Analyse et de Rescherche Economiques), Department of Economics, University of Bordeaux 1, France.
Daniel Goyeau	GRIEF, (Groupe de Rescherche en Intégration Économique et Financière), Department of Economics, University of Poitiers, France.
Boguslaw Grabowski	Institute of Economics, University of Lodz, Poland.

Dominique Lacoue-Labarthe	LARE (Laboratoire d'Analyse et de Rescherche Economiques), Department of Economics, University of Bordeaux 1, France.
Valayoudon Marimoutou	Professor of Economics, LARE (Laboratoire d'Analyse et de Rescherche Economiques), Department of Economics, University of Bordeaux 1, France.
Andy Mullineux	Director of Money, Banking and Finance Programmes, International Finance Group and Department of Economics, University of Birmingham, UK.
D. Mario Nuti	Professor Economics, London Business School, U. K.
Jerzy Pruski	Institute of Economics, University of Lodz, Poland.
Andrzej Raczko	Institute of Economics, University of Lodz, Poland.
Amine Tarazi	CRMM (Centre de Recherche en Macroéconomie Monétaire), Department of Economics, University of Limoges, France.

CHAPTER 1

FINANCIAL SECTOR REFORM IN CENTRAL AND EASTERN EUROPE: AN OVERVIEW

Andy Mullineux

Prior to adopting reform programmes designed to achieve a transition from centrally planned to 'market', but in reality 'mixed', economies, the 'Central and Eastern European' (CEE) countries, had developed into 'shortage economies' (Kornai, 1990). The key features of these economies were:

* prices too low to clear markets;
* repressed consumption/forced saving/'monetary overhang';
* repressed inflation;
* hidden unemployment;
* distorted (non 'world') relative prices
    - CMEA[1] oriented trade
    - planning and price subsidies;
* 'soft budget constraints' (Kornai, 1990)
    - macro (budget deficit/lax monetary (credit) policy
    - micro (investment capital allocated by plan/working capital on demand from banks);
* hoarding (alternative to bank deposits)
    - foreign exchange (useable on 'black markets'/special shops)
    - inventories (raw materials)
    - domestic currency ('monetary overhang');
* regional specialisation and large scale monopolies with product deficiencies in individual countries.

Many of these features were corollaries of others. The low, below market clearing, prices set under the 'plan', along with price subsidies, led to repressed consumption, given the bias towards investment under planning, a 'monetary overhang' and repressed inflation. The low, below market clearing, interest

[1] Council for Mutual Economic Assistance or 'Comecon'

rates encouraged heavy reliance on credits by 'state enterprises' and hoarding, and discouraged saving in the form of bank deposits.

Before embarking on 'transition' programmes in the 1990s, a number of countries, particularly Hungary in the 1970s and Poland in the 1980s, had tried to find a third way, between total reliance on central planning and 'capitalism', by retaining 'socialism' but making more use of market mechanisms. In the case of Poland, which is the CEE country studied in depth in this book, the 'reforms' led to heavy external indebtedness, a prominent role for 'workers councils' in enterprise management, and ultimately to hyperinflation in 1989. In Poland, the collapse of the 'Berlin Wall' in 1989 combined with hyperinflation, led to a political consensus in favour of more fundamental reform and the adoption of a 'Big Bang' reform programme on 1 January 1990. At the start of the transition the Polish economy was suffering from:

* Week 'corporate governance'
  - dominant workers councils and a strong unions (Solidarity)
  - weak management (appointed by workers councils) with poor incentives
* an underdeveloped financial system ('two-tier' banking system)
* distorted price structure and hyperinflation;
* stock problems
  - 'monetary overhang'
  - 'debt overhang'
* large budget deficit (flow problem)
* heavy foreign debt servicing requirements (flow problem).

There is continued debate over the significance of the monetary and debt overhangs given the pre-bang hyperinflation which obviously eroded their real zloty value substantially. It should be noted, however, that in response to high inflation in the late 1980s there had been substantial 'dollarization' in Poland. This can be regarded as repressed 'capital flight' given the non-convertibility of the zloty and the concomitant strict foreign exchange controls. It has been estimated that, by the beginning of 1990, 50% of the money circulating or being hoarded by households and enterprises was US dollars. The use of dollars afforded protection against domestic inflation and consequently the 'monetary overhang' was not entirely eroded and, to the extent that dollars were used for bank-enterprise and inter-enterprise transactions, the 'debt overhang' was not eliminated either.

The 'Big Bang' reform programme was designed to achieve 'macro economic stabilisation' (or to harden the macro-budget constraint), by first bringing the budget deficit and inflation under control and then reducing them, and to 'marketise' the economy. To stimulate 'marketisation', it was to be quickly followed by the implementation of a 'mass privatisation' programme. The 'Big Bang's' components were:

* trade and price (including the phasing out of subsidies) liberalisation;
* 'current account' convertibility of the zloty;
* fiscal and monetary restraint.

It contrasted with the 'gradualist' approach of Hungary; which elected to accelerate the more advanced reform programme it had in train and to go for piecemeal, rather than mass, privatisation. To date Hungary has in fact made more progress with privatisation because, partly due to political and partly due to organisational and infrastructural problems (discussed further below) Poland was unable to launch its mass privatisation programme until the second half of 1993. In both countries, 'small' privatisations (of shops, restaurants etc) were executed at an early stage and by 1992 over 50% of employment, exports and GDP were accounted for by the private sector in Poland. It should be noted, however, that in Poland the farming sector was never collectionised. The political instability associated with a series of unstable coalition governments in Poland seems to have had a significant impact and may explain its relative lack of success, compared to Hungary, in attracting foreign investment (Business International, 1992) and significant post 'Big Bang' (and convertibility) capital flight (Dickinson and Mullineux, 1993).

Trade and price liberalisation combined with 'current account' convertibility was designed to eliminate shortages and the associated queues, which they did remarkably quickly, and import 'world' prices, so that Poland could be integrated into the world trading system. This became all the more urgent as intra-CMEA trade collapsed in 1991. In Poland, convertibility was initially combined with a fixed exchange rate regime in order to support macro-stabilisation by providing a 'nominal anchor'. The choice of the initial exchange rate and the appropriate exchange rate regime (eg nominal-fixed, as opposed to floating, or real-fixed, or 'crawling peg' regimes) is clearly crucial in this respect and is the subject of Chapter 3.

In order to maintain fixed exchange rates under the high levels of political and economic uncertainty prevailing in the early stages of the 'transition', to discourage capital flight, and to generate domestic savings and encourage greater financial intermediation, high nominal and positive real interest rates are required. In addition, macro-stabilisation requires a tight monetary policy. Consequently, there is a risk of an overly restrictive monetary policy in the early phases of the transition and this may help to explain the unexpected depth of the 'transition recession'. These issues are discussed further in Chapter 2. In order to guage the restrictiveness of monetary policy a number of countries have employed monetary aggregates as 'indicators'. These have not always proved satisfactory, especially in times of rapid financial innovation, and alternative indicators have been sought. One such is P*, the performance of which is evaluated in the light of the experiences of France and Germany in chapter 4. Since transforming, formerly centrally planned, economies, are also introducing substantial charges to their financial sectors, it is possible that indicators, such as P* will prove to be more useful than monetary aggregates.

To the extent that the 'debt overhang' was not eliminated by the 1989 hyperinflation in Poland the banks inherited a debt problem which was soon exacerbated as the transition recession deepened. It was not widely appreciated at the outset that successful 'western' market economies are supported by an institutional infrastructure, which was woefully underdeveloped in the formerly centrally planned economies. As explained in Chapter 8, and more specifically in relation to Poland in Chapter 10, the move from central planning to a 'market' economy requires the development of alternative, to the plan, means of allocating capital. The degree of reliance on capital markets, as opposed to banking systems, varies considerably amongst OECD countries, but it is only in countries with highly developed financial sectors, such as the US and the UK, that capital markets have traditionally played a major role. This implies that bank dominated financial systems are most appropriate for transforming CEE economies.

The inherited, and rapidly accumulating, debt problem in the early phase of the transition in Poland was compounded by a growth in inter-enterprise indebtedness as banks were urged to restrict the supply of credit as part of the macro-stabilisation programme. Further, the worsening internal debt problem made it more and more difficult to launch the 'mass privatisation' programme and to privatise banks in particular. It also encouraged seemingly 'perverse' lending decisions by banks. They were unable to declare debtor enterprises bankrupt because another part of the institutional infrastructure was deficient, namely bankruptcy laws, and they were unwilling to do so anyway since, if they had, they would have revealed there own weak financial weakness and a banking crisis could have resulted.

The reasons for the 'perverse' bank lending behaviour in Poland are considered further in Chapter 11. The debt problem should have been tackled at the outset and banks should have been recapitalised, and perhaps privatised, at an early stage. The consequence of not doing so, as is now evident in Russia, is that 'micro-budget' constraints remain 'soft' and corporate governance remains weak. In the latter respect, and to the extent that it can weaken the power of workers councils, 'commercialisation' , which involves establishing German-style supervisory boards for enterprises, may be a useful interim step if privatisation has to be delayed.

Prior to the reforms, the governments in CEE economies relied heavily for their revenue on 'profits' generated by state-enterprises, and Poland was no exception. In the transition recession, as profits declined, the maintenance of an adequate flow of revenue, and success in containing the budget deficit, required the introduction of an alternative tax-system with a broader base (Chapters 2, 8 and 10). This is another example of the need to develop the institutional infrastructure and it clearly takes time to devise and introduce VAT and incomes tax systems. It was only in 1993 that income taxes became payable in Poland. Given the pressure on revenue, it is not surprising that CEE governments, including Poland, have felt unable to tackle the inherited and growing bank and inter-enterprise debt problems. Foreign assistance is, therefore, required at the outset, not only to help resolve the external debt problem and underwrite convertibility, as in the Polish case in 1991, but also to help resolve the internal debt problem of CEE countries and to recapitalise banks to facilitate their early privatisation.

Once recapitalised and relieved of their debt burden and bankruptcy laws are in place, banks should have the incentive to allocate credit more efficiently. There is a risk, however, that a moral hazard problem will emerge if banks expect to be bailed out again in future. To deal with this, another element of institutional infrastructure needs to be put in place, namely a bank regulatory and supervisory system. Banking risks during economic restructuring are the subject of Chapter 13 whilst Chapter 5 evaluates banking risks in the EC, which Poland and other CEE countries aspire to join. Chapter 14 discusses the evolution of banking regulation and supervision in Poland towards EC standards and Chapter 6 reviews more broadly issues involved in establishing safe and sound banking systems in CEE countries.

It should also be recognised that commercial and investment banking techniques were underdeveloped at the outset of the transition in the CEE countries, and hence bank managers lacked the skills to appraise risks and allocate credit efficiently. Early recapitalisation and privatisation thus risks relying on bank managers 'learning by doing'. Mistakes will inevitably be made and bad debts will therefore be accumulated. Worse, bank supervisors also need to learn on the job and the system may therefore be open to fraudulent exploitation which may also undermine confidence in the banking system.

The Polish 'two-tier' banking system was created at the end of 1988. As a result of the National Bank vested most of its commercial banking responsibilities under the former 'monobanking' system (Mullineux, 1987 Chapter 4) with 9 newly created state-owned, regionally orientated, commercial banks. This followed similar banking sector reform in other CEE countries (Mullineux, 1987, Chapter 4). In some cases (eg Bulgaria and Hungary) the commercial banks were allocated enterprise clients on an industrial sector, rather than regional, basis. In practice, given the regional concentration of industry, the difference was not substantial. The Polish commercial banks had therefore amassed little experience prior to the 'Big Bang'. To facilitate the reform process, early and substantial external assistance in training bank supervisors and managers is clearly essential. This, at least, has been recognised and training has been provided by central banks (especially the Bank of England, the Austrian National Bank and the Bundesbank, the German central bank) whilst the British 'Know-How' fund and the 'World Bank' (IBRD) has sponsored management training and the 'twinning' of Polish banks with Western banks. Similar training schemes are in operation in other CEE countries and Russia.

Following the 'Big Bang' in Poland, a 'third-tier' of 'private' banks, which provide commercial and investment banking services to enterprise clients and take deposits from households, emerged. A number of scandals broke in 1991/2 involving fraud perpetrated by some of the employees of these banks. The government responded by tightening bank regulations, including minimum capital requirements for authorisation, in 1992. Some rationalisation is therefore expected. Chapters 9, 10 and 14 chart developments in the Polish banking system, which remained dominated by the large state-owned commercial banks, in the first two years or so of the post Big-Bang transition period.

In Chapters 8 and 10 it is observed that the strong regional orientation of the Polish banks makes it necessary to develop an interbank market at an early stage to facilitate an efficient countrywide allocation of capital. The monetary authorities should therefore sponsor the development of a money market, which is part of the institutional infrastructure of OECD countries. An efficient payments system is also a key component of the commercial infrastructure and needs to be rapidly developed in 'transition economies', again with the guidance of the monetary authorities. In many OECD country banking systems the savings banks have a surplus which is lent, via interbank money markets, to commercial banks. In most CEE countries only the savings bank has a nationwide branch network and its surplus, derived from collecting household deposits, was, under the 'monobanking system', channelled into the National Bank for on-lending. This was the case in Poland too but the savings bank no longer has a surplus because it is saddled with bad, housing related, debts. The bad debt problems of savings banks in transition economies should, therefore, also be urgently addressed in order to stimulate the development of interbank money markets. With regard to the payments system, external assistance to provide 'know-how' and to encourage the adoption, and finance the development, of modern, electronically based, computerised systems is clearly required.

It is enlightening to contrast the experience of Poland, other CEE countries and Russia, with that of the Eastern Germany (the former GDR). This is done in Chapter 7, where it is noted that Eastern Germany had the advantage of a 'rich uncle' (namely Western Germany) to fund the transition; which has nevertheless proved more traumatic than expected largely due to pressure for wage equalisation between the Western and Eastern Länder (federal states). In addition the Eastern Länder could import a ready made institutional infrastructure; including well-run 'universal' banks, money markets and an efficient payment system. Universal banks have integrated commercial and investment banking capabilities (Mullineux, 1987, Chapter 3) and their staff are experienced in serving on supervisory boards and lending to small and medium sized enterprises (SMEs). Further, in Western Germany there is a postwar tradition of providing loan guarantees to SMEs and, partly as a result of this, the 'Mittelstand', as the SME sector is called in Germany, has thrived and made a major contribution to the country's post-war prosperity.

Most other OECD countries also provide state-backed loan guarantees to SMEs, though few have schemes as comprehensive as Germany. The reason for this seems to be that there is a market failure in the provision of finance to SMEs because lack of information about their financial position, uncertainty about their prospects, and lack of adequate collateral security leads banks to ration the supply of credit to this sector (Stiglitz and Weiss, 1981). The guarantees are needed to overcome the tendency of banks to ration credit. In Eastern Germany, the privatisation and restructuring agency, the Treuhandanstalt ('Treuhand'), has been a major supplier of loan guarantees along with the KfW, the development bank, and other institutions, as explained in Chapter 7. This suggests that Poland, other CEEs, and the former member states of the USSR would benefit from establishing investment or development banks or funds to dispense loan guarantees and that this too could be a focus for western financial and 'know-how' assistance. The reason that a thriving SME sector is crucial is that it provides a rapid route to privatising the economy, even if 'mass-privatisation' or de-nationalisation is stalled. It will also stimulate job creation at a time when the state-owned sector is being restructured and is shedding workers prior to privatisation and the already de-nationalised enterprises are rationalising their operations, and shedding workers. A growing SME sector is the key to containing the unemployment problem in transition economies.

It should be stressed that, the 'Treuhand' has well defined regional, employment and environmental *inter alia* objectives to guide its restructuring, rationalisation and privatisation activities. In Poland and other CEE countries governments have usually established a state ministry to oversee the process. The objectives of these ministries have not always been clear and their decisions have been the subject to political influence. The result has been little restructuring of enterprises prior to privatisation and repeated postponement of mass-privatisation programmes. The German experience seems to illustrate the advantages of vesting responsibility with a semi-autonomous privatisation (and restructuring) agency with well defined objectives. Such an agency could play a key role in the corporate governance of state-owned enterprises during the restructuring phase, prior to privatisation.

The mass-privatisation programme in Poland involves allocating shares in enterprises to workers and management, to ensure their cooperation and to provide incentives to improve the performance of enterprises, and to a number of national investment funds (NIFs). The NIFs are to be managed by expert 'western' fund managers and the public will be able to use vouchers, bought at a nominal cost, to 'buy' shares in the NIFs. As the stock market in Warsaw develops, the shares will become tradeable and institutions associated with the capital markets, including emerging 'institutional investors' (pension and investment funds) will begin to play a part in corporate governance. In the mean time, alongside the banks, the NIFs should also be encouraged to take an active role in corporate governance.

There is some evidence that, 'post-commercialisation', banks in Poland have adopted a more cautious and discerning approach to their lending and that managers in many enterprises have become less subservient to their workers (Mullineux and Belka, 1993). Micro-budget constraints, therefore, seem to be 'hardening' at last. The experience in Russia seems to demonstrate that a hardening of micro-budget constraints, which involves restricting the supply of bank credits and reducing the access of commercial banks to central bank refinancing, is a pre-requisite to macro-stabilisation, or the hardening of the macro-budget constraint. It is also clear from Poland's experience that too sharp a restriction of the supply of credit to enterprises can lead to an explosion of inter-enterprise indebtedness, and that this will make mass privation more difficult to achieve at an early stage. Worse still, it could lead to widespread bankruptcies and mass unemployment. Financial sector reform, involving bank recapitalisation and resolution of internal debt problems, and the provision of loan guarantees, with Western financial assistance and guidance, combined with 'commercialisation' at an early stage in the transition is, therefore, recommended for formerly centrally planned economies embarking on the transition to a 'market' economy.

Finally, 'convertibility', along with price and trade liberalisation and the phasing out of subsidies, should also be introduced at an early stage in order to: expose state monopolies to competition; import 'world' relative prices to reveal 'comparative advantages' and disadvantages; and perhaps also to provide a 'nominal anchor' (see Chapter 3). Again with the Western financial assistance, via a 'stabilisation fund', Russia should be encouraged to move to 'current account' convertibility as soon as it can credibly do so (Dickinson and Mullineux, 1993).

REFERENCES

Business International (1992) "*East European Investment Survey*", October, Business International and Creditanstalt, Vienna.

Dickinson, D G and Mullineux, A W (1993) "Currency Convertibility, Policy Credibility and Capital Flight in Poland and the CSFR, *Department of Economics Discussion Paper*, No. 93-4, University of Birmingham, (UK).

Kornai, J (1990) "*The Road to a Free Economy: Shifting from a Socialist Economy: The Example of Hungary*", New York: W.W. Norton.

Mullineux, A W (1987) "*International Banking and Financial Systems: A Comparison*", London: Graham and Trotman.

Mullineux, A W and Belka, M (1993) "Hardening Micro Budget Constraints: Bank Behaviour and Corporate Governance in Poland", *Birmingham Business School International Finance Group Working Paper (IFGWP-93-07)*, University of Birmingham.

Stiglitz, J E and Weiss, A (1981), "Credit Rationing in Markets with Imperfect Information", *American Economic Review*, 71, pp 393-410.

CHAPTER 2

HARD BUDGET CONSTRAINTS, CREDIT CRUNCHES AND CENTRAL BANK INDEPENDENCE

Andy Mullineux

INTRODUCTION

Reform programmes for economies wishing to switch from central planning to allocation of resources through markets normally emphasise the importance of macroeconomic stabilisation and the introduction of hard budget constraints on firms. The stabilisation programme is aimed at imposing a hard budget constraint on the government and entails reducing the government budget deficit substantially, or even producing a surplus. It also requires action to deal with the monetary overhang, which itself, at least in part, can be attributed to soft budget constraints. This is because enterprises facing soft budget constraints, in the sense that they have access to supplementary credit from the banks and other external assistance beyond credit allocated through the plan, will tend to develop a tendency to over-invest. This in turn creates a shortage of consumer goods which is compounded if a large part of the state expenditure is ear-marked for military expenditure. With prices centrally administered, household income tends to accumulate as 'savings', creating a monetary overhang. Clearly price liberalisation is likely to lead to inflation in the absence of 'monetary reform', which involves the state using its powers, at the risk of creating social unrest, to remove the overhang by calling in old currency and issuing new at an adverse exchange rate. As long as the government and firms continue to face soft budget constraints, however, inflationary pressures will remain.

FINANCIAL SECTOR REFORM AND HARD BUDGET CONSTRAINTS

The first step towards building a modern financial infrastructure to support the development of a market economy has usually involved replacing the 'monobanking system' with a system in which the State bank becomes more like a Western-style central bank and its commercial lending activities are distributed amongst a number of commercial banks. The latter commonly deal initially with specific sectors of the economy, or groups of firms, but are expected to compete, amongst themselves and with new banks, often created as joint ventures with foreign banks, over time.

To impose hard budget constraints, and remove inflationary pressures, it is necessary to ensure that the State does not rely on the central bank to fund its deficits. This can only be achieved if the State can fund its deficit in domestic or foreign capital markets. In the initial phases of the transformation it is likely to prove difficult to fund deficits by borrowing abroad unless the deficits are small. The domestic route will only be available once domestic bond markets are developed. This is likely to take time, although the faster it can be done the better, since it provides a route for absorbing some of the monetary overhang. In the short run, deficit reduction or elimination, by reducing (especially military) expenditure and raising taxes, therefore, seems essential.

If hard budget constraints are also to be imposed on firms, then commercial banks must be encouraged to adopt a much more cautious approach to lending, emphasising return on their capital; and firms, once privatised, should be encouraged to seek funding from the capital markets and subject themselves to market discipline, forcing them to focus on return on capital so raised. The privatisation programmes will contribute to the development of capital markets and, in so doing, will help to reduce the overhang by providing a reasonable return to investors thereby encouraging the overhang to be converted into genuine savings. It is, however, unrealistic to expect the privatisation programmes to be executed in their entirety in anything but the medium term and equity markets, like government bond markets, can only be expected to develop slowly.

As Lawrence Brainard pointed out in his excellent 1990 AMEX top prize winning essay, the banks are likely to be the key players in the financial sector in the first phases of transition. The question is, can they be expected to impose hard budget constraints? Brainard emphasised the need to recapitalise the banks before they can function efficiently as allocators of credit. This is because the whole system is riddled with debt. The commercial banks are indebted to the central bank, to which the state is effectively also indebted, and the firms have substantial outstanding, and often bad and doubtful, debts to commercial banks.

If the central bank were allowed to get too tough on the commercial banks and the State, then the macroeconomic consequences could be dire. As noted, the State would have to tighten fiscal policy substantially, although the scope of the tightening would depend on how rapidly it could run down military expenditure, adding to recessionary tendencies. Given the importance of the military sector, rapid reduction of military expenditure would itself clearly cause substantial dislocation, however. Further, if commercial banks no longer had access to central bank funding, then a credit crunch would be the most likely outcome. The severity of the crunch would depend on how adequately the banks had been recapitalised. If the recapitalisation is to be done in a non-inflationary manner, then the costs must be met out of the State budget, rather than through central bank funding. Given competing claims, including the need to provide transfer payments to the newly unemployed, a generous recapitalisation may, however, prove difficult; politically and practically, to achieve.

More realistically, the central bank can be expected to provide lender of last resort support to a banking system that will remain undercapitalised, saddled with substantial bad and doubtful debts, and will be operating in an extremely uncertain environment in which credit rating of clients, especially newly privatised ones or newly created small firms and co-operatives, is extremely difficult. The conditions under which and the terms on which the central bank provides such support will be a major factor determining how hard budget constraints are in reality. It should be born in mind that if 'marketisation' is to be combined with 'democratisation', as it has to be if financial support from Western governments and international agencies is to be secured, there will be limits to the extent of austerity that an electorate will bear. This means that the government, which will at some stage have to submit itself for re-election, may decide to relax its fiscal policy stance and rely on central bank funding, in the main, to make up the shortfall; and to encourage to cental bank to relieve the credit crunch.

An independent central bank, akin to the Bundesbank, might be in a position to refuse to accommodate the government, but the creation of a truly independent central bank in emerging democracies seems unlikely. Further, the Bundesbank is only able to sustain strict monetary discipline because of the soundness of the German banking system. If a banking system is fragile, it is very difficult for a central bank to impose monetary restraint because it might lead to bank failures and a systemic banking crisis, which would exacerbate the recession and possibly convert it into a major depression.

WHAT CAN THE EASTERN EUROPEAN ECONOMIES LEARN FROM THE WEST

What guidance can the Western industrialised economies give the emerging Central and Eastern European market economies about the imposition of hard budget constraints? More starkly, we might ask what the USSR can lean from recent US experience?

For most of the 1980s the US ran a sizeable budget deficit. It also experienced substantial financial reform, which started in the late 1970s with the de facto liberalisation of interest rates. Legislation at the beginning of the 1980s formally liberalised interest rates and allowed Savings and Loan Associations and other 'thrifts' to diversify into banking business. The budget deficit was funded largely by inflows of capital as domestic savings rates declined. This was done with little difficulty in most years, although at times foreign central banks effectively had to step in as inflows of private sector capital subsided, at the cost of pushing up real interest rates. The deficit remains large in dollar terms, but in 1991 a package which aims to reduce it substantially in the medium term was agreed and anyway, due to economic growth in the mid and late 1980s, the deficit declined substantially, as a proportion of GDP, to levels below that of many OECD countries. It remains possible that a world capital shortage might make US deficit funding from overseas more difficult in the 1990s. The shortage may be created by the decline (or elimination) of the German and Japanese trade surpluses, although the latter is showing signs of renewed expansion in 1991, and demands for reconstruction funding, in the Middle East and Eastern and Central Europe and the USSR, and restructuring finance, in Latin America and elsewhere.

One factor making deficit reduction increasingly difficult has been the rising cost of dealing with the 'Savings and Loans' crisis. There is no space to recount the origins and causes of the crisis in detail here and anyway it is only one manifestation of the fragility in the US financial system. There have also been problems amongst securities firms following the 1987 stock market crash and the collapse of the 'junk bond' market in early 1990. The incidence of bank failures also began to rise in the late 1970s. There are a number of causes of this phenomena too, which again cannot be discussed in detail here. The contrast between the US banking system and the traditional 'monobanking' system in the USSR cannot be starker. The US has literally thousands of the banks, many with single or just a few branches, as a result of strict branching restrictions. These restrictions have been eroded somewhat in the 1980s and the US Treasury tabled proposals in early 1991 which may lead, Congress permitting, to their removal in the near future. There are also severe restrictions on bank diversification. These have also been eroded in the 1980s and the Treasury proposals provide for their removal too.

In such a system, small local banks, and badly managed large banks, can easily become heavily exposed to particular sectors of the economy. As a result, in the mid 1980s, there were waves of failures amongst 'farm' and 'energy' banks. Latterly, a more widespread malaise has been caused by exposure to property markets, as property prices have gone into decline, and to highly leveraged debt, following the collapse of the mergers and acquisition boom in the late 1980s and the 'junk bond' market which grew on the back of it. The large US banks have, of course, also suffered from their exposure to major debtor countries, particularly in Latin America, in the 1980s.

The main response of the US bank regulators to the banks' problems has been to require banks to build up reserves against bad and doubtful debts and to raise capital ratios. This has been supported by the 1988 Basle Agreement on capital adequacy for international banks. The Basle Agreement, reached by the bank supervisors from the major Western industralised nations; requires a phased increase in risk related capital ratios to be completed by March 1992. The effect of the financial liberalisation and the trend towards securitised borrowing from the capital markets, leading to some disintermediation, has been to increase competition in the financial sector, leading to reduced interest rate margins and bank profitability. With the 1992 deadline approaching, many banks still have some way to go to hit the target capital ratios. They can meet the requirements either by raising new capital, which for troubled banks will prove expensive, or shrinking their balance sheets and restricting new lending. The most saleable assets are likely to be the least risky, however, so shrinkage may increase the average riskiness in the remaining portfolios, and increase fragility.

With the onset of the recession in the US in 1990, the US central bank (the Fed) came under pressure from the Presidential Administration to reduce interest rates. This was done cautiously at first in light of the weakness of the dollar and the fact that 'core' inflation remained stubbornly high. The Fed held out until an agreement to reduce the budget deficit was concluded and the severity of the recession became apparent, despite growing evidence of widespread problems in the banking sector. It has subsequently been able to reduce interest rates fairly aggressively; aided by renewed strength of the dollar following the successful conclusion of the war with Iraq in the Spring of 1991 and as a result of the weakness of the Deutschmark caused by unification problems and growing uncertainty about the future of the USSR. Despite the easing, there is some evidence that a credit crunch has developed in the US in 1991 and this in turn has encouraged further relaxation of monetary restraint in order to try to create conditions for an economic recovery.

Apart from the need to improve capital ratios and add to loan loss reserves in a recession, the cause of the reduced willingness of banks to lend, even to the supposedly creditworthy, is that in a recession creditworthiness itself has to be seriously scrutinised. It seems likely that in the 1980s banks became lax in their lending practices since rising asset prices made collatoralised lending appear relatively risk free. The collapse of the property market has undermined the value of assets most commonly used as collateral and the recession has reduced the cash flow of many firms, making a reappraisal of credit worthiness prudent and necessary. Further, as interest rates have fallen, banks have taken the opportunity to increase lending margins to restore profit ability. Increased profits can be retained to increase capital and make it possible to raise equity on the capital market more cheaply.

To some extent, the 'credit crunch' may also reflect an unwillingness to borrow at a time when interest rates are expected to fall further and cheaper loans may become available. A major difference between the US and the USSR is that commerce in the US relies heavily on firms granting each other credit whereas in the USSR firms rely much more heavily on bank credit. In a recession, as was particularly evident in the UK in the early 1990s, small firms can suffer disproportionately if their clients fail to pay their invoices on times. Larger firms frequently preserve their liquidity by paying bills less promptly. For the small firms, this can be fatal. Whilst this is a weakness that needs to be addressed in the UK and the US, it is clear that firms in the emerging market economies in Europe may be even more exposed to a 'credit crunch', in the form of a reduced willingness of banks to provide credit, than their Western counterparts.

Another feature of the US banking system is worth emphasising, namely its reliance on deposit insurance. Many of the problems in the banking and 'thrift' sectors stem from the liberalisation of interest rates without reforming the deposit insurance arrangements. Historically, comprehensive deposit insurance was introduced to bolster depositors' confidence in the light of the Fed's lack of credibility as lender of last resort to the banking system. It worked well until interest rates were liberalised and had the benefit of reducing recourse to lender of last resort intervention whilst forcing banks and thrifts to contribute to depositor protection. The funds are underwritten by the Treasury, and ultimately the taxpayer, rather than the central bank. It is for this reason that the 'thrift' rescue has required Congressional approval for its funding and the re-capitalisation of the banking fund (overseen by the FDIC), which has subsequently become necessary, is awaiting Congressional approval as part of, or possibly separate from, the aforementioned banking reform package proposed by the Treasury. It has been proposed that the burden of supporting the deposit insurance funds be transferred from the Treasury to the Fed, but the latter is resisting this strongly. If such a transfer occurs, then effectively the Fed, like most other central banks, will be the sole lender of last resort and its ability to impose monetary discipline may be compromised as a result.

The reason that interest rate liberalisation, in the presence of comprehensive deposit insurance, created problems in the US was because capital adequacy requirements and contributions to the deposit insurance funds were not risk-related. Following liberalisation, risk prone banks and 'thrifts' could therefore bid aggressively for deposits. This created an 'adverse selection' problem because depositors themselves were protected by the funds and tended naturally to place deposits where they earnt the highest returns. The net effect was an increase in financial fragility. To combat this a risk-related element needed to be introduced into the bank support schemes. This could have been done by introducing risk-related deposit insurance contributions, so that banks taking on more risk paid more for deposit protection. If, as seems likely, some of the costs were passed on to depositors, the adverse selection would have been curtailed. The move to risk-related capital adequacy requirements, which force banks with riskier portfolios to hold more capital, effectively places a tax on risk-taking and should help to resolve the problem. It is debateable whether both risk-related deposit insurance contributions and risk-related capital adequacy requirements are required to encourage prudence. What is required is that the whole support package, including deposit insurance, capital adequacy requirements, liquidity ratios or central bank deposits, and lender of last resort, contains an adequately large risk-related element. The Treasury banking reform proposals do entail a move towards risk-related deposit insurance, however, and some steps in this direction were taken when the 'thrift' fund was recapitalised and put under the administration of the FDIC in 1990. Because the 'thrifts' typically had lower capital ratios, they were required to pay more for deposit insurance than banks. Other Western industrial countries have much less comprehensive deposit insurance schemes and instead rely more heavily on lender of last resort support by the central bank to underwrite the stability of the banking system.

It is clear from the above discussion that Western democracies, do not find it easy to impose hard budget constraints. This was particularly true in the US in the 1980s and early 1990s, but is equally true in Italy and elsewhere. There is ample evidence that economic prosperity has a major influence on voting behaviour and that recessions are particularly bad for the re-election prospects of incumbent governments. There also seems to be a bias towards inflation, although, if inflation becomes excessive the electorate sometimes shows its displeasure through the ballot box. This has led some economists to postulate, without overwhelming empirical support, the existence of an electoral period conditioned economic cycle with pre-election booms and post election disinflationary purges. Even with 'rational' electorates an inflationary bias and 'political' business cycles may persist, according to some economic theorists. Further, inflation can be regarded as a tax, reducing the real value of income, which weak governments, unable to develop sufficiently wide tax bases, will levy (with the help of central bank 'lending') to fund their deficits.

CONCLUSIONS

The key to imposing hard budget constraints, on the government and on firms, seems to lie in establishing an independent central bank and a stable banking and wider financial system. The central bank may be involved, via regulation and supervision in assuring stability and prudence. Alternatively, this may be the responsibility of a separate banking commission. In the latter is the case, the central bank and the banking commission can be expected to co-ordinate activities fairly closely. This is because ince the central bank, as lender of last resort, may be called upon if the regulations are not rigorously administered and will need to be assured that applying the monetary brakes, as and when required, will not induce financial instability.

The growing interdependence of the financial sectors in various countries, as a result of the internationalisation of banking since the 1970s and the progressive removal of controls on international capital movements in the 1980s, has made co-ordination of regulatory arrangements essential. As noted above, the bank supervisors have successfully co-ordinated their arrangements. There is now considerable pressure on securities market regulators to follow suit.

The regulatory authorities in the emerging market economies in Europe will, therefore, get considerable advise, on best financial regulatory practices, from their Western counterparts, and those aspiring to EC membership will have to adopt similar arrangements to those currently being put in place in preparation for 1992. They will also have to prepare themselves for the rigours of central bank independence at a much earlier stage in their democratic lives than most Western democracies have had to do. Even some EC members with longstanding democratic credentials still baulk at the prospect, but, if hard budget constraints are indeed desirable, independent central banks with well defined anti-inflationary constitutional objectives seem to be the answer. The success of the Bundesbank was built on political consensus. It remains to be seen if German unification will undermine the concensus and whether the consensus in the EC is strong enough for the individual, member states to cede contral over monetary policy to an independent European central bank.

It seems a tall order to expect the emerging democracies in Central and Eastern Europe and the USSR to impose hard, rather than harder, budget constraints in the near future when many of their mentors, including the US, have yet to achieve the same goal.

CHAPTER 3

MONETARY AND EXCHANGE RATE POLICIES DURING EASTERN EUROPE'S TRANSITION: SOME LESSONS FROM FURTHER EAST

Maxwell J. Fry
and
D. Mario Nuti

INTRODUCTION

Over the past five years, Eastern Europe has embarked upon a transition from state ownership and central planning to a market system with private ownership and enterprise; this transition is now taking place in the former Soviet Union. Monetary institutions and policies, as well as trade and exchange regimes, played a major role in the collapse of the old system through open and hidden inflationary pressures and inefficiency insulated from world trade competition. Not surprisingly, they now constitute the centrepiece of this radical transformation.

A number of positive and negative lessons can be drawn from the transformation experience to date. Here, we outline the archetypical Eastern European economy, examine the prerequisites for effective, consistent and sustainable monetary and exchange rate policies, analyse the transitional problems with lessons from central Eastern European countries and draw additional lessons from some of the supremely successful Pacific Basin developing economies. We do not include the former Soviet Union in our analysis because of its unique features and because of the speed of current changes there.

The Eastern European countries started their stabilisation programmes from a position of repressed domestic imbalance and debilitating economic inertia. In our judgment, fiscal exigencies now dominate and constrain choice among macroeconomic policy options. Until Eastern European countries build the institutional structures to collect taxes, government deficits are likely to persist. We anticipate that deficits will be particularly large while GNPs continue to decline. To face the inevitable inflationary pressures with minimum distortion, monetary and exchange rate policies must be subordinate to and consistent with the fiscal stance. Use of a fixed exchange rate as an anti-inflationary device simply prices exporters out of world markets and leads back down the path to rationing. Similarly, keeping nominal interest rates artificially low in an attempt to support loss-making enterprises not only distorts factor prices and misallocates resources, but it also adds fuel to the inflationary fire by reducing the attractiveness of deposit money.

Until competitive banking systems are established, however, we believe that it would be a mistake simply to allow interest rates to be determined by the banks. Latin American experience suggests that financial liberalisation in the absence of a competitive financial system, sound prudential regulation and supervision, and macroeconomic stability can lead to financial crises. The opening of capital accounts should, in our view, also await the time when domestic financial systems are no longer subject to discriminatory taxation (for example, through high reserve requirements). But until capital accounts are opened, the best exchange rate regime appears to be a managed crawling peg with the domestic currency linked to some currency basket.

Under the second- and third-best settings in which macroeconomic policies must be set in Eastern Europe, an eclectic approach is essential. The purist may prefer a consistent set of policies based on neoclassical precepts, but he would be ignoring the enormous institutional lacunae in Eastern Europe which must be filled before market-based economic policies can be successful. In our opinion, the major institutional problems could well be solved within the next five years. Until some minimal set of institutional developments have occurred, however, some macroeconomic policies will have take the form of direct, nonmarket intervention. Provided such policies attempt to simulate market solutions, however, they need not present serious threats to the achievement of rapid economic growth. We draw upon the experience of Korea and Taiwan to support this view.

2 KEY FEATURES OF THE EASTERN EUROPEAN ECONOMIES

2.1 The Present Macroeconomic Setting

Some key macroeconomic features of the Eastern European countries are presented in Tables 1 and 2. Common characteristics of all the Eastern European countries at the outset of their transitions were acute external and internal (often repressed) imbalances, full (in some cases, overfull) employment and declining levels of GNP. Although overall government balances in Poland, Romania and Yugoslavia appeared sustainable, these figures conceal losses elsewhere in the public sector, including substantial central bank losses.

Table 1: Key Macroeconomic Variables in Eastern European Economies (Percentages).

	(1) Rate of Economic Growth			(2) Overall Government Balance/GNP	(3) Inflation Rate		(4) Unemployment Rate	
Country	1989	1990	1991	1990	1990	1991	1990	1991
Bulgaria	-0.4	-1.36	-23	-10	65	447*	1.6	10
CSFR	-0.7	-3.1	-14	-9	10	58	1.0	8
Hungary	-0.2	-5.0	-7	-2	30	38	1.7	8
Poland	-0.2	-12.0	-10	-4	250	60	6.1	11
Romania	-5.8	-7.9	-18†	-6	40	291*	1.3	4
Yugoslavia	-6.6	-8.0	-20	n.a	583	235	13.6	15

	(1) Current Account Balance/GNP	(2) Monetary Overhang		(3) Net Foreign Debt/Hard Currency Exports	(4) Foreign Exchange Reserves/Imports
Country	1990	Jan. 1990	June 1991	1990	1990
Bulgaria	-6.3	small	zero	497	31
CSFR	-2.5	small	zero	116	26
Hungary	0.3	zero	zero	328	19
Poland	1.1	significant	zero	408	53
Romania	-4.8	small	small	35	27
Yugoslavia	-7.1	small	significant	75	34

* November
† Industrial Output

Note: Data for this table have been compiled from the works cited below together with official national sources and ECE-UN, *Economic Bulletin for Europe*, 43, 1991. The 1990 inflation rates are point-to-point rates of change.

Source: Column 1, Williamson (1991), pp. 72, 74, 76, 78; Organisation for Economic Co-operation and Development (1991). Column 2, Kopits (1991), Table 2, p. 23; Organisation for Economic Co-operation and Development (1991); Williamson (1991), pp. 59, 74. Column 3, *International Financial Statistics*, June 1991; Organisation for Economic Co-operation and Development (1991); Williamson (1991), p. 79. Column 4, United Nations Economic Commission for Europe (1991). Column 5, Organisation for Economic Co-operation and Development (1991). Column 6, Cottarelli and Blejer (1991), Table 4. Column 7, Organisation for Economic Co-operation and Development (1991). Column 8, Bofinger (1990), Table 1, p. 11.

Table 2: Features of Stabilisation and Reform Plans in Easern Europe

Feature	Yugoslavia	Poland	Romania	CSFR	Bulgaria
Programme start	1 Dec. 1989	1 Jan. 1990	1 Aug. 1990	1 Jan. 1991	1 Feb. 1991
Price liberalisation	instant 90%	instant 90%	3 stages	instant 85%	gradual
Subsidy reduction, 1989--1991	yes	17.4--4%	partial	& 16.1--4.6%	16.7--3%
Fiscal squeeze	temporary	yes	no	yes	limited
Monetary restraint	temporary	yes	no	yes	limited
Currency devaluation	yes	yes	yes	yes	yes
Foreign trade liberalisation	extensive	extensive	v. limited	extensive	v. limited
Internal convertibility for firms	yes; aborted	yes	end--1991	yes; delayed	yes
Internal convertibility for households	yes; aborted	yes	no	no	no
Wages policy	yes; ignored	fiscal	no	yes	yes
Small-scale privatisation	yes	yes	yes	yes	slow
Sale of state enterprises	some	some	mostly land	slow	slow
Property restitution to former owners	no	yes	yes	yes	yes
Mass privatisation through vouchers	no	delayed	delayed	delayed	delayed
Capacity restructuring	no	little	no	little	no
Real anchoring		*M, r*		*M, r*	
Nominal anchoring	*W, i*	*W, e*		*W, e*	*M*

Note: *M*, money; *r*, real interest rates; *W*, wages; *i*, nominal interest rates; *e*, exchange rate.

Relocating losses from the central government to public enterprises or to the central bank is merely window dressing. The public sector deficit cannot be reduced by abolishing government subsidies if loss-making public enterprises have unfettered access to credit or to foreign exchange subsidies from the central bank.

While the 20--25 per cent of manufacturing firms in the Czech and Slovak Federal Republic (CSFR), Hungary and Poland now producing negative value added at international prices should be closed immediately, loss-making firms producing positive value added at world prices should be phased out more gradually. In the short run, therefore, they will require subsidies or tariff protection. Nevertheless, the longer-run goal of price stability requires hard budget constraints throughout the economy, applying indiscriminately to all levels of government, public sector enterprises and the emerging private sector.

By comparison with developing countries, Eastern European countries appear to have a relatively low level of international indebtedness.[1] Empirical evidence from developing countries suggests that debt accumulation creates more problems than it solves when government and government-guaranteed debt exceeds 50 per cent of GNP (Fry 1989). Although most Eastern European countries have foreign debts well below this threshold, their relatively small hard currency earnings (Table 1) create serious debt service difficulties. Indeed, these debt service ratios constitute major impediments to a rapid move to currency convertibility.

2.2 The Legacy of Centrally Planned Economies

Critics of capitalism place considerable emphasis on the pernicious role of the financial system that forms the hub of the capitalist economy. Karl Marx recognised the importance of the financial system in the process of capitalist economic development over a century ago. Lenin, impressed by the powerful political and economic influence of the European banks in the eighteenth and nineteenth centuries, also understood the crucial role of the financial system in a centrally planned economy (Garvy 1968).

The old-style central bank in centrally planned economies was shaped in the late 1920s as the counterpart of Soviet physical planning; it was usually described as a monobank for its monopoly of all short- and long-term credit in addition to central banking functions. Monetary policy was supposed to adapt passively to planned physical flows at centrally fixed and stable prices and wages. Investment credit was free to state investors, subject only to

[1] In relation to GNP, foreign debt represented 20 per cent in Bulgaria, 5 per cent in CSFR, 36 per cent in Hungary, 28 per cent in Poland, 2 per cent in Romania and 34 per cent in Yugoslavia in 1990 (Williamson 1991, Table 2.3, p. 12).

depreciation charges. Interest rates charged on state enterprise working capital and paid out on deposits were symbolic.

On the one hand, the exchange rate, ambitiously fixed at prestigious parities, was largely an irrelevance as trade transactions were conducted at world prices (or, in intra-CMEA trade, linked to world prices). On the other hand, domestic producers and users were subject to a cumbersome system of taxes and subsidies compensating for the difference between domestic and international prices at those exchange rates. Foreign exchange was available automatically for planned imports, while export revenues accrued to the central bank or one of its segments.

The banking system via the state budget reshuffled profits and losses throughout the economy. There was no effective difference between profits and taxes, as both were siphoned off as state revenue. Rather than being taxed, personal incomes were held down by controls and boosted in real terms by subsidies on a wide range of goods. Automatic credit for the execution of planned tasks covered not only investment finance but also those enterprise losses not already covered by state subsidies. In this sense enterprise budgets were ``soft'', as stressed by János Kornai (1980).[2] Protected from market discipline, state enterprises were basically administrative units managed by bureaucrats executing detailed central orders.

The state budget was made rather opaque by the all-pervasive nature of the state and by some obscure conventions. Traditionally, a surplus was envisaged, but any deficit was automatically funded by monetary expansion, given the absence of a market for state bonds. No other financial assets existed. A rigid link was established between money wages and budget balance via the profits of state enterprises, given price policy and low or absent income taxation. There was also a strong link between the budget deficit and monetary expansion due to the automatic monetisation of budget deficits. This rigidity made the system dependent on wage discipline and vulnerable to workers' demands.

In principle, this system should have insured domestic and external balance, including price stability. As a result of an ill-conceived and badly executed commitment to price stability, however, prices came, over time, to have no more economic significance than random numbers. They also differed between transactors and transactions, which aggravated the built-in inefficiencies of central planning. Balance was the exception, while the rule everywhere turned out to be an increasingly frequent and diffuse state of excess demand, first of a structural, then of an aggregate type. The basic causes were overambition, growthmanship, overoptimism and an inability to adjust to

---

[2] In reality, budget constraints were ``elastic'', not infinitely soft as Kornai seems to suggest.

external shocks. Thus Kornai (1980) could accurately label the system ``The Shortage Economy."

Endemic inflationary gaps, repressed by price controls in the state sector, cumulated over time to form large-scale monetary overhangs (Nuti 1989). While their size is debatable, their presence is revealed by the widening gap between state prices and prices of private sales (whether legal or illegal). These shortages and supply disruptions associated with the overhang did much to undermine the system. The CSFR and Hungary avoided large-scale overhangs, the former by maintaining its old tradition of monetary discipline, the latter by its early start (1968) in the reform process. In these two countries, systemic problems took the form of stagnation. In Yugoslavia, monetary overhang led to open hyperinflation (2,500 per cent in 1989, over 500 per cent in 1990). Poland succeeded in experiencing simultaneously shortages and hyperinflation in 1988--1989.

In Eastern Europe, domestic imbalance due to the failure to adjust to exogenous shocks spilt over into external imbalances and mounting foreign indebtedness. Secondary markets began to trade Eastern Europe's debt at a discount; agreed or *de facto* rescheduling took place. However, debt buildups were avoided in the former Soviet Union during times of booming oil prices and in Ceaucescu's Romania through the imposition of brutal deflations.

In our view, fiscal balance determines the parameters under which monetary policy can be set, while the monetary policy stance determines the appropriate exchange rate regime. However, of particular concern with respect to monetary policy implementation are the absence of a competitive banking system, the lack of expertise in loan appraisal and the inadequate legal recourse of lenders against delinquent borrowers. In the relatively closed economies of Eastern Europe, domestic prices constitute the dog that wags the exchange rate tail. Given the uncertainty of controlling inflation, a fixed exchange rate makes it impossible to influence the current account without returning to old-style controls. Hence, reliance on the exchange rate as *the* nominal anchor is dangerous in the extreme.

3 LESSONS FROM FURTHER EAST

3.1 High Growth Without Full Liberalisation

Economists have found the bold experiments in the economic opening of Latin America much more exciting than the gradual liberalisation in East and Southeast Asia. Nevertheless, rates of economic growth have been spectacular in the latter region but negative in the former. Hence, useful lessons of how to do things right might come from Asia even if lessons of how to avoid doing things wrong can be learnt from Latin America.

The fastest growing economies in East and Southeast Asia have placed emphasis on export promotion as their primary development strategy. However, implementation of outward-looking growth strategies in this region has taken a different form in each country. Hong Kong's relatively laissez-faire approach, for example, contrasts sharply with Korea's substantial interventionism. Nevertheless, two common policy characteristics can be detected: the complementarity between monetary and exchange rate policies, on the one hand, and the absence of any pressure for monetary expansion to finance government deficits on the other. Unlike the majority of developing countries, the high fliers of Asia have not allowed their currencies to appreciate in real terms *solely* as a result of domestic inflation and none of them has had any serious recourse to deficit finance.

Korea and Taiwan, in particular, have been cautious over liberalising their financial sectors and capital accounts. Their domestic institutional interest rates are still not determined by the free interplay of market forces. Gradually, Korea and Taiwan are liberalising capital account transactions. At some point, therefore, domestic interest rates will have to be market-determined. The main point is that high GNP and export growth rates are not dependent on financial or capital account liberalisation. However, the outward orientation of both economies has ensured that interest and exchange rates have been set close to competitive free-market rates.

As many developing countries have discovered, without stable domestic financial conditions, foreign borrowing can be treacherous: ``A healthy domestic financial market with a realistic exchange rate and positive real interest rates is a prerequisite [for successful foreign borrowing]. Otherwise, private investors responding to the perverse incentives offered will almost immediately find a way to ensure that the foreign exchange equivalent of foreign borrowing will flow out, preventing the accomplishment of a net capital inflow" (Black 1991, p. 5). In other words, if domestic financial conditions are unconducive to saving, savers will move their savings abroad. Even where prohibited, as in Eastern Europe at present, capital flight occurs simply through overinvoicing imports and underinvoicing exports. This ensures that foreign capital inflows do not finance productive domestic investment. Rather they facilitate portfolio diversification, which may improve the welfare of the residents of the capital importing country, but weaken the country's creditworthiness.

3.2 Korea's Stabilisation Programme

During the 1970s, the Korean government pursued an industrial policy of promoting heavy and chemical industries. To this end, it implemented directed credit policies to ensure that the favoured sectors received cheap and abundant credit from the government-owned banking system; one side effect was accelerating inflation. Most imported equipment for these industries was financed through foreign loans (Nam 1989, pp. 137--142).

With hindsight, it is clear that this strategy was a mistake. The favoured industries were inefficient and many firms were unable to repay their domestic-currency loans. In an attempt to alleviate their foreign debt service burdens, the government clung to a fixed exchange rate despite the evident overvaluation of the won. The ensuing economic crisis occurred in part because Korea had delayed vital reforms for too long.

The Korean stabilisation experience in the early 1980s provides some relevant lessons for Eastern Europe. After rising by 10 per cent annually over the previous two decades, Korea's real GNP fell by 5 per cent, inflation rose to 35 per cent, and the current account deficit reached 9 per cent of GNP in 1980. For Korea, the increases in oil prices and world interest rates in 1980 were equivalent to 6 per cent of GNP; a drought reduced agricultural output by an additional 4 per cent of GNP. Bijan Aghevli and Jorge Márquez-Ruarte (1987, p. 92) suggest that recession in the industrial countries compounded Korea's weak international competitiveness, substantially reducing export growth. Korea's total foreign debt, which includes long-term and short-term public and private foreign debt, fluctuated around a dangerously high 50 per cent of GNP between 1980 and 1985.

Korea embarked upon a stabilisation programme in conjunction with an IMF stand-by arrangement in March 1980. The main elements of the programme consisted of noninflationary financial policies, a substantial depreciation of the won and measures to reduce Korea's dependence on imported oil. During 1980, the real effective exchange rate depreciated by 7 per cent. Domestic energy prices were raised in step with the rise in world oil prices and restrictions were imposed on energy use. As international oil prices subsequently fell, Korea raised its oil import duty and passed through only 30 per cent of the oil price decline to consumers (Aghevli and Márquez-Ruarte 1987, pp. 94--101).

During 1981--1982, Korea initiated a programme of structural adjustment encompassing public sector investment, a comprehensive tax reform, and trade liberalisation. An important feature of the investment plan was to reduce dependence on imported oil by expanding domestic coal, gas and nuclear-powered electricity generation. The tax reform increased tax on interest and dividend income, simplified corporate tax and extended VAT. Trade liberalisation was aimed at increasing competition in the industrial sector and at stabilising prices.

Having negotiated another stand-by arrangement with the IMF in July 1983, Korea intensified its adjustment efforts. The government deficit fell from 4.5 per cent of GNP during 1981--1982 to 1.5 per cent of GNP during 1983--1984. Credit expansion was halved between the same periods, in large part by restricting policy loans to fewer priority sectors. Real interest rates on bank deposits and loans rose to positive levels from the negative levels of the late 1970s (Nam 1989, Table 2, p. 151). The real effective exchange rate depreciated by 7 per cent in 1983, subsequently remaining stable. During the 1983--1984 period, trade liberalisation was accelerated and tentative steps taken towards financial reform.

These structural adjustments and policy reforms revived Korea's highly successful strategy of export-led growth. They produced an annual economic growth rate of 8 per cent during 1983--84, reduced inflation to 2 per cent, and reduced the current account deficit to less than 2 per cent of GNP. As a percentage of GNP, Korea's foreign indebtedness started to fall sharply. Over the five-year period 1985--1989, Korea's economic growth accelerated to just over 10 per cent annually and the current account posted an annual surplus averaging over $4 billion or over 4 per cent of GNP. By 1989 Korea was on the verge of becoming a net creditor nation. Korean exports grew from 35 to 41 per cent of GNP, an increase of over 200 per cent in real terms, between 1980 and 1988.

4 THE POLICY ISSUES

4.1 Transition and Stabilisation Programmes

The first institutional change required for transition in Eastern Europe is the transformation of the monolithic monetary and banking system of the communist system into a multi-level, competitive and pluralistic system, with a measure of currency convertibility. The second is the development of an articulated tax system, replacing diversified (*ad hoc* and often enterprise-specific) tax and subsidy rates with uniform rates of income and value-added taxes. The third is the development of asset markets, accompanied by substantial privatisation of state property. The model of transition now emerging along these lines is based on the experience of Hungary, which started reform in 1968 and gradually implemented over the years both reform and stabilisation.

The other central Eastern European countries now undertaking reform and stabilisation do not face the same option of gradual transformation: internal and external imbalances have cumulated to far greater levels than Hungary's in 1968, the trading arrangements of the CMEA have disintegrated and conditions in international trade and financial markets are less favourable. Recent literature has focused on appropriate sequencing. Some authors have pinpointed the high degree of interdependence and concluded that everything has to be done simultaneously, while others have proposed a sequential critical path. Most agree, however, that speedy action is of greater importance than orderly procrastination.

Rightly, internal and external stability---prerequisites for the viability of any system---have been given priority in the transformation. Where price controls still exist and rationing is prevalent, excess monetary expansion creates a monetary overhang rather than inflation. In Bulgaria and Poland, the monetary overhang has been eliminated through inflation. Romania and Yugoslavia have the worst of both worlds---monetary overhang and high inflation. Demonetisation or open inflation can eliminate monetary overhangs;[3] both are confiscatory. An alternative to demonetisation is compulsory conversion of ``excess'' money holdings into bonds. This could involve some element of confiscation in that the market value of the bonds exchanged for money balances might fall below the face value of the bonds. In any event, the aim of the conversion is to remove the monetary overhang in a noninflationary manner. Fiscal exigencies will dictate the extent of expropriation involved in the conversion. In the limit, a comprehensive currency reform could be used to tax away the entire overhang.

By and large, stabilisation packages have followed the pattern of the Polish stabilisation plan of January 1990: almost instant introduction of price and trade liberalisation, nominal anchoring to money wages and the nominal exchange rate, targeting the real money supply and real interest rates, monetary and fiscal austerity, large devaluations and internal convertibility, extreme fiscal pressure on the state sector, taxes on excess wage increases and, in the longer run, privatisation and capacity restructuring.

Yugoslavia started a similar stabilisation plan a month before Poland on 1 December 1989. However, the Yugoslav programme was fairly conventional because Yugoslavia had virtually no monetary overhang, a considerable degree of economic decentralisation, reasonably free trade and a reasonable degree of currency convertibility, as well as experience with restructuring and unemployment. The Yugoslav programme was rapidly aborted because of inflationary pressures caused in part by Republican failure to comply with wage

---

[3] In February 1991, large-denomination rouble notes were demonetised in a misguided attempt to address the monetary overhang problem in the former Soviet Union. In the end, only 15 per cent of these notes (1.5 per cent of GNP) were actually confiscated. Undoubtedly, however, the ensuing panic reduced the demand for money by a much larger amount. Hence, the measure must have been counterproductive.

guidelines. Convertibility was suspended in late 1990 and civil war broke out in 1991.

Thus, the Polish stabilisation plan remains the prototype for Eastern Europe. After Poland, stabilisation plans were introduced in Romania on 1 September 1990, the CSFR on 1 January 1991 and Bulgaria on 1 February 1991. Table 2 highlights the main features of these plans. The Polish approach has worked in some respects but not in others. It has been accompanied by overshooting and has been costly in terms of employment and output. Many of the details of the Polish-style programme require reconsideration. Privatisation and restructuring have progressed much more slowly than expected. Widespread recession prevails throughout the area.

One lesson from the Polish experience is that ``shock therapy" stabilisation can bring an instant end to shortages, through a large but tolerable hike in prices, after which the rate of inflation can be brought down. This may seem obvious now, but at the time it was not at all clear in view of the unprecedented features of Polish stabilisation. Purely administrative price increases, below the market clearing level, of the kind introduced by the Romanian government and in the former Soviet Union on 2 April 1991, aroused popular resistance and discontent without eliminating shortages.

In Poland, it was a mistake to let real wages and the real rate of exchange float at random with the vagaries of inflation, to excessively overdevalue the zloty, to effectively tax old loans by raising their interest rates, to neglect farmers' incomes and supply response, to neglect the state sector, to postpone further institutional changes, not to make clear announcements about further developments and to make no provision for possible overshooting. The inability to recognise mistakes and to learn from them was a major drawback of the old system. It is depressing that it should also be a feature of the new system.

4.2 Fiscal Reform

A major lesson from the Polish experience is that budgetary and monetary discipline are indispensable. Otherwise the round of price increases involved in stabilisation is wasted and inflationary pressures reemerge. Again, this may seem obvious enough but it is a lesson which is lost, for instance, on Romanian (and Russian) leaders. In this respect, Kornai (1980, 1986, 1990) has been proved both right and wrong: wrong in that state enterprise budget constraints can be hardened, right in that this takes a noncommunist government aiming at restoring a private market economy.

Ronald McKinnon (1991, Ch. 11) argues that Eastern European countries must secure adequate fiscal and monetary control *before* decontrolling prices, floating exchange rates, privatising state enterprises and decentralising economic decision-making. Furthermore, monetary and fiscal discipline necessitate radically new tax and banking systems. As pointed out in section 2, the traditional method of tax collection in Eastern Europe is through the appropriation of surpluses of state-owned enterprises. This automatic source of government revenue has been eroded by privatisation in agriculture, financial incentives introduced in private manufacturing and the decline in profitability of the still-dominant state sector. In other words, the dismantling of the communist system of public ownership and control over the means of production has reduced government revenue at an alarming rate. Although price liberalisation can eliminate the burden of product subsidies, the budget is now charged with providing a ``safety net'' for the newly unemployed and the other involuntary losers from the transition process. The upshot is that government expenditure has not declined in step with the fall in government revenue. In the absence of functioning bond markets, government deficits are monetised and monetary control is destroyed.

Fiscal changes parallelling the transformation of the monetary system thus need to include the introduction of income taxes, the replacement of the (largely residual) turnover tax at enterprise- and product-specific rates by a value-add tax (VAT) at a uniform rate and the funding of budget deficits by bond issues to whatever extent possible. Hungary was a pioneer in this respect, gradually developing a thriving market in government and state enterprise bonds in the second half of the 1980s. Hungary also introduced VAT in 1988 but, confusingly, called it a ``generalised'' turnover tax. These changes would permit the three variables, wages, the budget deficit and monetary expansion, which were formerly rigidly linked, to be decoupled. This, in turn, would allow greater latitude in the conduct of monetary and fiscal policies, as well as greater flexibility for response to exogenous shocks.

4.3 Reform of the Banking System

In addition to deficit finance, the traditional Soviet-style system of banking and credit leads to a further loss of monetary control. Under the passive credit system of a centrally planned economy, credit flows automatically to finance plan-approved expenditures. With decentralisation, enterprises start to make autonomous decisions. Many have large money balances, others can borrow at trivially low interest rates. Hence, effective budget constraints are almost nonexistent and the inflationary potential is limitless.

Hard budget constraints are, therefore, essential if price liberalisation is not to escalate into hyperinflation. This, in turn, means that banks must be in a position not only to refuse new loan requests but also to enforce payment of interest on existing loans. The *efficient* allocation of a limited volume of credit is crucial, but clearly requires institution-building that cannot possibly be accomplished overnight. In the meantime, *inefficient* credit allocation through some form of rationing may be the only viable, noninflationary alternative.

The pattern of change in monetary and financial institutions is exemplified by the pioneering Hungarian reform of 1987; it has now been followed throughout Eastern Europe. The monobank is stripped of all its functions other than central banking. Commercial banking is transferred to new independent units, in part by splitting up the former central bank, in part by establishing new banks of a state, cooperative or private nature. In some cases, commercial banks are established with partial or even exclusive participation of foreign capital. The intention is that these new institutions should compete in attracting deposits and in lending to state enterprises---now more independent-and private enterprises on the basis of their creditworthiness, instead of automatically financing their projects and validating their losses. This presupposes the achievement of a degree of independence and autonomy of state enterprises, freed from the tutelage of sectoral ministries and other central bodies, as well as legalisation and encouragement of private property and enterprise.

The central bank exercises monetary policy through reserve ratios and by setting the scale and rate of refinancing. Markets or policies lift real interest rates near to or above zero in real terms. Liberalisation of most external trade is accompanied by a measure of currency convertibility, at least for most imports required by producers. Major problems encountered at this stage include: the recapitalisation of those sections of the banking system that have inherited bad loans and guarantees in their portfolios from the previous system; the inertia of the state enterprise system, most of which is subject to constraints and negative incentives; and the accompanying inelasticity of supply.

4.4 Privatisation and Corporate Control

An essential component of the transition must be the establishment of capital markets to be extended from government bonds to enterprise bonds and shares, including shares in state enterprises, and a wide set of assets ranging from options and futures to foreign capital, land and physical assets. An uncontroversial first step is the transformation of state enterprises into joint stock companies, as a preliminary to private ownership. The idea is that the shares are then transferred to public investors (e.g., pension funds taking over state liabilities for pensions as well as assets, insurance companies and state holding companies) and to the wider public, including foreign investors.

Ideological obstacles have now been largely overcome, but there is still controversy over the desirable pace and mode of privatisation of state assets (Grosfeld and Hare 1991, Nuti 1990). Political expediency has led to restitution of state assets to former owners, subsidised sales to employees (partly in return for the loss of self-management powers and profit-sharing rights) and (except in Hungary) to schemes for the free distribution to the whole adult population of vouchers entitling them to shares or to certificates in investment funds managed by professional investors.

It seems that the possibility of instant capitalism through these means has been grossly overstated: transfer of ownership can be instantaneous but the transfer of control to the public, which is necessary for ownership change to set in motion the desired constraints and incentives, cannot be hurried. It depends on the development of well-established and well-functioning capital markets, efficient development banks or other soundly based institutional arrangements to absorb nonmarketable debt.

4.5 Monetary Policy

Given the enormous changes taking place in the Eastern European economies, effective monetary and exchange rate policies will have to rely on a range of techniques. Not only are the effects of each technique uncertain, but their impact will also undoubtedly change during the transition. Hence, diversification could reduce the risk of large policy errors. Even to the extent of appearing to control both quantity and price, the monetary authorities may be well advised to set interest rates and attempt to control the quantity of money at the same time. The minor disequilibrium that may result could well be far less damaging than major instability.

In the main, Korea and Taiwan have not been greatly disadvantaged by targeting money and credit volumes, while at the same time setting institutional interest rates by administrative fiat. Nevertheless, Korea's deliberate manipulation of interest and exchange rates to keep unsuccessful heavy and chemical industries afloat in the late 1970s was disastrous. The lesson is that exchange rate policy must be consistent with monetary conditions; high inflation caused by expansionary monetary policy must be accompanied by appropriate adjustments in the nominal exchange rate. Neither exchange rate nor monetary policy should be used in an attempt to prop up inefficient and unprofitable industries.

Monetary and exchange rate policies are dependent on the fiscal balance, broadly defined to include the consolidated budget of all levels of government, as well as the budgets of central and state-owned commercial banks. If the central bank has to bail out insolvent commercial banks or provide excessive loans to republics or local governments, the monetary consequences are identical to inflationary central government budget deficits. Hence, stability necessitates insulating the central bank from automatic demands for cash from all quarters. Although its three major commercial banks are operated by provincial authorities, Taiwan's central bank has been well insulated by the simple device of fining or imprisoning bank loan officers who make bad loans (Patrick 1990, p. 34).

Where such insulation is impracticable or impossible, interest and exchange rate policies must be made consistent with and subordinate to the consequent inflation generated by excessive monetary expansion. The worst response to such fiscal exigencies is to suppress the inflationary consequences through price controls or to ameliorate them by clinging to a fixed and overvalued exchange rate and fixed interest rates that become increasingly negative in real terms. Open inflation is much less detrimental to the economy than repressed inflation.

The two prices over which administrative control has traditionally been exercised in capitalist countries are interest rates and exchange rates. While interest and exchange rate liberalisation has occurred in the developed countries and in some of the developing countries of Latin America, developing countries of the Pacific Basin have been much more cautious in abandoning these controls. Eastern Europe may well find that control over these two prices for another decade or so would be prudent. Such control certainly does not thwart economic growth, as the experience of Korea and Taiwan makes quite clear. In general, however, the developing countries of the Pacific Basin have maintained positive real institutional interest rates and competitive exchange rates.

Experience, particularly in Latin America, suggests that successful interest rate liberalisation requires a competitive financial sector, strong prudential regulation and supervision of financial activities, and adequate legal support for debt recovery and bankruptcy. The Latin American experience suggests that, in the absence of these prerequisites, distress borrowing can easily drive real interest rates so high that normally viable enterprises are forced out of business. Hence, interest rate liberalisation should be delayed until financial institutions are functioning efficiently and the necessary legal support is in place.

Experience in East and Southeast Asia also suggests that interest rates that are fixed at realistic levels may constrain adverse selection and moral hazard problems that have plagued many OECD and Latin American countries since financial deregulation occurred in the early 1980s. When market-determined bank loan rates exceed the inflation rate by more than 10 percentage points, pathological banking behaviour is often the cause. A loan rate ceiling 6 percentage points above the inflation rate is unlikely to constrain ``normal'' banking activity, while a floor on deposit rates equal to the inflation rate could be used to combat oligopolistic collusion.

There is no doubt that administratively set loan rates impede efficient financial intermediation when they lie below the inflation rate by more than a few percentage points. Positive real interest rates are a prerequisite for improving the efficiency of investment and hence for raising the rate of economic growth without increasing the level of investment.[4] One reason for this that, when real interest rates are negative, there is no incentive to use capital efficiently. If financial intermediaries allocate investible funds more efficiently than other allocative mechanisms, then greater financial depth caused by higher real deposit rates of interest itself improves the quality of investment.

The effect of raising institutional interest rates towards their competitive free-market equilibrium level on the rate of economic growth in the medium run can be calculated indirectly from the estimated effects of real deposit rates on saving ratios and on investment efficiency. It can also be estimated from reduced-form equations of the growth rate. Estimates for a sample of 14 developing countries in Asia and the Pacific show positive and significant relationships between the incremental output/capital ratio and the real deposit rate of interest and also between the rate of economic growth and the real deposit rate of interest (Asian Development Bank 1985, pp. 10--11, 48--49). Jacques Polak (1989, pp. 66--70) reports econometric estimates for a sample of 40 developing countries over the period 1965--1985 in which an increase in the real interest rate of 10 percentage points is associated with a rise in the rate of economic growth by between 2 and 3 percentage points. He concludes that a reduction in the real interest rate below its equilibrium level by 1 percentage point requires an increase in the investment ratio by 1 percentage point in order to maintain a fixed rate of economic growth.

Even if all this is accepted by policy makers in Eastern Europe, fiscal exigencies may preclude any optimal choices. Given the almost inevitable problem of deficit finance that will continue to plague Eastern Europe until tax reform can be completed, we enumerate here some basic principles of less inefficient deficit finance:

1. Try to keep the annual inflation rate at under 20 per cent. Inefficiencies multiply exponentially when inflation exceeds this rate, in part because *stable* inflation rates of over 20 per cent a year have never been observed.

2. Limit the proportion of domestic credit appropriated by the government to about 25 per cent of total domestic credit. Higher ratios of government

---

[4] Fry (1991, pp. 29--33) provides empirical support for this proposition in the case of 10 Asian developing countries.

credit to total credit are typically accompanied by high inflation and low rates of economic growth (Harberger 1981; Harberger and Edwards 1980).

3. Abolish selective credit policies and remove artificial specialisation within the financial sector. Selective credit policies distort allocative efficiency and reduce domestic resource mobilisation without producing any measurable benefits.

4. Ensure that interest rates are set close to ``normal'' competitive market equilibrium levels.

5. Manage capital account transactions to deter capital flight and excessive short-term inflows. Some intervention can be justified due to the fact that reserve requirements impose negative protection on domestic financial intermediaries. To prevent potential disintermediation, private capital inflows should be taxed at the same rate as local loans through the imposition of similar reserve requirements. Deposits denominated in dollars, if permitted at all, would carry reserve requirements *in local currency* identical to domestic currency deposits. This would drive the same wedge between dollar deposit and loan rates of interest (McKinnon and Mathieson 1981).

6. Develop a treasury bill or some other short-term direct financial market to promote competition within the financial sector (Fry 1988, Ch. 17).

One lesson from the Polish experience is that interest rates should never be raised on old credit contracts, because this is equivalent to an inefficacious tax on loans. It is also unfair and perhaps unconstitutional. There are better taxes, including a tax on nominal capital gains. Retroactive interest rate rises were disastrous for Polish farmers and literally stopped their supply response. The same mistake is being repeated in Bulgaria, where raising interest rates on old contracts is being discussed by Parliament.

Hungarian policy has been better. The interest rate on enterprise payment arrears *vis-a-vis* other enterprises and the banking system has been increased to a maximum of twice the 22 per cent basic bank rate.[5] More generally, if the government expects to get inflation down during the year, it should underpin that expectation by lending over the medium term at interest rates which embody that expectation of lower inflation and therefore lower

[5] However, in Hungary the marginal cost of borrowing to enterprises is of the order 30--40 per cent and therefore automatic borrowing at 44 per cent through cumulating arrears may still be preferred to negotiated borrowing at 40 per cent. Twice the actual borrowing rate would be a preferable penal rate.

subsequent monthly rates of interest, instead of lending mostly on variable monthly rates as was done in Poland.

4.6 Exchange Rate Regimes and Exchange Rate Policies

Joshua Greene and Peter Isard (1991, p. 9) identify four prerequisites for successful currency convertibility: ``(1) an appropriate exchange rate; (2) an adequate level of international liquidity; (3) sound macroeconomic policies, including the elimination of any monetary overhang; and (4) an environment in which economic agents have both the incentives and the ability to respond to market prices, from which all major distortions should have been eliminated." Paul Seabright (1991) shows that the fourth condition was not satisfied when East Germany and Poland adopted a convertible currency. Managers of state-owned firms have little or no incentive to respond appropriately to changes in market signals.

Given that Eastern European countries are likely to adopt or have already adopted convertible currencies before satisfying these preconditions, some restrictive transitional measures are essential. Since large inflows or outflows of foreign capital can be destabilising, there is certainly a case for delaying liberalisation of capital account transactions for a decade or so, as recommended also in the case of interest rate liberalisation. Indeed, interest rate liberalisation must precede capital account liberalisation. Assuming that government budgets in all Eastern European countries will be under strain for the next five years or so, there is likely to be some reliance on implicit taxes on the financial sector through reserve requirements, etc. Until Eastern Europe can afford to relinquish this easily and cheaply collected revenue source, financial sectors will suffer from negative effective protection. Hence, competition from aboard should be restrained if healthy domestic financial systems are to be developed.

Although the exchange rate should be pegged until capital account liberalisation occurs, this does not imply that the exchange rate should also be used as the nominal anchor. In the dislocated economies of Eastern Europe, the exchange rate is far from the pervasive price that it is thought to be in the West. Even in the West, vast price variations still exist despite conditions of relatively free trade. In other words, the exchange rate can hardly be relied upon to anchor an economy in which competition is limited, marketing nonexistent and communications appalling. This segmentation in the economies of Eastern Europe also implies that monetary and exchange rate policies are not nearly so tightly intertwined as they are in the West. Not only are capital controls in place in most Eastern European countries, but the effects of monetary policy do not ripple smoothly across the economic pond; the ripples are absorbed by many dense clumps of weed.

With surprising speed, four of the seven Eastern European countries have adopted convertible currencies and liberalised interest rates as part of dramatic reform programmes. Without substantial official foreign exchange reserves or liberalised capital transactions, however, exchange rate policy faces inherent difficulties. Without a credible level of official foreign exchange reserves, the exchange rate inevitably has to float. Without a liberalised capital account, which enables stabilising speculation, the ensuing exchange rate fluctuations can be destabilising.

The Polish experience suggests that internal convertibility for current account transactions is within closer reach than previously thought. This does not imply that, in the words of the CSFR Minister of Finance Václav Klaus: ``The only problem with convertibility is to declare it." Obviously there is no point in any exchange rate manoeuvre unless there are market-clearing prices, subsidies have been eliminated or very substantially reduced on tradable goods and services, and there are significant elasticities of demand and supply with respect to prices (Nuti 1991). In Poland, the simultaneous price liberalisation and reduction of subsidies, together with the presence of a significant private sector and the hardening of budget constraints in the state sector, ensured that these preconditions were satisfied. They were also satisfied in the CSFR on 1 January 1991 when limited convertibility was also introduced, without a private sector and therefore with more limitations than in Poland.

Caution dictates the choice of general current account convertibility for residents only. Peter Bofinger (1991, p. 245) argues that current account convertibility is indispensable for the following reasons:

1. It is the only rapid way of achieving an undistorted price structure.

2. It enables foreign competition to stimulate competition in domestic markets without prior internal structural adjustments. The elimination of monopoly profits puts downward pressure on the price level. This should not be confused with any anticipated effects of a fixed exchange rate on the rate of change in the price level.

3. It provides a temporary substitute for privatisation by enabling hard budget constraints to be imposed.

4. It enables regional trade flows to be maintained without establishing a new administered payments system.

5. It enables the exchange rate to be used as a nominal anchor.

In our view and in the light of the Polish experience, the use of the exchange rate as a nominal anchor should be excluded as an argument in favour of current account convertibility.

Having opted for general current-account convertibility for residents after domestic price liberalisation has occurred, we turn to the choice of exchange rate regime. In our view, priority must be given to export promotion. Hence, exporters must be assured of a reasonably conducive and stable real exchange rate. Under certain circumstances, however, real exchange rate rules can destabilise domestic prices (Aghevli, Khan and Montiel 1991, p. 11). If a real exchange rate rule is adopted, there is one less nominal anchor. Rather than sacrifice exporters and potential exporters at the altar of price stability, we believe that other nominal anchors should be strengthened. In other words, monetary policy and fiscal discipline should be assigned to stabilise domestic prices, while the exchange rate is used to foster an export response. Logically, only one nominal anchor is needed. However, there is no denying that in certain circumstances a commitment to manage the exchange rate flexibly to provide confidence to exporters may undermine credibility in the government's commitment to price stability.

If a fixed exchange rate system is adopted to reduce inflationary expectations, gross exchange rate misalignment must be avoided. As the recent Polish experience shows, devaluation should not be postponed simply as part of an anti-inflationary strategy. By the time devaluation is warranted, it is too late to use the exchange rate as a nominal anchor. In our view, a crawling peg is preferable to a fixed exchange rate subject to disruptive devaluation. The choice of currency for the exchange rate peg is undoubtedly of second-order importance. Weight should be given to the predominant currencies of invoice and to risk-reduction through the use of a currency basket. A peg to some currency basket has the advantage of removing the exchange rate from the limelight, since small exchange rate changes occur continually against all currencies. In the present circumstances of most Eastern European countries, the precise content of such a basket really does not matter.

Finally, there is the issue of the initial exchange rate level. We argue that a moderate overdepreciation is preferable to underdepreciation. Some undervaluation of the domestic currency may be necessary to establish the credibility of convertibility.[6] Hence, the initial exchange rate should err on the side of undervaluing the domestic currency, but not by an excessive amount.[7]

---

[6] Seabright (1991) points out that in 1990 an undervalued exchange rate in Poland and an overvalued exchange rate in East Germany both produced perverse responses by state-owned firms. In the German case, however, the real wage was fixed by reference to the federal level because of labour mobility. Hence, the German exchange rate had wealth effects but could not have affected East German competitiveness.

[7] The exchange rate may have to be set at a rate that depreciates the domestic currency considerably more than the purchasing power parity (PPP) rate. In fact, PPP is not a good guide to the initial

The ensuing crawl can then proceed at a slower rate than the inflation rate, thus appreciating the currency in real terms until it finds its equilibrium level. Credibility of convertibility with respect to domestic holders of dollars as well as foreign and domestic firms is initially low, but it grows as convertibility is maintained. This gradual credibility enhancement allows real appreciation of the currency, which would not be possible were the currency initially pegged at a more appreciated rate; the equilibrium rate rises because of increasing confidence. Yugoslavia fixed a realistic exchange rate which could not have been maintained, even in the absence of civil unrest, precisely because it was not undervalued. There is no point in introducing convertibility if it cannot be maintained.

Notwithstanding the need for some undervaluation of the domestic currency for the sake of credibility, the exchange rate for hard currency should not be pitched at the level prevailing in the free market. The free price in a two-tier free/controlled market is always more depreciated than the single price which would prevail in a completely free market. Some undervaluation is necessary but is expensive because it leads to distress exports, worsens the terms of trade, raises domestic inflation and unnecessarily reduces real wages. In any case, a nominal exchange rate is a bad anchor if, as in the Polish case, further inflation is expected and, moreover, cannot be controlled. A combination of a real wage policy and a floating exchange rate (as in the Bulgarian programme of February 1991) or, better, a crawling peg, appears to be preferable. The Polish crawling peg introduced in September 1991 appears too rigid and slow to eliminate inflation-induced real exchange rate fluctuations in the future.

4.7 Trade Liberalisation

Trade liberalisation and financial stability are arguably the two most crucial elements in all successful structural adjustment programmes. After comparing East Asia with Latin America, Bernardo Villegas (1990, p. 16) concludes: "It is not enough ... to invest new capital efficiently; the economy must also be able to generate the foreign exchange needed to carry the international borrowing. Heavy borrowing from international markets can rarely be sustained without a strong export program in a country's development strategy."

The most effective way to stimulate exports is to liberalise imports. After surveying the evidence, Max Corden (1987, p. 260) finds: "In general,

---

exchange rate for three reasons: the equilibrium rate is affected by stock equilibrium, which in Polish-type conditions may require a more depreciated rate than flow equilibrium; PPP includes nontradables; more important, PPP is an average concept whereas competitiveness is a marginal one, i.e., what counts are the elasticities of supply and demand for tradables at the margin.

trade liberalization requires devaluation. It is thus particularly important to think of trade liberalization and exchange rate adjustment as representing a policy package." Import liberalisation raises the demand for the foreign exchange earned by exporters. Under a floating exchange rate system, import liberalisation automatically depreciates the domestic currency so increasing export profitability and competitiveness. Under a managed exchange rate system, import liberalisation necessitates the adoption of a realistic exchange rate policy to prevent the depletion of foreign exchange reserves. Indeed, wherever the premium in the black market for foreign exchange exceeds 10 per cent, substantial export growth should be possible through the liberalisation of the foreign trade and payments systems.

With respect to the importance of the real exchange rate, Peter Quirk (1990, p. 121) concludes: ``Successful structural adjustment in East Asian economies has been widely associated with the competitiveness of their export industries. Exchange rate policies in this region have had one major element in common over the past two or three decades: regardless of whether the official exchange rates have been pegged or flexibly managed, they have deviated little from rates in domestic free or black markets for foreign exchange." In other words, official exchange rates have been kept at or close to their market equilibrium levels in these countries.

CONCLUSION

Major changes have already occurred in the central Eastern European economies in transition. Of crucial concern for the conduct of monetary and exchange rate policies are the exploding government deficits in these countries. Not only are state-owned firms no longer providing government revenue as before, but also their management has not been given incentives to react appropriately to market signals. Both the inflationary potential of rising government deficits and the poor performance of state-owned firms constrain the choices of appropriate monetary and exchange rate policies.

In the present circumstances, we have suggested that monetary and exchange rate policies in Eastern Europe should be both subordinate to and consistent with the fiscal stance. An inflationary fiscal position dictates a crawling peg exchange rate to ensure continued competitiveness of export industries. It also necessitates an interest rate policy that actively maintains positive real interest rates on deposits and new loans from the banking system. Given that the financial sector will be subject to negative effective protection both from reserve requirements and from old low-interest earning loans (not to mention the increasing burden of nonperforming assets), we are dubious of any rapid adoption of currency convertibility for capital account transactions.

Looking on the brighter side, however, the lessons from East and Southeast Asia suggest that postponing liberalisation of both financial systems and foreign exchange regimes does not necessarily hinder economic growth. Provided monetary and exchange rate policies simulate competitive free-market prices under an outwardly orientated trade regime, full currency convertibility and financial liberalisation can be introduced gradually as stability is achieved and maintained. Letting the real side dictate the speed of financial liberalisation and the opening of the capital account appears eminently sensible.

REFERENCES

Aghevli, Bijan, Mohsin S. Khan and Peter J. Montiel (1991), *Exchange Rate Policy in Developing Countries: Some Analytical Issues* (Washington, DC: International Monetary Fund, Occasional Paper 78, March 1991).

Aghevli, Bijan and Jorge Márquez-Ruarte (1987), ``A Case of Successful Adjustment in a Developing Country: Korea's Experience During 1980--84" in *Economic Adjustment: Policies and Problems* edited by Frank Holmes (Washington, DC: International Monetary Fund, 1987), pp. 91--113.

Asian Development Bank (1985), *Improving Domestic Resource Mobilization through Financial Development* (Manila: Asian Development Bank, Economics Office, September 1985).

Black, Stanley W. (1991), ``External Resources for Development and International Capital Markets," *Asian Development Review*, 9(1), 1991, pp. 1--14.

Bofinger, Peter (1990), ``The Role of Monetary Policy in the Process of Economic Reform in Eastern Europe" (London: Centre for Economic Policy Research, Discussion Paper No. 457, August 1990).

Bofinger, Peter (1991), ``Options for the Payments and Exchange-Rate System in Eastern Europe," *European Economy: The Path of Reform in Central and Eastern Europe*, Special Edition No. 2, 1991, pp. 243--261.

Corden, W. Max (1987) *Protection and Liberalization: A Review of Analytical Issues* (Washington, DC: International Monetary Fund, Occasional Paper No. 54, 1987).

Cottarelli, Carlo and Mario Blejer (1991), ``Forced Savings and Repressed Inflation in the Soviet Union: Some Empirical Results" (Washington, DC: International Monetary Fund, March 1991).

Fry, Maxwell J. (1988), *Money, Interest, and Banking in Economic Development* (Baltimore: Johns Hopkins University Press, 1988).

Fry, Maxwell J. (1989), ``Foreign Debt Instability: An Analysis of National Saving and Domestic Investment Responses to Foreign Debt Accumulation in 28 Developing Countries," *Journal of International Money and Finance*, 8(3), September 1989, pp. 315--344.

Fry, Maxwell J. (1991), ``Domestic Resource Mobilization in Developing Asia: Four Policy Issues," *Asian Development Review*, 9(1), 1991, pp. 15--39.

Garvy, George (1968), *Money, Banking, and Credit in Eastern Europe* (New York: Federal Reserve Bank of New York, 1968).

Greene, Joshua E. and Peter Isard (1991), *Currency Convertibility and the Transformation of Centrally Planned Economies* (Washington, DC: International Monetary Fund, Occasional Paper 81, June 1991).

Grosfeld, Irena and Paul Hare (1991), ``Privatisation in Hungary, Poland and Czechoslovakia," *European Economy*, (48), May 1991, pp. 131--146.

Harberger, Arnold C. (1981), ``In Step and Out of Step with the World Inflation: A Summary History of Countries, 1952--1976" in *Development in an Inflationary World* edited by M. June Flanders and Assaf Razin (New York: Academic Press, 1981), pp. 35--46.

Harberger, Arnold C. and Sebastian Edwards (1980), ``International Evidence on the Sources of Inflation" (Chicago: University of Chicago, Department of Economics, December 1980).

Kopits, George (1991), ``Fiscal Reform in European Economies in Transition" (Washington, DC: International Monetary Fund, WP/91/43, April 1991).

Kornai, János (1980), *Economics of Shortage* (Amsterdam: North-Holland, 1980).

Kornai, János (1986), ``The Hungarian Reform Process: Visions, Hopes, and Reality," *Journal of Economic Literature*, 24(4), December 1986, pp. 1687--1737.

Kornai, János (1990), *The Road to a Free Economy* (New York: Norton, 1990).

McKinnon, Ronald I. (1991), *The Order of Economic Liberalization: Financial Control in the Transition to a Market Economy* (Baltimore: Johns Hopkins University Press, 1991).

McKinnon, Ronald I. and Donald J. Mathieson (1981), ``How to Manage a Repressed Economy," *Princeton Essays in International Finance*, (145), December 1981.

Nam, Sang-Woo (1989), ``Liberalization of the Korean Financial and Capital Markets" in *Korea's Macroeconomic and Financial Policies* edited by Korea Development Institute (Seoul: Korea Development Institute, 1989), pp. 133--171.

Nuti, Domenico Mario (1989), ``Hidden and Repressed Inflation in Soviet-Type Economies: Definitions, Measurements and Stabilisation" in *Models of Disequilibrium and Shortage in Centrally Planned Economies* edited by Christopher Davis and Wojciech W. Charemza (London: Chapman and Hall, 1989), pp. 101--146.

Nuti, Domenico Mario (1990), ``Privatisation of Socialist Economies: General Issues and the Polish Case" in *The Transformation of Planned Economies* edited by Hans Bloomenstein and Michael Marrese (Paris: Organisation for Economic Co-operation and Development, 1990), pp. 51--68.

Nuti, Domenico Mario (1991), ``How Quickly Should Convertibility bBe Introduced? A Comment on Jacques J. Polak and Friedrich Levcik" in *Currency Convertibility in Eastern Europe* edited by John Williamson (Washington, DC: Institute for International Economics, 1991), pp. 48--55.

Organisation for Economic Co-operation and Development (1991), ``Transition Issues in Central and Eastern Europe" (Paris: Organisation for Economic Co-operation and Development, Economics and Statistics Department, September 1991).

Patrick, Hugh T. (1990), ``The Financial Development of Taiwan, Korea, and Japan: A Framework for Consideration of Issues" (Taipei: Academia Sinica, Institute of Economics, Conference on Financial Development in Japan, Korea and Taiwan, 27--28 August 1990, August 1990).

Polak, Jacques J. (1989), *Financial Policies and Development* (Paris: Development Centre of the Organisation for Economic Co-operation and Development, 1989).

Quirk, Peter (1990), ``Exchange Rate Policies and Management: A Model for Successful Structural Adjustment" in *Strategies for Structural Adjustment: The Experience of Southeast Asia* edited by Ungku A. Aziz (Washington, DC: International Monetary Fund, 1987), pp. 99--126.

Seabright, Paul ``Exchange Rate Management When There Are Failures of Corporate Control: Dilemmas for Reforming Economies in Eastern Europe" (Cambridge: Churchill College, 1991).

United Nations Economic Commission for Europe (1991), *The ECE Economies in Mid--1991* (New York: United Nations Commission for Europe, July 1991).

Villegas, Bernardo M. (1990), ``Economic Adjustment, Financing, and Growth in Southeast Asia During the 1980s" in *Strategies for Structural Adjustment: The Experience of Southeast Asia* edited by Ungku A. Aziz (Washington, DC: International Monetary Fund, 1990), pp. 16--38.

Williamson, John (1991), *The Economic Opening of Eastern Europe* (Washington, DC: Institute for International Economics, Policies Analyses in International Economics 31, May 1991).

CHAPTER 4

P* AND INFLATION CONTROL: LESSONS FROM FRANCE AND GERMANY

Christian Bordes, Eric Girardin and Velayoudom Marimoutou

INTRODUCTION

Central banks of the so-called "emerging market oriented economies" [EMEO] must be provided with the tools necessary to conduct monetary policy in a way that gives central attention to monetary stability [see, for example, Crow (1990)]. There are two ways in which this objective can be attained : 1) membership of a fixed exchange rate system where the nominal anchor is provided by a virtuous foreign central bank; 2) the use of domestic monetary targeting emphasizing the role of domestic indicators and intermediate targets.These two solutions are not exclusive from each other. For example since 1979 the French strategy of fighting inflation has been based on its membership of the ERM and the regular publishing of monetary targets.

The role of exchange rate policy as a means of ensuring price stability has been the subject of several studies (see other contributions to this volume). We will examine here the contribution of monetary targeting to the achievement of this objective. More precisely, we propose an evaluation of P-star, which is one of the main candidates to the function of monetary indicator. Indeed, P-star is very attractive since it is the monetary indicator used by the Bundesbank, whose success in fighting inflation constitutes a reference. Under such conditions, one must consider whether this monetary indicator could be used as well by other central banks. The answer lies mainly on the empirical side. This represents a major difficulty as far as former planned economies are concerned since they are now experiencing substantial economic and institutional transformations. At the present time it would be rather difficult to try and establish long term econometric relationships between monetary variables and prices. Therefore, we decided to focus our analysis of the robustness of P-star as a monetary indicator on a careful investigation of the experience of countries which can be considered

* comments from participants at a workshop at the University of Birmingham where this paper was originally presented helped to improve it. We remain solely responsible for all remaining errors.

as representative of the future functionning of EMOE. We thus examine two West-Europan countries : Germany and France. The choice of Germany is obvious as far as price stability is concerned. The choice of France is due to the fact that it represents the example of a country which succeeded during the eighties in ending a long tradition of high inflation.

Recently Hallman, Porter and Small (1989) suggested to use a measure of the long run level of prices, named P-star, as an indicator of monetary conditions. This indicator should enable to evaluate the inflationary or deflationary character of monetary conditions prevailing in a given economy. More specificaly, P-Star should provide a forecast of future movements in the aggregate price level. The same study contains an application to the U.S. case which emphasizes the relevance and the fruitfulness of such a concept. Subsequently, similar works were implemented for the U.K., Japan and Germany, showing also the fruitfulness of P-star as an indicator of monetary conditions.

The present study offers a new approach to the measurement of P-Star and its application to the French and German cases. In the first section we introduce this concept by setting it up in the general context of a monetary explanation of inflation. The specification adopted here is more general than the usual one and leads to an explanation of price increases in the long run as well as in the short run. In the second section we implement econometric tests which imply that the gap between the equilibrium value of the aggregate price level generated by the model and its actual value can be used as a basis for a forecast of future movements in the overall price level.

1. The model

The P - Star concept is part of the Quantity Theory of money (QT) according to which [see Humphrey (1989)] long term movements in the aggregate price level are determined by long term movements in the excess supply of money as measured with respect to real income. The QT acknowledges that price movements are also a function of the velocity of circulation of money, but the latter depends in the long run on institutional factors and changes only slowly. In the short run the aggregate price level can deviate from this equilibrium relationship, but forces then come into play to bring back prices towards their long term equilibrium level.

1.1 The Quantity Theory of money

In its general form the Quantity Theory model can be expressed as follows [1]:

$$(1)\quad p_t = m_t - q_t + v_t$$

$$(2)\quad v_t = \beta_0 + \beta_1 i_t + \varepsilon_t$$

we note p the aggregate price level, m the money supply, v the velocity of circulation of money, and i the rate of interest. All variables, except the rate of interest are in logarithm. The residuals (ε_t) are assumed to be stationary, with zero average.

The combination of these two equations gives the reduced form of the model :

$$(3)\quad p_t = \beta_0 + \beta_1 i_t + m_t - q_t + \varepsilon_t$$

The QT implies that there exists a long term relationship between the movement of the aggregate price level and the variation in the supply of money, real income and the rate of interest. Thus, the QT implies a cointegrating relationship between the aggregate price level, money supply, real income and the rate of interest. It is thus possible to use an error correction model (ECM) to represent short term movements in prices [Engle et Granger (1987)]. We have :

$$(4)\quad \Delta p_t = v_0 + v_1 \varepsilon_{t-1} + \sum_{j=1}^{n} v_{j+1} \Delta p_{t-j}$$

where Δ p refers to the rate of inflation.

1.2. The P-Star Model

The P-Star model is a specific case of this general QT model. It relies on the assumption that in the long run the velocity of circulation of money is

---

1 On the Quantity Theory of money, see for instance Fry (1990) or Laidler (1991).

independent of the rate of interest and fluctuates randomly, around a constant mean. Equation (2) is transformed as follows :

$$(5)\quad v_t = v^* + \varepsilon_t$$

The long term price equation then becomes :

$$(6)\quad p_t = v^* + m_t - q_t + \varepsilon_t$$

The long run equilibrium value of the overall price level, p*, is then obtained by replacing in equation (5) the actual value of output and velocity by their "long run value" [Hallman, Porter and Small (1989)]. It is thus assumed that the overall price level tends in the long run towards the P* value corresponding to the following equation :

$$(7)\quad P^* = \frac{M \, . \, V^*}{Q^*}$$

where M measures the supply of money, Q* long run output, V* the long term velocity of money. Thus, P* is the long run equilibrium value of the aggregate price level for given values of the money supply and of long run output. We have :

$$(8)\quad \frac{V^*}{Q^*} = k$$

where k is a constant term. This implies that movements of P* are strictly proportional to those of M. In the long run, the actual value of P tends to come closer to P* and the ratio (P*/P) is an indicator of future movements of prices. If it is durably greater than one, we should expect an acceleration in inflation; otherwise, we should anticipate its deceleration.

In order to analyse the short term movements in prices, the following model is used :

$$(9)\quad \Delta p_t = \nu_0 + \nu_1 \left[p_{t-1} - p^*_{t-1}\right] + \sum_{j=1}^{n} \nu_{j+1} \; \Delta p_{t-j}$$

where p* is the log of the long term equilibrium value of the overall price level defined by equation (10) :

$$(10)\quad p^*_t = m_t + v^*_t - q^*_t$$

1.3. Empirical studies on the measurement and the performance of P*

1.3. 1 Approaches to the measurement of P*.

To measure the long run value of output, Q*, Hallman, Porter and Small (1989) use potential GNP with alternative estimates from the Federal Reserve Board and the Bureau of Economic Analysis. Noting that the GNP velocity of M2 was relatively trendless over the last thirty years, Hallman, Porter and Small then determine V* by computing the mean of V2 over their sample period (1955:1-1988:1), which implies that V* is a constant (equal to 1.6 for the U.S.) in their model, or that P* is proportional to M2 per unit of potential output. [2]

Three series of difficulties are raised by such estimates of V* and Q*. The first two stem from the fact that these estimates leave aside the time series properties of these variables. The third one has to do with the use of independent estimates of V* and Q*.

A number of studies have tried to abandon the assumption of a constant V*. Thus at the Federal Reserve itself, Kole and Leahy (1991) have departed from this assumption in their study of Germany and Japan, since in the latter two countries the income velocity of the key monetary aggregate seems to exhibit a downward trend. Indeed, for Japan, the Bank of Japan (1990) computed V* as a simple deterministic trend [having checked for the stationarity of velocity around it by an Augmented Dickey-Fuller test].[3] In their study of the United Kingdom, Hannah and James (1989) use segmented deterministic trends for V*, with a trend rate of growth of velocity equal to 3% per year from 1961 to 1973 and to 4.25% thereafter. In a different setting, not directly related to the P* model, Bohmhoff (1991) uses a Kalman filter technique to estimate a relationship between the level of V and the level of the interest rate for M1 and M2 in all the Group of seven countries with annual data from the 1950's to the end of the 1980's. This specification points to a non-constant trend in velocity. Pecchenino and Raasche (1990) emphasize that the assumption made by Hallman et alii on the stationarity of V2 -i.e. that V2 reverts to a constant mean- implies to assume that shocks on V2 are transitory. By contrast, one often

---

2 However they acknowledge that this assumption cannot be taken for granted. Indeed in the U.S., "since the end of 1982, the velocity of M2 has almost always been below the mean for the full sample period" [Hallman et alii (1989) p. 4]. This is explained by financial innovations.

3 Ebrill and Fries (1991) implement unit root tests for different monetary and real variables for the U.S. economy.

uses as a working hypothesis that the velocity of the money supply is a random walk, i.e. that its behavior is affected by permanent shocks to its level, which prevent it from reverting to a trend or its average.

The second difficulty with the Hallman-Porter-Small (HPS) approach, that is shared by the studies refered to above, is the fact that it provides estimates of Q* which are not based on the same method as the one used to compute V*. Thus Hannah and James (1989) for the UK use a deterministic time trend for the growth of output (supposed to be constant at the average over the period , i.e. 2.25%) as well as for the growth of velocity. However, the use of the same methodology is not sufficient since the time series properties of Q have to be taken into account, alongside those of V. Having checked for the existence of a unit-root in both series, and the absence of a deterministic trend, Hoeller and Poret (1991) then draw the logical consequence of this finding by using the Hodrick-Prescott detrending method, and compare its results with the usual fitting of a deterministic trend. They deal with all O.E.C.D. countries but give very little detail about the specification of their filters, making it difficult to evaluate their contribution.

The third difficulty with the HPS and related studies' methodology has to do with the independent estimates of V* and Q*. This difficulty was perceived by HPS who mention that estimating an ECM on inflation (or its acceleration) with P-P* as the error correction term, implies that in the long run this gap vanishes. Allen and Hall (1990) emphasize on a theoretical level that for HPS's ECM model to be valid, the difference between P and P* must be stationary. Along the same lines, Kole and Leahy (1991) empirically have difficulties in showing the existence of such a cointegration for Germany, and even more for Japan, with quarterly data over the period 1970:1-1989:4.

1.3.2. The performance of P-Star in different countries

The evaluation of the forecasting performance of P* has been the subject of numerous empirical studies. For the U.S. case, Hallman, Porter, and Small (1989) find that this performance is very good over the 1955-1988 period with M2 as a measure of money supply. The coefficients of the error correction model are stable over the whole period. When the gap between P and P^* widened, one could record, with a variable lag, an upward or downward movement in inflation. Hannah and James (1989) examined the forecasting performance of P^* in the U.K. case after 1961 using M0 as a measure of money supply Their main conclusion is that M0 represented a good leading indicator of inflation. (P*/P) was greater than one at the beginning of the seventies, anticipating the acceleration in inflation in 1972 and at the end of this same decade.

Subsequently, (P*/P) fell under one announcing the subsequent disinflation. The application of P - Star to Japan [Bank of Japan (1990)] generates two conclusions (i) movements in P* are very similar to observed movements in the overall price level ; (ii) P - Star can be considered as a simple though useful and complete indicator of potential pressures on prices. Recently, the Bundesbank suggested an application of P-Star to the German economy [Bundesbank (1992)]. A number of transformations were made to the model. Thus the error correction model is specified in yearly variations and not in quarterly ones. Moreover, the rate of inflation depends not only on monetary conditions but also on production costs. "The comparison between $(P^* - P)$ and the rates of variation of the overall price level suggests that the gap $(P^* - P)$ is an indicator of future movements of prices and announces their turning points" [Bundesbank (1992), p. 24].

2. Implementation of the approach for France and Germany

The previous theoretical analysis generates three main teachings to be used in implementing an empirical analysis :

- First, one should study the time series properties of the price level, of money supply, output and the rate of interest by implementing unit-root tests;
- In case these series were non-stationary in level, one could consider as a second stage a representation of the long term movement of prices conforming to equation (3) leading to a cointegration test between these variables.
- In case the cointegration hypothesis is accepted, one could use a specification similar to equation (4), where the gap between the long run equilibrium value of the overall price level and its actual value plays a leading role.

This modelling strategy is applied in the following in turn to the French and German experience over the seventies and the eighties. Apart from the very general comparative study by Hoeller and Poret (1991) mentioned above, to this day this has not been attempted for France . The most widely used explanations of French inflation rely on non-monetary factors and the Bank of France never considered using an indicator such as P-Star for its monetary policy[4] . However, in the perspective of European Monetary Union, and given the interest raised by P-Star among German monetary authorities, it seems worth while to try and get

---

4 A critical analysis P^* was made in a technical note of the Bank of France [Raffin (1989)]

some indication of the way in which this indicator performs in France as well as in Germany, when consistently constructed along the lines suggested above.

2.1. The French case

2.1.1. Unit-root tests

The first stage of the procedure consists in examining the statistical properties of the different time series used. Table 1 gives the results of unit-root tests implemented for real GDP (y), its deflator (p), the rate of interest on government bonds (i), and money supply (M1). According to studies of money demand in France, [see Bordes and Strauss-Kahn (1989)], M1 indeed seems to be the best definition of money supply.

All variables are I(1) as required by the procedure used here. Moreover, the joint hypothesis of unit-root with no constant and no trend is accepted for all variables except economic activity and the M1 monetary aggregate.

Table 1 : Unit-root tests for France (1971:2 - 1990:4)

$$\Delta X_t = a + bT + cX_{t-1} + \Delta \sum_{j=1}^{4} d_j X_{t-j} + \varepsilon_t$$

X_t	τ_τ	Φ_2	Φ_3
p	0.10	2.18	2.82
y	– 3.04	6.59	5.10
i	– 1.49	1.03	1.53
m1	0.19	5.13	5.22

$$\Delta^2 X_t = \alpha + \beta\ T + \varphi\ \Delta X_{t-1} + \omega\ \Delta^2\ X_{t-1} + \nu_t$$

	p	q	i	m1
τ	- 3,37	- 4,81	-4.19	-8.35

Note : p is the GDP deflator ; y is GDP at constant prices ; m1 corresponds to money supply ; i is the long term interest rates on government bonds ; all variables, except for interest rates are in logarithm ; τ_τ is the value of the statistic suggested by Dickey and Fuller (1979) to test the hypothesis c = 0 , the critical values of which, computed by Mac Kinnon are -4.07 (1%) ; -3.46 (5%) ; -3.15 (10%); Φ_2 is the value of the statistic suggested by Dickey and Fuller (1981) to test the hypothesis a = b = c = 0, the critical values of which are given in Table V of Dickey-Fuller (1981, p.1063) ; Φ_3 is the value of the statistic suggested by Dickey and Fuller (1981) to test the hypothesis b = c = 0, the critical values of which are given in Table VI in Dickey and Fuller (1981, p. 1063).

However, for the latter two variables, the joint hypothesis of unit-root and no trend is accepted. The lower part of Table 1 shows that our variables are stationary in first differences.

2.1.2 Cointegration

Results of the single equation estimation of the long term price equations are given in Table 2. . The cointegration test is first implemented with the Augmented Dickey-Fuller (ADF) : the absolute value of the statistic is smaller than critical values corresponding to the 5 % level (part (iii) of table 2). However, an F test implies that taking into account laggged values of the variation in residuals of the long term equation is illegitimate; it is thus better to test the cointegration hypothesis using a simple Dickey-Fuller (DF) test. This assumption cannot be rejected at the 5 % level. Then we can accept the existence of a long term relationship between money supply and the equilibrium value of the overall price level.

Estimated values of coefficients have expected signs and size. The money supply coefficient implies that in the long run a higher rate of growth of money supply is linked with an increase in inflation. The activity coefficient is nearer from minus unity, which implies that in the long run an increase in real growth is disinflationary about one for one. The long term rate of interest exerts a positive effect on prices. One may then consider that the interest rate coefficient reflects the influence on prices of long term movements in the velocity of money. A permanent increase in the rate of interest would generate a permanent decrease in the desired value of money balances, i.e. an increase in the velocity of money with inflationary implications. This equation is thus in line with a P-star model where the interest rate is taken into account in order to explain long term movements in velocity. More specificaly, it confirms that movements of P* are a good indicator of long term movements in the overall price level. We now have to see whether (P-P*) can also be considered as a good indicator of the short run movements in the price level. This requires to estimate an error correction model.

Table 2: Cointegration tests for France: 1971:2-1990:4
(M1 monetary aggregate)

i) estimated values of the coefficients of long term equations[a] **:**

$$p = \omega_0 + \omega_1 m + \omega_2 q + \omega_3 i + \omega_4 T + \omega_5 D1 + \omega_6 D2 + \omega_7 D3 + \varepsilon_t$$

ω_0	ω_1	ω_2	ω_3	ω_4	ω_5	ω_6	ω_7
1.819	0.849	-0.981	0.008	0.006	0.049	0.035	0.043

T = linear trend; Di = seasonal dummy (i=1,..,3) for first, second and third quarter.

ii) Autocorrelation coefficients of ε_t **:**

1	2	3	4	5	6	7	8	9	10
0.402	0.003	-0.09	-0.06	-0.17	-0.05	0.027	-0.18	-0.02	-0.18

iii) Dickey-Fuller test :

$$\Delta\varepsilon_t = \phi\,\varepsilon_{t-1} + \sum_{j=1}^{4} \delta_j\,\Delta\varepsilon_{t-j} + \nu_t$$

Statistics	ϕ	t	F
ADF	–0.772	-4.05	0.77
DF	–0.557	-5.14	

Note : The critical value of the Augmented Dickey-Fuller test is given in Table III of Engle and Yoo (1987). In the present case it is 3.23 at 5%. F values enable to test the nul hypothesis : $\Sigma\delta_j=0$; the critical value is between 2.53 and 2.45. The critical value of the simple Dickey-Fuller test corresponds to test 2 in Engle et Granger (1987). In the present case it is 3.50 at 5%.

(a) $H_0 : \omega_0 = 0$: $F(1,71) = 20.77^*$; $H_0 : \omega_4 = 0 : F(1,71) = 41^{**}$.

Figure 1: The price gap in France : 1971:2-1990:4
(P-P* in %)

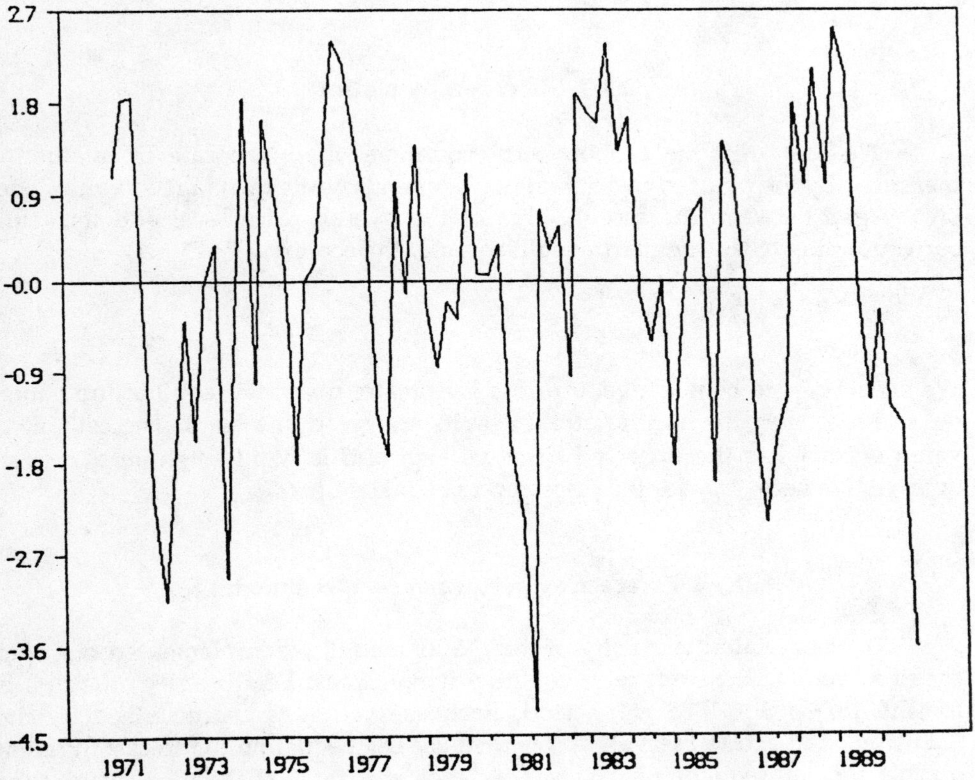

Figure 1 shows that the actual French price level was higher (or around) its long term level (P*) in 1971, and in 1975-76. Inflationary tendencies were present from early 1972 to mid 1974, and again from the end of 1977 to the end of 1979. The two following years saw the succession of deflationary (1980) and inflationary (1981) conditions, which is in line with the change in the orientation of the ruling parties. Then prices were around the P* level for about a year. A change occured at the end of 1982 with monetary conditions becoming much more restrictive until early 1984. This is particularly noticeable since traditionnaly one rather emphasizes in France the shift to wage disindexation at about the same time (see Bordes and Girardin, 1992; or Blanchard and Muet, 1993). It may be that restictive monetary conditions were as much important a factor of disinflation as wage disindexation. After a period of neutral monetary conditions, substantial restrictive ones reappeared in mid 1986, followed by expansionary conditions in 1987. Then until mid 1989 they turned quite restrictive. The last year and a half of the sample saw a build up in inflationary pressures from monetary policy.

2.1.3 Short run dynamics

We now estimate a short term equation where the rate of inflation - measured by the quarterly variation in p- depends on its own lagged values and on the gap between the actual value of the overall price level and its value corresponding to the long term equilibrium of the economy (P-P* $=\varepsilon_t$):

$$\Delta p_t = \nu_0 + \nu_1 \varepsilon_{t-1} + \sum_{j=1}^{n} \nu_{j+1} \Delta p_{t-j}$$

We expect υ_1 to be negative: if prices are greater than their equilibrium value, we expect a slowdown in inflation. Results are given in table 3. The estimated value of υ_1 has the expected negative sign and is highly significant. Seven quarters are necessary for the price gap to be made up.

2.1.4 Forecasting performance of the model

To appreciate the quality of the P-Star model, we implemented one step ahead forecasts : the short term equation is reestimated eight times : the first is for the 1971 : 3 - 1988 : 1 period. Each estimation is characterised by the inclusion of an extra observation. We then use each equation to forecast inflation during the subsequent year[5]. Forecasts of the rate of inflation were thus generated between 1989 : 1 and 1990 : 4. Results of these forecasts are given in Table 4. Over 1989-1990, the actual rate of inflation was on average 0.237 % higher than what the monetary inflation model led us to expect. This model thus gives a quite acceptable characterisation of the inflation process in the French economy.

---

[5] This method prevents us to give the usual statistics to assess the quality of the forecasts.

Table 3: Error correction mechanism for France (1971: 3 - 1990 : 4)

$$\Delta p_t = \nu_0 + \nu_1 \varepsilon_{t-1} + \sum_{j=1}^{n} \nu_{j+1} \Delta p_{t-j}$$

Coefficient	Value	t
$\upsilon 0$	0.0014	0.74
$\upsilon 1$	- 0.135	-2.87
$\upsilon 2$	0.401	3.88
$\upsilon 3$	0.235	2.08
$\upsilon 5$	0.282	2.75
R^2	0.613	
F(4,70)	28.92	
DW	2.13	
Residual autocorrelation	F (8,62) = 0.81	
ARCH	F (8,54) = 0.60	
Normality	χ^2 (2) = 0.56	
Heteroskedasticity	F(8,64) = 0.72	
Functional form	F(14,58) = 0.92	
Omitted variables (reset)	F(3,67) = 0.00	

Table 4: Actual and forecasted values of the French inflation rate
Inflation (annual rates in %)

year up to	actual (1)	forecast (2)	gap (2)-(1)
1989 : 1	3.21	2.45	0.77
1989 : 2	2.92	2.64	0.28
1989 : 3	2.55	2.37	0.19
1989 : 4	3.30	2.52	0.78
1990 : 1	2.60	3.13	-0.53
1990 : 2	3.26	3.27	-0.01
1990 : 3	2.91	3.92	-1.00
1990 : 4	2.03	4.40	-2.37
		average	-0.237

2.2. The German case

2.2.1. Unit-root tests

Unit root tests were implemented for each variable entering the long term equation with Augmented Dickey-Fuler tests. According to studies of money demand in Germany (see Trehan, 1988), M3 seems to be the best definition of money supply. We use a long term interest rate rather than a short term one. Results are presented in Table 5. For the level of each variable it is not possible to reject the hypothesis of a unit-root. However all variables are stationary in first differences.

Table 5: Unit-root tests for Germany (1975:1 - 1990:2)

$$\Delta X_t = a + bT + cX_{t-1} + \Delta \sum_{j=1}^{4} d_j X_{t-j} + \varepsilon_t$$

X_t	τ_τ	Φ_2	Φ_3
p	−0.74	5.28	1.76
y	−2.24	4.78	2.54
m3	−2.87	4.58	4.14
i	−2.23	2.07	3.10

$$\Delta^2 X_t = \alpha + \beta\ T + \varphi\ \Delta X_{t-1} + \omega\ \Delta^2\ X_{t-1} + \nu_t$$

X_t	P	y	m3	I
τ_τ	- 7,39	- 6,15	- 6,32	- 5,20

Note : p is the GDP deflator ; y is GDP at constant prices ; m3 corresponds to money supply + quasi-money ; i is the long term interest rate on government bonds ; all variables, except interest rates, are in logarithms;

τ_τ is the value of the statistic suggested by Dickey and Fuller (1979) to test the hypothesis c = 0 , the critical values of which computed by Mac Kinnon are - 4,0 (1%) ; - 3,46 (5%) ; - 3,16 (10%). Φ_2 is the value of the statistic suggested by Dickey and Fuller (1981) to test the hypothesis a = b = c = 0, the critical values of which are given in Table V of Dickey-Fuller (1981, p.1063) ; at 5% : 4.98. Φ_3 is the value of the statistic suggested by Dickey and Fuller (1981) to test the hypothesis b = c = 0, the critical values of which are given in Table VI of Dickey and Fuller (1981, p. 1063) ; at 5% : 6.58.

2.1.2. Cointegration

Results of the estimation of the long term equation for Germany[6] over the period 1975:1 - 1990:4 are given in Table 6. Estimated values of coefficients have expected signs : a higher growth of money supply and a durable increase in the short term interest rate are linked with an increase in inflation. By contrast, an increase in real growth is deflationary The cointegration test is implemented with the Augmented Dickey-Fuller (ADF). An F test indeed implies that taking into account lagged values of the variation in residuals of the long term equation is legitimate. The absolute value is smaller than critical values corresponding to the 1%, 5% and 10% levels. Then we can accept the existence of a long term relationship between money supply and the equilibrium value of the overall price level.

Table 6: Results of cointegration tests for Germany. (1975 : 1 - 1990 : 4) (monetary aggregate M3)

i) estimated values of the coefficients of the long term equation :

$$p = \beta_0 + \beta_1 m + \beta_2 q + \beta_3 i + \varepsilon_t$$

$$\beta_0 = 1.06 \ ; \beta_1 = 0.797 \ ; \quad \beta_2 = -0.717 \ ; \quad \beta_3 = 0.454$$

ii) Autocorrelation coefficients of ε_t ***:***

1	2	3	4	5	6	7	8	9	10
0.52	0.07	0.14	0.28	-0.38	0.25	-0.14	0.35	0.05	-0.00

iii) Dickey-Fuller test :

$$\Delta\varepsilon_t = \phi\, \varepsilon_{t-1} + \sum_{j=1}^{4} \delta_j \Delta\varepsilon_{t-j} + \nu_t$$

Statistic	ϕ	t	F
ADF	– 0.34	- 2.24	2.53
SDF	– 0.47	- 4.21	

Note : Critical values of the Augmented Dickey-Fuller test are given in Table III of Engle et Yoo (1987). F values enable to test the nul hypothesis : $\Sigma\ \delta_j = 0$; the critical value is between 2.53 and 2.45. The critical values of the simple Dickey-Fuller test correspond to test 2 in Engle and Granger (1987).

---

[6] In the German case, contrary to the French one, no deterministic trend appears significant

Figure 2: The price gap in Germany: 1975:1-1990:4.
(P-P* in %)

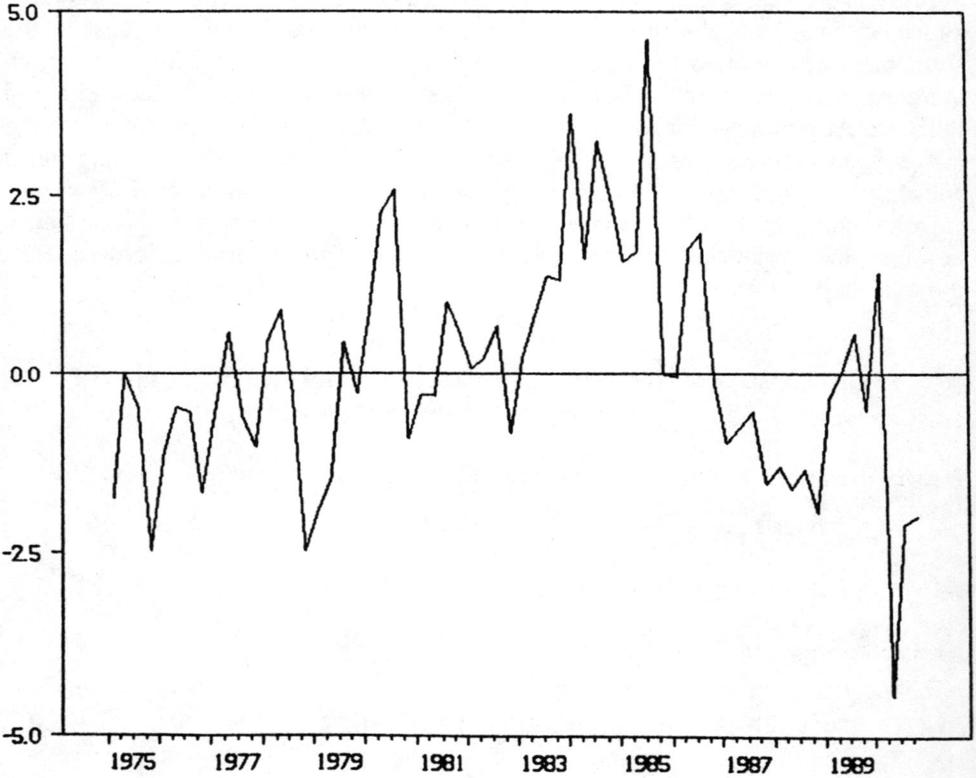

Figure 2 illustrates how the German price level was lower than its long term level from early 1975 to the end of 1977, indicating the presence of inflationary conditions. Deflationary conditions set in early 1978, and reappeared in 1980 and from mid 1981 to the third term of 1986. Inflationary pressures were present subsequently until early 1989, and again very strongly in 1990. It thus seems that there is much more persistence in the orientation in monetary conditions (i.e. in the P-P* gap) in Germany than in France.

2.2.3 Short run dynamics of German inflation

We now estimate for Germany a short term equation where the rate of inflation - measured by the yearly variation in p- depends on its own lagged values and on the lagged value ot the simple average of the gap between the actual value of the overall price level and its value corresponding to the long term equilibrium of the economy over the four previous quarters [This specification follows the work of the Bundesbank (1992)] . Results are given in Table 7. The estimated value of υ_1 has the expected negative sign and is significant at the 10% level.

Table 7: Short term equation : (1977:1 - 1990:4)

$$(1-L^4)P_t = \theta_0 + \theta_1 \left[(1/4)\sum_{i=1}^{4} \varepsilon_{t-i} \right]_{t-1} + \sum_{j=1}^{n} \theta_{j+1} (1-L^4)\, p_{t-j}$$

Coefficient	Value	t
θ_0	0.095	3.04
θ_1	- 0.132	-1.65
θ_2	0.574	4.73
θ_3	0.442	3.36
θ_5	- 0.303	-2.76
R^2	0.662	F (4, 51) = 24.9 [0.00]
DW	1.94	
Residual autocorrelation	F (4,47) = 1.35	
ARCH	F (4,43) = 1.71	
Normality	χ^2 (2) = 1.01	
Heteroscedasticity	F(8,42) = 2.49	
Functional form	F(14,36) = 2.83	
Omitted variables (reset)	F(1,50) = 0.19	

2.2.4 Forecasting performance of the model

To appreciate the quality of the P-Star model for Germany, we implement one-step ahead forecasts : the short term equation is reestimated eight times ; the first is for the 1977 : 1 - 1988 : 1 period. Each estimation is characterised by the inclusion of an extra observation. As the German model uses yearly differences each equation is then used to forecast inflation during the subsequent year ; forecasts of the rate of inflation were thus generated between 1989 : 1 and 1990 : 4. Results of these forecasts are given in Table 8. Over 1989-1990, the annual inflation rate was on average smaller by 0.3 % than what the monetary inflation model led us to expect.

Table 8: Actual and forecasted values of the German inflation rate.
Inflation (annual rate in %)

	actual	forecasted	gap	t
year up to	(1)	(2)	(2)-(1)	
1989 : 1	2.33	2.81	-0.48	-0.59
1989 : 2	2.5	3.09	-0.59	-0.73
1989 : 3	2.86	3.24	-0.38	-0.49
1989 : 4	3.01	3.29	-0.28	-0.36
1990 : 1	3.08	3.36	-0.27	-0.36
1990 : 2	3.24	3.33	-0.09	-0.12
1990 : 3	3.83	3.5	0.33	0.43
1990 : 4	3.10	3.99	-0.89	-1.14
		average	-0.331	
Forecast	$\chi8$ (8) = 0.41			
Chow	F(8,43) = 0.29	[0.96]		

Conclusion

We have suggested here to locate the P-Star model as a specific case of a more general Quantity Theory model of inflation. This relies on the fact that the usual procedure relying on an error correction model to generate a forecasting equation with the price gap as the error correction term, assumes a cointegrating relationship between P* and its determinants.

The empirical approach we implemented thus consisted in first testing for the existence of such a cointegrating relationship, so as to be allowed to estimate the error correction mechanism. The results obtained from the estimation of such a model for France and Germany over the seventies and the eighties indicate that its forecasting performance is quite accurate for both countries.

However, these results remain preliminary in as much as the forecasting performance of this model of inflation should be compared to alternative ones, built for instance along keynesian lines, and the approach should be applied to other European countries in order to assess the extent of their generality. It would also be useful to replicate the present tests in a VAR, enabling to test for weak exogeneity in the relationship between money supply and prices.

Source of the data

The source of the quarterly data used for France and Germany is OECD National Accounts (price and volume of GDP) and Main Economic Indicators (interest rates and money supply). In the French case, the OECD series for money supply shows a break in definition at the end of 1977. Preliminary tests using these series showed that they bias the results. We then used here series given to us by the SEMEF (Bank of France). These series were obtained from quarterly flow of funds accounts (MEFISTO data bank).

References

Allen, C. and Hall, S.G. (1990) : "Money as a Potential Anchor for the Price Level : A Critique of the P* Approach". *London Business School.*

Bank of Japan (1990) : "A Study of Potential Pressure on Prices : application of P* to the Japanese Economy". *Research and Statistics Department. Special Paper* n°186. February.

Blanchard, O.J. and Muet, P.A. (1993) " Competitiveness through disinflation : an assessment of the French macroeconomic strategy". *Economic Policy,* vol. 16 , April, pp. 11-56.

Bohmhoff, Eduard, J. (1991) : "Stability of Velocity in the Major Industrial Countries". International Monetary Fund, *Staff Papers.* September. Vol 38, n°3. pp. 626-642.

Bordes, C., Girardin, E (1992) : "The achievements of the ERM and the preconditions for monetary union : A French perspective", in *Monetary Union after Maastricht,* R. Barell ed, Saige Publications.

Bordes, C. and Strauss-Kahn, M.O. (1989) "Cointégration et demande de monnaie en France" *Cahiers Economiques et Monétaires,* Banque de France, 34, pp. 161-97.

Bundesbank (1992) : "The correlation between monetary growth and price movements in the Federal Republic of Germany," *Monthly Report of the Deutsche Bundesbank,* Vol. 44, No. 1, pp. 20-28.

Christiano, L.J. (1989) : "P * is not the inflation forecaster's Holy Grail," Federal Reserve Bank of Minneapolis, *Quarterly Review,* Fall, pp.3-18.

Crow, J.W. (1990) "Monetary policy and the control of inflation" in *Central Banking issues in emerging market-oriented economies,* Federal Reserve Bank of Kansas City.

Dickey, D.A. and Fuller W.A. (1979) : " Distribution of the estimators for autoregressive series with a unit root," *Journal of the American Statistical Association,* 74, pp. 427.431.

Dickey, D.A. and Fuller W.A. (1981) : "Likelihood ratio statistics for autoregressive time series with a unit root," *Econometrica,* 49, pp. 1057-1072.

Ebrill, L.P. and Fries, S.M. (1991) : "Broad money growth and inflation in the United states". International Monetary Fund, *Staff Papers.* vol. 38, n° 4. December, pp. 736-750.

Engle, R. F. and Granger, C. W. (1987) : "Co-integration and error correction : Representation, estimation, and testing, " *Econometrica,* 55, pp. 251-276.

Engle, R.F. and Yoo, B.S. (1987) : "Forecasting and testing in co-integrated systems," *Journal of Econometrics,* 35, pp. 143-159.

Fry, M.J. (1990) "Money - hard and soft", The University of Birmingham, *Inaugural Lecture,* December 5th.

Hallman, J.J., Porter R.D. and Small D.H. (1989) : "M2 per unit of potential GNP as an anchor for the price level," *Board of Governors of the Federal Reserve System,* Staff Sudy, No.157.

Hallman, J.J., Porter, R.D. and Small, D.H. (1991) : "Is the price level tied to the M2 monetary aggregate in the long run", *American Economic Review,* September, pp. 841-858.

Hannah, S. and James, A. (1989) : "P - Star as a monetary indicator for the UK," *National Westminster Capital Markets Report.*

Hendershott ,P.H. (1968) : *The neutralized money stock : An unbiased measure of Federal Reserve policy actions,* Richard D. Irwin Inc. Homewood, Illinois, 1968.

Hoeller, Peter and Poret, Pierre, (1991) : "P-Star as an Indicator of Inflationnary Pressure". *OECD Economic Review.* n°17. Autumn. pp. 7-32.

Humphrey, T.M. (1989) : "Precursors of the P - Star model," Federal Reserve Bank of Richmond, *Economic Review,* July - August, pp. 3-9.

Kole, Linda, S. and Leahy, Michael, P. (1991) : "The Usefulness of P* Measures for Japan and Germany". Board of Governors of the Federal Reserve System. *International Finance Discussion Papers.* n°414. November.

Kuttner, K. N. (1990) : "Inflation and the rate of growth of money," Federal Reserve Bank of Chicago, *Economic Perspectives,* January - February, pp. 2-10.

Laidler, D. (1991) : "The quantity theory is always and everywhere controversial - Why ?" *The Economic Record,* December, pp. 289-305.

Mehra, Y.P. (1989) : "Cointegration and a test of the quantity theory of money," *Federal Reserve Bank of Richmond, Working Paper 89 - 2.*

Pecchenino, R.A. and Rasche, Robert, H. (1990) : "P* Type Models : Evaluation and Forecasts". *NBER Working Papers*. n°3406. August.

Raffin, J. (1989) : "Un nouvel indicateur pour la politique monétaire américaine: P* ", *Banque de France,* Direction Générale des Etudes, Service des Economies Etrangères, *Internal Memo,* August, 18th.

Trehan, B. (1988) "The practice of monetary targeting : a case study of the west German experience", Federal Reserve bank of San Francisco, *Economic Review,* Spring, n°2, pp. 30-44.

CHAPTER 5

AN EMPIRICAL INVESTIGATION OF BANKING RISKS IN EC COUNTRIES

D. Goyeau
and
A.Tarazi

INTRODUCTION

The purpose of this paper is the investigation of bank risk in Europe in the light of european monetary union. The need for a homogeneous banking system in order to ensure similar reactions to shocks is broadly recognized. Using accounting data concerning individual british, french, german, italian, and spanish banks, a measure related to the probability of failure is computed to assess bank risk. The main feature of the measure used is that it simultaneously deals with both the effect of asset risk and the effect of leverage on default risk. Moreover compared with traditional measures, the effect on risk of asset and liability structure is also taken into account. Empirical evidence indicates changes in the level of risk of european banking systems throughout the 1980s. Our findings show similar levels of failure risk in the early 80s, and point out an increase in risk for France, Spain and the U.K. and a decrease in risk for Germany and Italy later on. However the case of Germany can be differentiated from that of Italy on the basis of the nature of the decrease in default risk. Indeed, whereas both lower asset risk and lower need for capital explain the decrease in the probability of failure of german banks, the decrease in failure probability for italian banks is only due to lower leverage asset risk having rather increased.

The new financial environment of the 80's has undoubtedly lead to an increase in bank risk which makes the profitability of banking institutions more uncertain. Higher competition resulting from deregulation of financial services has also narrowed margins and the development of new banking activities and products seems insufficient to counterbalance income losses. Overall the result is an increase in bank vulnerability. The chart presented in appendix 1 shows the tremendous increase in the number of bank failures in recent years in the USA. Even though less outstanding the situation of other industrialized countries appears worth worrying about.

To counter higher risk exposures regulators reacted by imposing more severe prudential rules to banks and mainly by enforcing stronger capital requirements. However the development of off-balance sheet activities cast doughts on the effectiveness of such prudential rules. Moreover the effect of an increase in capital on bank default (failure) risk may be opposite to what expected if banks react by increasing asset risk (Blair and Heggestad (1978) and Koehn and Santomero (1980)).

In the case of the USA empirical studies show that in spite of improvements in capital positions the risk of failure of american banks has significantely increased since the early 80's (Furlong (1988)). It is possible that the results obtained for the USA also hold for Europe. However because of structure differences in european banking systems the extent of risk changes could differ from one country to the other. Now, in the light of european monetary union and of a single banking market the need for a homogeneous banking system in order to ensure similar reactions to shocks is broadly recognized.

The aim of this study is to carry out an assessment of the fragility of different european banking systems. The first part of this paper introduces a method to assess fragility which simultaneaously takes portfolio risk and leverage into account. The second part presents empirical results obtained on a sample of large banks belonging to several european banking systems.

I) PORTFOLIO RISK, LEVERAGE AND RISK OF FAILURE

Analysing bank failure risk

Traditionnally the analysis of bank risk is carried out using a set of financial ratios which are the most significant of banking activity. Computing ratios from balance sheets and income statements the task is then to compare average measures obtained for banks on the individual level on a purely arbitrary basis. The aim is here to compare the riskiness of banks on the european level. Since the significance of financial ratios may vary from one country to the other because of different accounting rules and accounting traditions such a method has here its limits. Moreover this approach relies on no theoretical foundations and it is on this basis severaly critisized by modern finance theory and mainly with mean-variance analysis (Markowitz (1952)). Indeed, even under the most sophisticated version of ratio analysis the effects of diversification (of asset portfolio) on risk are not taken into account. In other words ratio analysis ignores the covariances between the returns on the different assets held in portfolio.

In modern finance theory risk is commonly measured by the fluctuations (variance) of the rate of return on the entire asset portfolio. By considering the variance of the return on total assets the variances of the return on all assets as well as the covariances in the return on assets are simultaneously taken into account.

Concerning a banking institution portfolio risk is the outcome of different types of risks : interest rate risk, exchange rate risk, credit risk, sovereign risk, liquidity risk, operating risk .... Measuring each type of risk separately is possible however it then becomes difficult to assess the overall risk of bank asset and liability portfolio. A measure of overall or global risk cannot be obtained by simply adding the different risk components. A weight would have to be assigned for each type of risk but of course on a purely arbitrary basis only. Also one should not neglect possible trade-offs between different risks that is the possible gains from diversification. For instance Santomero (1983) shows that higher interest rate risk taking may allow bank companies to reduce credit risk.

The simultaneous management of those different risks can nevertheless be traced through the bank's financial statements. The variation in the return on its portfolio reveals to be an indicator of overall risk which does not require the explicit assessment of each risk or defining an arbitrary weighting for each source of risk. Thus if the variability in the return on portfolio is measured by its variance, the weight (proportion) of each asset and liability category is taken into account as well as risk trade-offs between different assets (covariances in the return on assets), between different liabilities (covariances in the return on liabilities) and between assets and liabilities (covariances in the return on assets and liabilities)[1] .

However portfolio risk, however measured, does only provide a partial assessment of bank default (or failure) risk that is of bank vulnerability. An appropriate measure of bank vulnerability should also take into account the ability of a bank to honour its liabilities. Indeed, an increase in risk -- resulting from a riskier management of asset and liabilities or from a more volatile environment -- does not necessarily imply higher failure risk if counterbalanced by an increase in capital. In other words the risk of failure must be considered as the result of two opposite effects : positive effect of

---

[1] The variance of the return on the portfolio can be written :

$$\sigma_R^2 = \sum_{i=1}^{p} x_i^2 \sigma_{R_i}^2 + \sum_{i=1}^{p}\sum_{j=1}^{p} x_i x_j \sigma_{R_i R_j}$$

where x_i : proportion of asset i in total assets for i = 1,...,a and proportion of liability i in total assets for i = a+1,......,p

σ_{RiRj} : covariance between rate of returns Ri et Rj for i and j = 1,...p and for j≠i

r_i : return on asset i (i = 1,...a) or cost of deposit (liability) i (i = a+1,...p)

$R_i = r_i$ for i = 1,...,a et $R_i = - r_i$ for i = a+1,...p risk level and negative effect of the hedge provided by the level of capital held (leverage)[2].

Since it is easier for regulators to affect bank leverage than to control bank asset structure, throughout the 80's capital standards have been tightened for banks on an international level. Improvements in capital positions (decrease in bank leverage) can be considered as a positive development since it should normally serve to reduce default risk among the banking institutions. However decreasing leverage may not be sufficient to control risk if accompanied by increases in asset or portfolio risk. For instance higher volatility in financial markets in the 80's may have offset part (if not all) of the beneficial effects of the higher levels of bank capital. Also on a theoretical level it can be shown that banks that are required to meet higher capital ratios may react by increasing asset or portfolio risk in order to offset the decrease in return on equity related to lower leverage (Kahane (1977), Koehn and Santomero (1980), Kim and Santomero (1988)...)[3]. This incentive to take higher portfolio risk can only be stronger if moral hazard considerations are taken into account within a fixed rate (flat premium) deposit insurance system (Kane (1986)). Since simple capital standards (capital-to-asset ratios) seemed less efficient in containing bank failure risk regulators progressively began to require risk related capital ratios (Cooke ratios) in most OECD countries (BIS (1987)). The aim was to reduce the incentive to turn to riskier assets and to allow a coordinated and more efficient supervision of bank risk on the international level.

Measuring bank failure risk

The net effect portfolio risk / leverage on default (failure) risk can be obtained by estimating the probability of failure of the bank. Specifically an institution fails when its market value V is negative :

$$V = \tilde{A} - D(1+\tilde{c}) < 0$$

---

[2] Appendix 5 presents return on asset measures as well as capital to asset ratios estimated for a sample of european banks described later on. The differences observed among countries are not easy to analyse. For instance french banks are reputated to hold relatively low levels of capital at the international level. This does not necessarily indicate higher failure risk for french banks since interbank activities (low risk activities) stand for a relatively high portion of their assets (IBCA (1987)) (see appendix 5 for other examples of misinterpretation)

[3] Within a mean-variance markowitz portfolio model it is shown that more stringent capital requirements can cause a risk averse bank to increase asset risk. Such a point of view has been seriously critisized on the basis that the possibility of bankruptcy is usually ignored in such models and that the latter are thus internally inconsistent (Furlong and Keeley (1987) and Keeley and Furlong (1990)).

where $\tilde{A}$ represents the market value of assets, D stands for liabilities and $\tilde{c}$ is the cost of liabilities (here and throughout a tilde ~ denotes a random variable).

$$\tilde{A} = (E + D)(1 + \tilde{r})$$

where E is total equity and $\tilde{r}$ is the future rate of return on assets.

Failure occurs when :

$$\tilde{\Pi} = (\tilde{r} - \tilde{c})D + E < -E$$

where $\tilde{\Pi}$ is the bank's net profit

The bank's probability of failure is thus the probability that losses exceed capital in other words that its net wealth becomes negative (Roy (1952), Blair and Heggestad (1978), Boyd and Graham (1986)). Formally :

$$\text{Probability of failure} = \text{Prob.}\,(\tilde{\Pi} < -E) \qquad (1)$$

Dividing both terms of the inequality by equity E the probability of failure becomes :

$$\text{Prob.}\left(\frac{\tilde{\Pi}}{E} < \frac{-E}{E}\right) = \text{Prob.}(\tilde{r}_e < -1) \qquad (2)$$

where $\tilde{r}_e$ is the rate of return on equity.

Assuming that $\tilde{\Pi}$ is distributed as a normal variable[4] then :

$$\text{Prob.}\left(\frac{\tilde{r}_e - \bar{r}_e}{\sigma_{re}} < \frac{-1 - \bar{r}_e}{\sigma_{re}}\right) = \text{Prob.}\left(\frac{\tilde{r}_e - \bar{r}_e}{\sigma_{re}} < -Z\right) = \text{Prob.}\left(\frac{\tilde{r}_e - \bar{r}_e}{\sigma_{re}} > Z\right) \qquad (3)$$

where $\bar{r}_e$ and σ_{re} are respectively the mean and the standard deviation of the rate of return $\tilde{r}_e$ and

---

4 In fact the normally distributed profit assumption is not essential. One can also refer to the Bienaymé-Tchebycheff inequality (see Blair and Heggestad (1978)).

$$Z = \frac{1 - \bar{r_e}}{\sigma_{re}} \tag{4}$$

The variable Z can thus be considered as a measure of the risk of failure of a bank. Higher Z values indicate a lower probability of failure. However with this kind of measure it is difficult to explicitely distinguish between the effect of asset or portfolio risk and the effect of leverage on failure risk. This distinction can be obtained when either return on asset (Boyd et Graham (1988) or profit levels are considered.

- By considering net return on assets instead of return on equity equation (2) can be rewritten :

$$\text{Prob.}\left(\frac{\tilde{\Pi}}{A} < \frac{-E}{A}\right) = \text{Prob.}\left(\tilde{r_a} < \frac{-E}{A}\right) \tag{2'}$$

where $\tilde{r_a}$ is the net rate of return on assets and A stands for total assets

Equation (3) then becomes :

$$\text{Prob.}\left(\frac{\tilde{r_a} - \bar{r_a}}{\sigma_{ra}} < \frac{-\lambda - \bar{r_a}}{\sigma_{ra}}\right) = \text{Prob.}\left(\frac{\tilde{r_a} - \bar{r_a}}{\sigma_{ra}} > Z'\right. \tag{3'}$$

where $\bar{r_a}$ et σ_{ra} are respectively the mean and the standard deviation of the rate of return r_a, λ is the equity to assets ratio (E/A), and

$$Z' = Z'1 + Z'2 \tag{4'}$$

$$\text{with } Z'1 = \frac{\bar{r_a}}{\sigma_{ra}} \quad \text{and} \quad Z'2 = \frac{\lambda}{\sigma_{ra}}$$

Breaking up Z' makes the distinction between portfolio risk (Z'1) and the effect of leverage (the hedge of portfolio risk with equity) (Z'2) possible.

Note that Z'1 is nothing but a commonly used risk measure in Finance theory which simultaneously takes into account return volatility and return level, that is the inverse of the coefficient of variation of return (an increase in volatility does not necessarily imply higher risk as long as it is followed by higher returns).

With Z'2 the extent to which a given level of equity can cover losses is compared to the extent of risk : with identical equity to asset ratios the portion of portfolio risk that is hedged is lower when portfolio return volatility is higher.

- When considering the level of profit the probability of failure can be written :

$$\text{Prob.}(\tilde{\Pi} < -E) = \text{Prob.}\left(\frac{\tilde{\Pi} - \bar{\Pi}}{\sigma_{\Pi}} > \frac{E + \bar{\Pi}}{\sigma_{\Pi}}\right) \qquad (1'')$$

$$= \text{Prob.}\left(\frac{\tilde{\Pi} - \bar{\Pi}}{\sigma_{\Pi}} > Z''\right) \qquad (2'')$$

where $\bar{\Pi}$ and σ_{Π} are respectively the mean and standard deviation of profit $\tilde{\Pi}$ and :

$$Z'' = Z''1 + Z''2 \qquad (3'')$$

$$\text{with} \quad Z''1 = \frac{\bar{\Pi}}{\sigma_{\Pi}} \qquad \text{and} \qquad Z''2 = \frac{E}{\sigma_{\Pi}}$$

Again we obtain a measure that allows the distinction between portfolio risk (Z"1) and leverage (Z"2).

Using either Z, Z' or Z" it becomes possible to compare the risk of failure of different banks and to classify banks on the basis of their risk of failure. With Z' and Z" measures the causes of failure risk can be pointed out. By computing both Z1 and Z2 it can be shown whether the risk of failure is mostly due to high portfolio risk (Z1) or essentially because of insufficient capital holding (Z2).

Z and Z' are alternatively used in the literature as indexes of failure risk. However as noted by Furlong (1988) both measures rely on the strong assumption that regulators always close a bank when the latter is found to have negative net worth upon examination. Since as noted by Kane (1989) the failure of banking institutions is more the result of a decision taken by regulators then by the market the indexes provided by Z measures should be interpreted with care. In other words to the extent that banks are allowed to operate with negative market net worth the so obtained Z measures would tend to overstate the "effective" probability of the bank to fail.

Z'2 or Z"2 here defined can be compared to Cooke ratio type measures. However whereas Cooke ratios only consider asset risk and on an arbitrary basis (the amounts invested in different asset categories are weighted with arbitrarely defined risk coefficients and summed) with Z'2 or Z"2 risk is measured by the variability of portfolio return (see appendix 7). Thus compared to the risk weighted capital to asset Cooke ratio Z'2 (or Z"2) takes into account not only the level of risk of the different assets held but also the level of risk resulting from the confrontation of earnings (on assets or off-balance sheet activities) and the cost of liabilities. In other words, as mentionned above Z'2 (or Z"2) takes into account the covariances between the returns (costs) on the different assets and liabilities included in the bank portfolio. Thus Z'2 (or Z"2) is consistent with the results obtained by Kim and Santomero (1988)[5]. Of course such Z'2 or Z"2 measures can be considered less performing than Cooke ratios on a prudential ground since risk is only measured its sources remaining unknown. Nevertheless from a risk valuation rather than a risk control point of vue Z measures seem more appropriate to assess risk since they include factors ignored in Cooke ratios.

Moreover, this global approach of bank risk does not take into account the possible support provided by central banks (lender of last resort) which is considered in the ratings provided by rating agencies. Thus the indexes and classifications here obtained will be of less interest to individuals than to monetary authorities concerned with the supervision of individual banks. Also from a single banking market point of view with this method banks are somehow insulated from their institutional environment. Since the aim of this paper is to measure the degree of homogeneity of european banking systems on a risk or fragility basis this general approach seems more accurate for detecting possible divergences among different systems.

II) EMPIRICAL RESULTS

To compute risk measures for banks either market (share price) or accounting (book) data can be used. In the literature authors do not seem to have reached a conclusion concerning the superiority of either approach. On the one hand a widely recognized problem with accounting data is for example the intentional smoothing of reported profits leading to an understatement of risk. On the other hand the volatility of market returns may reflect random noise which are unrelated to the true profitability of the bank leading to an overstatement of risk. Boyd and Graham (1988) carry out a comparative study on a sample of american banks confronting the results obtained with market data and accounting data with the results obtained by rating agencies which integrate all available information (market information as well as accounting information). Their results point out the superiority of accounting data in assessing risk. Though this kind of test does not seem very powerful to discriminate between both approaches in what follows our measures are all computed using accounting data only. Our choice

5 Using a portfolio model Kim and Santomero (1988) show that the weights defined in risk related capital ratios (Cooke ratios) should depend on the expected return on assets and on liabilities, on their variance-covariance structure and on the level of failure risk tolerated by regulators.

is also essentially guided by the lack of sufficient market data, specially in the case of France (nationalised banks).

The analysis of the fragility of european banking systems is carried out using IBCA[6] annual bank data. IBCA data appear to be the most appropriate for our analysis for at least two reasons. First, the data concern banks at the individual level. The use of aggregated data (as that published by the OECD) can lead to an offsetting of risk among banks and neglects the possibility of domino effects within the banking system. Second IBCA data are frequently adjusted[7] and homogenized which makes international comparisons easier.

The analysis is carried out for the British, French, German, Italian and spanish banking systems. For the three first ones the data are available for the years 1979-1988, and for the remaining two, for the years 1981-1988. For each country our sample includes the largest number of banks that could be available. Those banks generally correspond to the largest and main banks operating in each system which is essential for our analysis (see appendix 2 for the number of banks, their size, and other information ..., and appendix 6 for a detailed composition of our samples). Our samples cover 20 banks for France, 11 banks for Germany, 10 for Spain and 9 banks for the UK. Although most of the major banks in each country are included in our samples sample size differences from one country to the other can be critisized. Therefore for each country the obtained estimations were rerun once again on the basis of the following criterion : for each country we have included a given number of banks such that the smallest bank (asset size in 1988) showed asset size at least greater than 1% of global assets held by all the banks present in the sample. Such a criterion has the effect of eliminating banks with relatively small asset size and provides comparable and harmonized samples. Only the sample of french banks is affected by this method (12 banks instead of 20) and our results are thereby not significantely affected.

In what follows for reasons mentioned above Z' and Z" measures are privileged to Z. However in order to compare the results obtained with those obtained with Z, computations are also carried out for Z. The results are in general approximatively equivalent. Thus only the results obtained with Z" appear throughout the text and those relative to Z and Z' can be found in appendix.

For each risk measure (Z, Z' and Z") an empirical estimation is carried out for each bank for the entire period and also for two sub-periods (1979-84

---

[6] International Bank Corporate Analysis is a rating agency based in London which systematically carries out analysis (and not only on request of clients as it is the case for the main world agencies) on a growing number of banks at the international level.

[7] For instance results published by scandinavian banks are frequentely adjusted from reserves (accounting rules and local habits encourage banks to publish excessively low profits for tax purposes).

and 1983-88 for France, Germany and the UK, and 1981-85 and 1984-88 for Spain and Italy) in order to trace possible changes in failure risk. Mean returns and their standard deviations are computed for the just mentioned three periods. Bank failure risk or fragility is assessed estimating Z, Z' and Z" mean measures for each period. And the fragility of each banking system is then measured by the inter-bank mean of individual bank risk measures in each country. Homogeneity tests are then carried out to compare risk levels among countries and changes in risk. Both the study of changes in risk and comparison of the level of risk seem necessary. Indeed, level differences on their own do not necessarily reflect significant differences in risk since they may only be the result of different accounting rules and habits in each country (profit smoothing, reserve carrying over...). Therefore this type of analysis should also be completed by that of the changes witnessed in those level differences across time. Concerning this time analysis, because of the too few number of observations available, it seemed preferable to us to define two overlapping sub-periods. Note that this contributes to enhance the power of homogeneity tests.

Three variables need to be defined for the computation of the different measures. From the data available from IBCA the following were chosen :

- Equity : core capital plus equity reserves excluding subordinated debt.
- Net profit : published after tax net income (before dividend distribution)
- Assets : balance sheet total

Before carrying out any comparison it seems important to us to analyse contagion (domino) and size effects. In a banking system if large and small banks do not show the same level of fragility small and large banks should not be considered on an equal basis. In other words if the fragility of a banking system is merely measured by a simple arithmetical mean of individual bank risk levels then fragility would be understated if large banks show higher risk levels than small banks or overstated if small banks are found riskier than large banks.

To analyse these contagion effects we have computed two types of mean measures : a simple arithmetical mean ($\bar{Z}$, $\bar{Z}'$ or $\bar{Z}''$) and a weighted average where the weights are the relative sizes of balance sheet totals for each bank ($\bar{Z}P$, $\bar{Z}'P$, or $\bar{Z}''P$). The spread between both kind of measures then reveals possible contagion effects. When the weighted average is greater (lower) than the simple mean than it follows that small banks are generally more fragile (less fragile) than large banks.

Table 1 shows average values of Z" ($\bar{Z}''$ and $\bar{Z}''P$) computed for the global period and changes from one sub-period to the other [8] and Table 2

[8] Results obtained for each bank individually are presented in appendix 6.

presents t-statistics relative to the inter-country comparisons of the $\bar{Z}''$ measures obtained in Table 1.

Table 1: level of fragility and changes

Country	Global period		1st sub-period(1)		2nd sub-period(2)		Difference (2)-(1)	
	$\bar{Z}''$	$\bar{Z}''p$	$\bar{Z}''$	$\bar{Z}''p$	$\bar{Z}''$	$\bar{Z}''p$	$\bar{Z}''$	$\bar{Z}''p$
Spain	15,00	15,91	42,07	52,12	21,56	21,37	-20,51 (-1,44)	-30,75
France	19,49	20,87	42,56	44,71	26,00	27,55	-16,56 (-1,81)	-17,16
Italy	32,96	28,87	33,84	30,62	44,79	39,44	+10,95 (+1,03)	+8,82
Germany	35,35	36,33	56,20	60,65	59,21	64,17	+3,01 (+0,23)	+3,67
UK	14,91	15,82	49,69	49,34	17,5	15,63	-32,19* (-4,98)	-33,71

( ) : t-statistic , * : Significant difference at the 95% level

Table 2: homogeneity tests of different systems ($\bar{Z}''$)

Country[1]	G[2]	1st[3]	2nd[4]	Country[1]	G	1st	2nd
FR/GER	-3,00*	1,01	-3,89*	FR/UK	1,03	-0,75	1,10
FR/ITA	-1,94	0,83	-2,03*	FR/SPA	1,00	0,03	0,76
GER/UK	5,06*	0,53	5,17*	GER/ITA	0,35	1,7	1,38
GER/SPA	4,97*	0,79	3,86*	UK/ITA	-2,98*	1,75	-2,98*
UK/SPA	-0,03	0,51	-0,46	ITA/SPA	2,95*	-0,9	2,27*

1: if X/Y<0 then higher risk in X , 2: global period,
3: 1st sub-period, 4: 2nd sub-period.

*: Significant difference at the 95% level

The results obtained with the weighted and unweighted averages give approximatively the same classification of fragility levels concerning the different countries under study. Only a weak spread seems to indicate higher failure risk for larger banks in the case of Italy and the UK (the measures shown in appendix confirming this result). A similar situation could be that of Spain for which a higher increase in risk for large banks can be observed in the late 80's. If the banking systems in this countries are effectively characterized by a higher failure risk of the relatively largest banks then they may be threatened by a relatively higher exposure to global failure (size effects, contagion effects) justifying the need for a greater support from the authorities. However, these differences in fragility levels relative to bank size can not be significantely highlighted and therefore only the results obtained from simple arithmetical means are used to assess the fragility of banking systems in what follows.

Considering the period of analysis as a whole[9] homogeneity tests (Table 2) lead to the distinction between two groups of countries : Germany on one side and France, Italy, Spain and the UK on the other side the case of Italy remaining ambiguous. Sub-period analysis shows that the different banking systems formed a homogeneous group (non significant difference tests) in the early 80's and that they progressively presented differences afterwards. Increases in bank risk failure can be noted for France, Spain and the UK, whereas decreases can be witnessed for Germany and Italy. Even though those changes do not appear to be significant[10] (Table 1) except for the UK (or for Italy and Spain on the basis of Z (see appendix 3)), the levels of risk for those two groups of countries appear to be significantely different in the second sub-period (Table 2).

These results are confirmed by those obtained with Z and Z' (see appendix 3). Note that with Z' : Germany shows a significantely different level of risk since the early 80's; Spain initially shows a similar level to that of germany with an increase in risk later on. And note that with Z : Italy shows a higher level of risk (relatively to all other countries) in the early 80's and a level similar to those of France, Spain and the UK later on.

These three exceptions suggest that the increase in risk witnessed for spanish banks may be relatively high and that the decrease in risk for italian banks may be quite important. Note that this conclusion is supported

---

9 Note that the measures computed over the global period may well give lower values than those computed over each sub-period since when $\bar{\Pi}_1 \quad \bar{\Pi}_2$, $\sigma_{\Pi_1} + \sigma_{\Pi_2}$ and thus $\sigma_{\Pi} > \sigma_{\Pi_1}$ and $\sigma_{\Pi} > \sigma_{\Pi_2}$.

10 The use of overlapping sub-periods may explane why the differences are not found to be significant.

by the results obtained with Z since statistically significant changes are only observed for those two countries.

Thus, according to the results outlined above it appears that throughout the 80's the fragility of european banking systems has evolved. The questions are then the following. Are those changes mostly related to higher or lower exposure to risk? In other words with the development of new types of risks (interest rate risk, exchange risk, operation risk, ...) is it possible to differentiate between bank risk exposure from one country to the other? Or is it more the development of capital (or the hedge of risk exposure) that explains the changes witnessed in the degree of fragility of european banking systems?

To answer those questions Z"1 and Z"2 are estimated and homogeneity tests are carried out again. As explained above Z"1 (the coefficient of variation of profit) represents the risk incurred by a bank or its risk exposure and Z"2 (capital divided by the standard deviation of profit) is the hedge of its risk exposure. Dividing capital by the variability of profit allows assessing the hedge provided by capital taking risk considerations into account and also makes interbank comparisons easier. Estimations are also carried out using Z'1 and Z'2 and are presented in appendix 4.

Table 3: risk exposure and risk hedging

Country	global		1st subperiod (1)		2nd subperiod (2)		Difference (2)-(1)	
	$\bar{Z}''1$	$\bar{Z}''2$	$\bar{Z}''1$	$\bar{Z}''2$	$\bar{Z}''1$	$\bar{Z}''2$	$\bar{Z}''1$	$\bar{Z}''2$
Spain	1,47	13,53	4,07	38,00	2,08	19,48	-1,99	-18,52
							(-0,56)	(-1,44)
France	1,52	17,97	2,89	39,67	1,95	24,06	-0,94	-15,61
							(-1,5)	(-1,78)
Italy	3,9	29,06	4,92	27,78	4,56	40,24	-0,36	12,46
							(-0,56)	(1,35)
Germany	2,34	33,01	3,56	52,63	4,19	55,01	+0,63	+2,38
							(+0,73)	(+0,19)
UK	1,56	13,35	4,77	37,87	1,78	15,72	-2,99*	-22,15*
							(-3,81)	(-3,87)

( ) : t-statistic, * : Significant difference at the 95% level

Table 3 shows $\bar{Z}''1$ and $\bar{Z}''2$ measures for each country and their changes from one sub-period to the other. The exposure to risk ($\bar{Z}''1$) appears more important during the first sub-period for all countries except for Germany. The hedge provided by capital ($\bar{Z}''2$ has increased for both Germany and Italy. However those changes appear significant only for the UK for which both higher risk exposure and weaker hedging explain the increase in fragility.

Tables 4 and 5 present t-statistics relative to the comparison of Z"1 and Z"2 among the different countries for the different periods and sub-periods. If the different banking systems could not significantely be differentiated in the early 80's (on the basis of either Z"1 or Z"2), only Germany shows lower portfolio risk (Z"1) later on. However concerning hedging (Z"2), in the late 80's, the same group of countries obtained above for failure risk (Z") can again be put forward : Germany and Italy on one side and France, Spain and the UK on the other side.

Table 4: homogeneity tests of different systems ($\bar{Z}''1$)

Country[1]	G[2]	1st[3]	2nd[4]	Country[1]	G	1st	2nd
FR/GER	-2,29*	0,74	-3,94*	FR/UK	-0,11	-2,16*	0,33
FR/ITA	-1,44	-1,57	-2,40*	FR/SPA	0,13	-0,82	-0,29
GER/UK	2,4*	-1,20	4,08*	GER/ITA	-1,84	-0,98	-0,32
GER/SPA	2,7*	-0,33	3,90*	UK/ITA	-2,73*	-0,11	-1,85
UK/SPA	0,26	0,46	-0,64	ITA/SPA	2,84*	0,49	1,88

1: if X/Y<0 then higher risk in X , 2: global period,
3: 1st sub-period, 4: 2nd sub-period.

*: Significant difference at the 95% level

Table 5: homogeneity tests of different systems ($\bar{Z}''2$)

Country[1]	G[2]	1st[3]	2nd[4]	Country[1]	G	1st	2nd
FR/GER	-3,02*	1,02	-3,86*	FR/UK	1,53	0,20	1,53
FR/ITA	-1,80	1,23	-1,95	FR/SPA	1,07	0,11	0,84
GER/UK	5,21*	1,29	5,47*	GER/ITA	0,66	2,07*	1,55
GER/SPA	5,08*	0,9	4,95*	UK/ITA	-3,00*	1,29	-3,28*
UK/SPA	-0,07	-0,01	-0,91	ITA/SPA	2,41*	-0,7	2,29*

1: if X/Y<0 then higher risk in X , 2: global period,
3: 1st sub-period, 4: 2nd sub-period.

*: Significant difference at the 95% level

-Thus over the recent period german banks show lower risk exposures than banks operating in the 4 other countries under study. This lower exposure to risk as well as stronger capital positions (lower leverage) both explain why the german banking system appears less fragile than others. As for italian banks only higher capital ratios account for the decrease in fragility their exposure to risk having rather increased than decreased.

CONCLUSION

This study highlights that european banking systems have experienced different changes in the degree of risk during the 80's. Showing similar levels of failure risk in the early 80's different changes are pointed out later on. Empirical evidence indicates an increase in failure risk for France, Spain and the UK and a decrease for Germany and Italy. However the case of Italy differs from that of Germany. Whereas both lower portfolio risk and lower need for capital explain the decrease in the probability of failure of german banks the decrease for italian banks is only due to lower leverage the riskiness of assets held by banks having rather increased.

Appendix 1

Bank failures (USA)

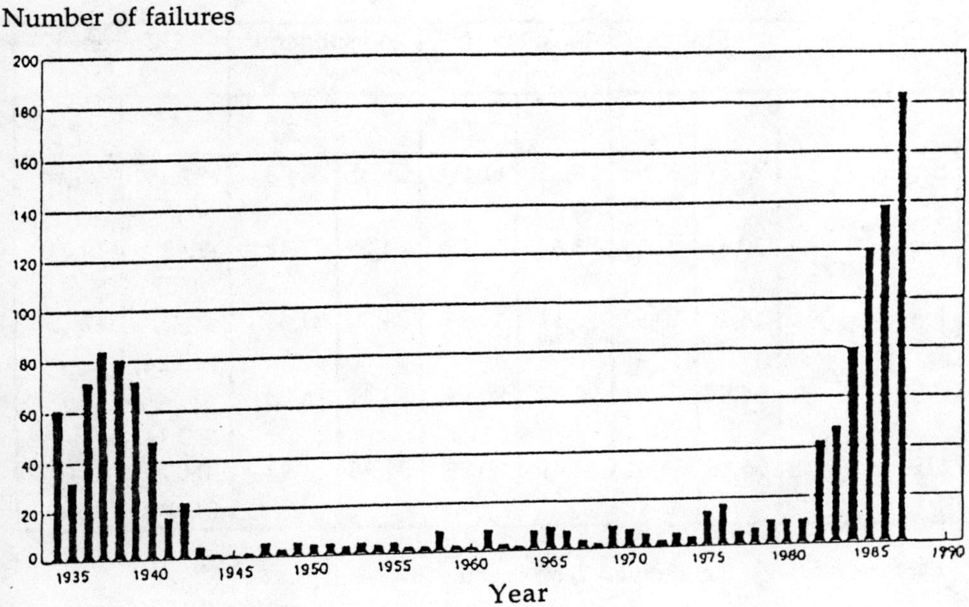

SOURCE: *New England Economic Review* (July–August 1987):38.

Appendix 2

Table 0: the sample
(computed from IBCA data)

Country	number of banks	(1)	total assets	median	max.	min
			(in billions of national currencies)			
Spain	10	0,16	17705	2026,4	4056	243,9
France	20	0,11	7116,96	168,70	1193,35	13,4
Italy	14	0,09	669828	57851,7	90297,5	7114,8
GER	11	0,15	1276,11	133,27	297,55	3,06
UK	9	0,20	375,69	51,83	104,65	2,23

(1): Herfindahl concentration index

Appendix 3

Table 1': level of fragility and changes

Country	Global period		1st subperiod (1)		2nd subperiod (2)		Difference (2)-(1)	
	$\bar{Z}$	$\bar{Z}P$	$\bar{Z}$	$\bar{Z}P$	$\bar{Z}$	$\bar{Z}P$	$\bar{Z}$	$\bar{Z}P$
Spain	25,81	32,91	50,81	60,00	28,35	30,44	-22,46* (-2,04)	-29,56
France	30,63	44,19	53,68	52,93	44,25	57,14	-9,43 (-0,57)	+4,21
Italy	14,1	10,97	15,11	10,99	38,53	31,51	+23,4* (+3,24)	+20,5
GER	64,85	71,91	79,87	90,59	83,41	98,55	+3,54 (+0,14)	+7,96
UK	26,15	21,46	32,81	30,35	31,38	21,94	-0,93 (-0,16)	-8,41

( ) : t-statistic , * : Significant difference at the 95% level

Table 1": level of fragility and changes

Country	Global period		1st subperiod (1)		2nd subperiod (2)		Difference (2)-(1)	
	$\bar{Z}'$	$\bar{Z}'p$	$\bar{Z}'$	$\bar{Z}'p$	$\bar{Z}'$	$\bar{Z}'p$	$\bar{Z}'$	$\bar{Z}'p$
Spain	31,37	38,78	57,97	53,84	34,14	37,31	-23,83	-16,53
							(-1,75)	
France	24,36	30,75	37,01	42,52	31,55	35,15	-5,46	-7,37
							(-0,61)	
Italy	22,53	19,57	26,93	20,01	35,83	33,42	+8,90	+13,41
							(+1,12)	
GER	71,09	79,41	74,92	84,22	105,02	131,65	+30,1	+47,43
							(+0,99)	
UK	24,82	19,98	27,95	24,35	34,36	22,87	+6,41	-1,48
							(+0,69)	

( ) : t-statistic , * : Significant difference at the 95% level

Table 2': homogeneity tests of different systems ($\bar{Z}$)

Country[1]	G[2]	1st[3]	2nd[4]	Country[1]	G	1st	2nd
FR/GER	-2,09*	0,99	-2,51*	FR./UK	0,61	1,53	1,45
FR/ITA	2,89*	2,87	0,48	FR./SPA.	0,69	0,17	1,56
GER/UK	2,79*	2,03*	3,62*	GER/ITA	3,88*	2,81*	3,27*
GER/SPA	2,85*	1,16	4,34*	UK/ITA	2,16*	3,73*	-0,69
UK/SPA	0,05	-1,65	0,31	ITA/SPA	-2,26*	-3,30*	1,09

1: if X/Y<0 then higher risk in X , 2: global period,
3: 1st sub-period, 4: 2nd sub-period.

*: Significant difference at the 95% level

Table 2'': homogeneity tests of different systems ($\bar{Z}'$)

Country[1]	G[2]	1st[3]	2nd[4]	Country[1]	G	1st	2nd
FR/GER	-2,48*	-1,99*	-2,91*	FR./UK	-0,09	1,18	-0,27
FR/ITA	0,42	1,00	-0,67	FR./SPA.	-1,09	-1,24	-0,35
GER/UK	2,49*	2,64*	2,69*	GER/ITA	2,58*	2,53*	2,76*
GER/SPA	2,04*	0,96	2,80*	UK/ITA	0,43	0,14	-0,15
UK/SPA	-0,92	-2,14*	0,02	ITA/SPA	-1,36	-2,01*	0,26

1: if X/Y<0 then higher risk in X , 2: global period,
3: 1st sub-period, 4: 2nd sub-period.

*: Significant difference at the 95% level

Appendix 4

Table 3': risk exposure and risk hedging

Country	Global period		1st subperiod(1)		2nd subperiod(2)		Difference (2)-(1)	
	$\bar{Z}'1$	$\bar{Z}'2$	$\bar{Z}'1$	$\bar{Z}'2$	$\bar{Z}'1$	$\bar{Z}'2$	$\bar{Z}'1$	$\bar{Z}'2$
Spain	3,31	28,06	6,11	51,86	3,47	30,67	-2,64	-21,19
							(-1,51)	(-1,62)
France	2,10	22,26	2,86	34,15	2,42	29,13	-0,44	-5,02
							(-0,7)	(-0,59)
Italy	2,91	19,62	4,03	22,90	3,62	32,21	-0,41	+9,31
							(-0,32)	(1,37)
GER	4,72	66,37	4,73	70,19	7,6	97,43	+2,87	+27,14
							(+0,15)	(+0,96)
UK	2,79	22,03	3,25	24,70	3,63	30,73	0,38	6,03
							(0,39)	(0,72)

( ) : t-statistic , * : Significant difference at the 95% level

Table 4': homogeneity tests of different systems ($\bar{Z}'1$)

Country[1]	G[2]	1st[3]	2nd[4]	Country[1]	G	1st	2nd
FR/GER	-2,04*	-1,48	-2,91*	FR/UK	-1,08	-0,55	-1,17
FR/ITA	-1,35	-0,94	0,54	FR/SPA	-1,61	-1,89	-1,54
GER/UK	1,42	1,23	2,00*	GER/ITA	1,35	0,43	2,15*
GER/SPA	0,99	-0,68	2,26*	UK/ITA	-0,16	-0,66	0,01
UK/SPA	-0,59	-1,7	0,14	ITA/SPA	-0,47	-1,04	0,18

1: if X/Y<0 then higher risk in X , 2: global period,
3: 1st sub-period, 4: 2nd sub-period.
*: Significant difference at the 95% level

Table 5': homogeneity tests of different systems ($\bar{Z}'2$)

Country[1]	G[2]	1st[3]	2nd[4]	Country[1]	G	1st	2nd
FR/GER	-2,51*	-2,02*	-2,90*	FR/UK	0,05	1,29	-0,17
FR/ITA	0,70	1,23	-0,52	FR/SPA	-1,02	-1,27	-0,23
GER/UK	2,50*	2,73*	2,74*	GER/ITA	2,66*	2,70*	2,80*
GER/SPA	2,12*	0,9	2,84*	UK/ITA	0,52	0,28	-0,17
UK/SPA	-0,95	-2,20*	0,01	ITA/SPA	-1,47	-2,14*	0,27

1: if X/Y<0 then higher risk in X , 2: global period,
3: 1st sub-period, 4: 2nd sub-period.
*: Significant difference at the 95% level

Appendix 5

Country	std deviation of return on assets		Capital ratio (E/Total Assets)	
	early 80's	late 80's	early 80's	late 80's
Spain	0,0025	0,0023	0,0560	0,0560
France	0,0017	0,0020	0,0224 *	0,0231*
Italy	0,0020	0,0012	0,0324	0,0384
GER	0,0006*	0,0005 *	0,0291	0,0313
UK	0,0027	0,0036	0,0638	0,0581

*: statistically different from all other countries at the 95% level.

Among the problems that appear with this kind of analysis the following can be mentioned :

- What to say about the net effect on failure risk of the increase of both standard deviation and capital ratio for France ?
- How to compare the case of Spain (high standard deviation and high capital ratio) with that of Germany (low standard deviation and low capital ratio) ?

Appendix 6

FRANCE

		Z(3)			
Bank(1)	weight(2)	global period	1st sub-period	2nd sub-period	+ or - risk Z
B.N.P.	0,1680	56,94	57,38	60,98	-
Crédit Lyonnais	0,1523	52,55	43,07	78,47	-
C.N.C.A.	0,1477	23,47	18,15	57,21	-
S.G.	0,1324	56,05	108,90	44,08	+
Groupe Paribas	0,1035	47,25	57,7	41,74	+
Banque Paribas	0,0622	36,12	62,31	35,02	+
C.I.C.	0,0537	28,28	23,88	26,55	-
Banque Indosuez	0,0410	31,04	25,00	74,08	-
C.C.F.	0,0330	58,56	52,14	61,16	-
B.F.C.E.	0,0304	93,6	78,48	208,84	-
C.N.	0,0170	9,24	19,84	7,88	+
C.C.B.P.	0,0167	18,21	110,01	16,94	+
Banque union europ.	0,0095	4,95	4,94	9,73	-
Banque Worms	0,0087	4,64	3,49	3,45	+
U.B.A.F.	0,0071	31,80	64,98	31,83	+
Banque Sudameris	0,0048	11,47	9,88	53,14	-
B.A.I.I.	0,0046	16,69	42,75	13,70	+
B.N.S.M.	0,0043	26,23	20,73	56,09	-
Europ. de Banque	0,0019	1,35	0,84	0,96	-
B.sté financière europ.	0,0012	4,17	269,09	3,09	+
	Σ = 1				

(1): ordered by decreasing asset size in 1988 , (2): \f(assets/Σassets) , (3): measure of failure risk

SPAIN

Bank[1]	weight[2]	$Z^{(3)}$ global period	$Z^{(3)}$ 1st sub-period	$Z^{(3)}$ 2nd sub-period	+ or - risk Z
Banco central	0,2291	49,69	90,73	38,54	+
Banco de Santander	0,1877	34,1	74,49	31,66	+
B.Hispano Americano	0,1767	15,91	18,82	12,19	+
B.Exterior de Esp.	0,1374	49,08	72,78	44,80	+
B.Popular Esp.	0,1144	28,65	48,85	27,35	+
B.intercont. Esp.	0,0461	18,63	82,83	16,97	+
B.Atlantico	0,0422	8,91	6,84	50,51	-
B.Urquijo Union	0,0319	6,06	5,05	15,89	-
B.Zaragozano	0,0206	32,23	82,95	26,23	+
B.Arabe Esp.	0,0137	14,87	24,79	19,35	+
	Σ=1				

ITALY

Bank[1]	weight[2]	$Z^{(3)}$ global period	$Z^{(3)}$ 1st sub-period	$Z^{(3)}$ 2nd sub-period	+ or - risk Z
B.Naz.Lavoro	0,1348	9,34	7,71	25,81	-
Ist.B.S.P.Torino	0,1217	5,79	5,41	49,14	-
B.Com.Ital.	0,1099	9,16	8,43	25,32	-
B.di Napoli	0,1084	9,52	8,26	8,33	-or=
Credito Ital.	0,1059	8,12	7,76	30,79	-
B.di Roma	0,0986	6,09	5,69	20,51	-
M.D.P.S.	0,0864	10,74	13,75	16,5	-
B.di Sicilia	0,0573	29,98	32,43	30,43	+
B.Naz.Agric.	0,042	6,89	6,11	39,13	-
B.Pop. di Novara	0,0352	13,67	12,63	74,01	-
B.Santo Spirito	0,0341	10,72	10,68	34,27	-
B. pop.Milano	0,0323	28,53	25,42	104,99	-
Cred. Romagnolo	0,0224	24,65	37,87	21,89	+
B. d'Amer. e D'ital.	0,0106	24,19	29,34	58,23	-
	Σ=1				

(1): ordered by decreasing asset size in 1988 , (2): $\frac{\text{assets}}{\sum \text{assets}}$, (3): measure of failure risk

GERMANY

Bank(1)	weight(2)	Z(3) global period	Z(3) 1st sub-period	Z(3) 2nd sub-period	+ or - risk Z
Deutsche Bank	0,2332	50,11	69,41	52,17	+
Dresdner Bank	0,1776	75,6	62,41	148,15	-
Commerzbank	0,1400	29,55	33,22	97,7	-
Bayer. Vereinsbank	0,1258	181,71	307,73	158,25	+
Hypo-Bank	0,1044	91,16	87,56	110,7	-
Deutsche genoss. B.	0,1009	47,54	51,21	84,17	-
B.f.Gemeinwirschaft	0,0499	23,10	20,21	38,67	-
Berliner Bank	0,0258	56,14	54,50	60,87	-
B.H.F.	0,0256	69,56	60,73	75,63	-
Vereins u Westbank	0,0154	68,48	104,93	56,40	+
B.H.L.	0,0024	19,95	26,68	34,54	-
	Σ=1				

UNITED KINGDOM

Bank(1)	weight(2)	Z(3) global period	Z(3) 1st sub-period	Z(3) 2nd sub-period	+ or - risk Z
Barclays	0,2785	20,69*	22,70	20,61**	+
Nat. West.B.	0,2626	28,73	28,89	30,57	-
Midland B.	0,1483	9,69	16,88	8,02	+
Lloyds B.	0,1380	8,5*	52,23	6,19**	+
Standard Chartered	0,0631	8,02	31,87	6,2	+
Royal B. Scotland	0,0375	53,63	43,50	71,99	-
B.of Scotland	0,0375	53,63	43,50	71,99	-
Yorkshire B.	0,0085	27,37	26,59	28,53	-
Cooperative B.	0,0059	33,68	25,59	68,88	-
	Σ=1				

(1): ordered by decreasing asset size in 1988 , (2): $\frac{\text{assets}}{\sum \text{assets}}$,

(3): measure of failure risk

*: computed over 1979-89 , **: computed 1984-89

Appendix 7

The Cooke ratio can be defined as :

$$\frac{E}{\sum_{i=1}^{a} p_i A_i} = \frac{E/A}{\sum_{i=1}^{a} p_i A_i / A} = \frac{\lambda}{\sum_{i=1}^{a} p_i x_i}$$

The bank's profit can be written :

$$\Pi = \sum_{i=1}^{a} r_i A_i - \sum_{i=a+1}^{p} r_i D_i$$

return :

$$R = \frac{\Pi}{A} = \sum_{i=1}^{a} r_i x_i - \sum_{i=a+1}^{p} r_i x_i$$

and the variance of the return on the portfolio:

$$\sigma_R^2 = \sum_{i=1}^{p} x_i^2 \sigma_{R_i}^2 + \sum_{\substack{i=1 \\ i \neq j}}^{p} \sum_{j=1}^{p} x_i x_j \sigma_{R_i R_j}$$

and note that:

$$Z2 = \lambda / \sigma_R$$

Where E: Equity
A: assets
p_i: risk weight coefficient in the Cooke ratio
x_i: proportion of asset i in total assets for i = 1,...,a and proportion of liability i in total assets for i = a+1,.....,p
σ_{RiRj} : covariance between returns Ri and Rj for i and j = 1,...p and for j≠i
r_i : on asset i (i = 1,...a) or cost of deposit i (i = a+1,...p)
$R_i = r_i$ for i = 1,...,a and $R_i = - r_i$ for i = a+1,...p
note that with the Cooke ratio each asset proportion is arbitrarely weighted by a risk weight (p_i) whereas with Z2 each asset proportion is weighted by a usual risk measure of that asset (σ Ri) .

Moreover with Z2 the proportion of each liability is taken into account as well as the covariances of asset returns, the covariances of liability costs and the covariances of asset returns and liability costs.

REFERENCES

Artus, P. (1989) "Le ratio Cooke et le comportement des banques", *Revue française d'économie* .

Artus, P. et Pollin, J.P. (1989) "les effets de la réglementation et le comportement des banques", article présenté au colloque de la *S.U.E.R.F.*, sept.

Bank of international settlements (1986) *Recent innovations in international banking*, Basle, (the Cross report) april .

Bank of international settlements (1987) : " Proposal for the international convergence of capital measurements and capital standards " Dec..

Barnea, A. et al (1981) "An equilibrium analysis of debt financing under costly tax arbitrage and agency problems", *Journal of Finance* , 36.

Benston G.J., Eisenbis R.A., Horvitz P.M., Kane E.J., Kaufman G.G. (1986) : "*Perspectives on safe and sound banking, past, present, and future*", MIT Press .

Blair R.D. and Heggestad A.A. (1978) "Bank portfolio regulation and the probability of bank failure", *Journal of Money Credit and Banking,* Feb. vol.10

Boyd, J.H. and Graham, S.L. (1986) "Risk, regulation, and bank holding company expansion", Federal Reserve bank of Minneapolis, *Quarterly Review* , spring.

Boyd, J.H. and Graham, S.L. (1988) "The profitability and risk effects of allowing bank holding companies to merge with other financial firms : a simulation study", Federal Reserve bank of Minneapolis, *Quarterly Review* , spring.

Commission Bancaire (1987) Livre blanc : "les nouveaux instruments financiers et le risque bancaire", *Banque de France* , mars .

Dermine J. (1987) : "Les banques et le risque d'intérêt", *Analyse financière,* 2ème trimestre .

Furlong, F.T. (1988) "Changes in bank risk taking", Federal reserve bank of San Fransisco *Economic Review*, spring .

Furlong, F.T. and Keeley, M. (1987) "Bank capital regulation and asset risk", Federal reserve bank of San Fransisco *Economic Review,* spring .

Galy M. (1989) : "L'exposition des banques au risque de marché", *Revue d'économie financière* n° 10, septembre.

IBCA, (1987) "*Statistical comparisons : France* ".

James C. (1987) : "Off-Balance Sheet Banking", Federal Reserve Bank of San Fransisco, *Economic Review*, Fall.

Kane , E.J. (1984) "Deregulation and changes in the financial services industry", *Journal of Finance* , 39.

Kane E.J. (1985) : "*The gathering crisis in deposit insurance*", Cambridge : MIT Press
Kane, E.J. (1986) "Appearance and reality in deposit insurance", *Journal of Banking and Finance* , 10.
Kane, E.J. (1989), "*The S. and L. insurance mess : how did it happen ?* Cambridge; MA :MIT Press.
Kaufman G.G. (1984 (a)) : "Measuring and managing interest rate risk : a primer". Federal Reserve Bank of Chicago, *Economic Review,* jan./fev.
Kaufman G.G. (1984 (b)) : "Consequences of deregulation for commercial banking" *Journal of Finance* , Juillet Vol 39.
Keeley M.C., Furlong F.T. (1990) : " A reexamination of Mean-Variance analysis of bank capital regulation ", *Journal of Banking and Finance,* 14.
Kim, D. and Santomero, A.M. (1988) "Risk in banking and capital regulation", *Journal of Finance,* 63.
Koehn M. and Santomero, A.M. (1980) "Regulation of bank capital and portfolio risk", *Journal of Finance* , 35.
Koehn M.and Stangle B. (1980): "The effect of deposit-rate ceilings on bank risk : a comment", *Journal of Banking and Finance,* Vol 4.
Komarnicki R. et Gil G. (1987) : "Gestion du risque de taux d'intérêt des opérations de marché", *Analyse Financière* , 2ème trimestre.
Lacoue-Labarthe D. (1990) : "Les crises financières internationales", Journées AFSE-GRECO "EFIQ", *LARE,* Université de Bordeaux I, mai.
Markowitz, H. (1952) "Portfolio selection", *Journal of Finance,* March .
Miller, M. (1977) "Debt and taxes", *Journal of Finance,* 32.
Mingo J. (1978) : "The effect of deposit-rate ceilings on bank risk", *Journal of Banking and Finance,* Vol 2.
Modigliani, F. and Merton M. (1958) "The cost of capital, corporation finance and the theory of investment", *American Economic Review,* 48.
Paroush, J. (1988) "The Domino effect and the supervision of the banking system", *Journal of Finance,* 63.
Roy A.D. (1952) "Safety first and the holding of assets", *Econometrica,* 20
Smirlock M. (1984) : "An analysis of bank risk and deposit-rate ceilings", *Journal of Monetary Economics,* Vol 16.
Wall, L.D. (1986) "Nonbank activities and Risk", Federal Reserve bank of Atlanta, *Economic Review,* October.

CHAPTER 6

SETTING UP A SAFE AND SOUND BANKING SYSTEM IN CENTRAL AND EASTERN EUROPEAN COUNTRIES

Dominique Lacoue-Labarthe

INTRODUCTION

When the institutional framework of a country cannot provide either legal mechanisms and statutes for competition, privatisation of firms, unconstrained distribution of goods and services, or financial intermediaries independent from regulatory authorities, it is hardly possible for economic agents to respond to macro-economic incentives. This is the kind of situation one can meet in Central and Eastern Europe (hereafter CEE) today, where a dozen of newly independent and free republics are engaged in a transition towards a market economy. For a couple of years or so, these countries have initiated a macro-economic adjustment process, some of them even administering a shock therapy in order to reduce the length of this troubled period. Most of them have succeeded in reducing the inflation rate from a two or three-digit level to an almost tolerable rate of, say, 15-25% a year, within a very short period of time. As most energies were mobilised towards this target, time and resources devoted to institutional reforms were scarce. However, it is important to realize how an efficient financial and banking system is essential to the implementation of an operational monetary mechanism during the length of the adjustment period. Financial reform must proceed without delay.

Most of these transition economies are over-industrialized and their financial system is far from being adequately designed for a market mechanism. Such is the case of Poland where only nine banks were created in 1989, as an end product of the dissolution of the former central financial office which enforced the government policies. The new banks which are large enough to collect deposits all over the country are presently hindered by non performing loans transmitted by the former central financial office (Calvo and Frenkel, 1991). In addition to these banks, more than ninety new financial intermediaries have emerged suddenly everywhere in the country, most of them poorly capitalized, collecting very few deposits and making loans out of their own resources without serious guarantees. In these conditions, one can hardly speak of actual banks or of a genuine and complete credit market. Besides, there exists no bonds market, not even a possibility for intermediaries to borrow in an interbank market or from the Central Bank. Finally, the very instruments of credit operations like bills, discounting, acceptances, etc, are still unknown. Firms prefer to rely on informal inter-entreprise credits, simple leads and lags in the payments process or implicit agreements to postpone settlements. Much work lays ahead before a performing market-compatible financial system can be set up.

Following several pioneering contributions, (Brainard (1991), De Cecco (1989), Saunders and Walter (1991)), the present paper addresses the narrower question of defining the conditions for building a safe and sound banking sector in a transition economy. Clearly, one first has to choose, among different financing processes, the role to be played by indirect finance through financial intermediation as opposed to direct finance in the capital market. Then we have to cope with the problem of organizing the financial services industry and the banking sector, defining activities allowed to various types of intermediaries, establishing what sort of barriers to entry, recommending what development strategies banks should follow. Finally, we shall try and define the minimum set of rules and regulations necessary to prevent systemic risk, i.e. that a single insolvent bank failure degenerate by contagion of fear in a general panic capable of causing severe damages and high social costs to the payments system and, possibly, a debt deflation collapse of the whole economy.

1. DESIGNING A NEW FRAMEWORK FOR THE FINANCIAL SYSTEM

A few years after engaging in the transition process, CEE economies have already dismantled the former centralized financial structures and institutions but the new ones have not yet come to maturity. Financial reform has multiple objectives. One is primarily concerned with elaborating a system that fits into the future European Economic and Monetary Union (EMU), in compatibility with the risk-based capital regulation and the "home country rule" applying to banks. There also exists a willingness to design a modern and efficient financial system, which implies avoiding errors experienced previously in foreign countries. A tendency to deregulate the financial system too rapidly might be harmful. The process of financial transition might well be slower than the real sector transition to a market economy. Some regulation and monitoring might prove necessary in order to avoid financial disorder and systemic risk. This could result in a fairly important and durable discrepancy between the financial systems of EMU and CEE countries

1.1 The roles of direct and indirect finance

National financial systems are sometimes divided into two separate stylized reference models. The first one relies upon a process of direct finance; the capital market, essentially a bond market, plays the essential role in the financing process. Firms issue bonds to finance their borrowing requirements. So does the government in case of a budget deficit. Households face a choice of holding cash balances or bonds, which depends positively on their income and negatively on the rate of interest paid on bonds, viewed as the opportunity cost of holding cash. Since loans are perfect substitutes for bonds of the same maturity, there is no need to separate them in the analysis, therefore banks are treated as pure brokerage firms in the securities market.

By contrast, the process of financial adjustment can be analysed from a credit market and financial intermediation perspective. In this case, the bond market is supposed to be too small to play a significant role, or to satisfy the sole borrowing requirement of the government, the private sector being systematically rationed. Banks then collect sight deposits and lend funds to firms for longer terms, providing a transformation function to the economy. In the process, banks have to refinance their loans; it is admitted that the Central Bank accepts to lend funds at an interest rate level that it defines through its reaction function.

Indeed, these two polar cases should not be viewed as real world descriptions. The type I model does not strictly apply to the U.S. or U.K. economies, nor does the type II model to the German or the French financial systems. Each and every national system has its own combination of both direct and indirect finance. It is true however that in some economies, the emphasis is put on the capital market rather than on financial intermediation, or the reverse in other countries.

Is it possible to conceive of a certain margin for choosing financial structures in transition economies? Answering this question is mostly a matter of welfare economics, that is, of comparisons between benefits and costs associated with each type of organization. In the case of CEE countries, we argue that relying on a direct finance process in the course of transition to a market economy might prove less efficient and more costly than extending bank credit.

1.2 Costs of building up a capital market

In an economy in transition, it is clear that shares and equities are more attractive to the general public than bonds or securities. Privatisation of firms distributes property rights that have long been kept off from the hands of individuals. In contrast, underwriting securities only offers a succession of future coupons, possibly of negative real value, and practically no possibility of further trading due to the absence of a secondary bond market.

However, industrial and commercial activities might well keep being risky for a long period because of a maintained residual inflation and a declining production. As a result individuals can be afraid of freezing their savings in equities, and of taking excessive risk in case the failure of firms induces them to withdraw their funds unexpectedly.

When real growth is back, firms are prompt to engage in new investment opportunities promising high yields and implying a high degree of risk. This attitude results in the multiplication of anticipated failures. It is often mentioned that excessive risk taking can be masked by collusion between managers and their creditors, notably by extending inter-firm credit. Finally, the capital market appears to be excessively constrained by the volume of available funds and the number of agents accepting to maintain their participation in the capital of firms on a stable basis. A clear priority should be given to capitalizing banks who could, in turn, acquire shares in the capital of firms and supply them with loans for financing their borrowing requirement.

The other component of the capital market is the securities market. Unfortunately, there seems to be no easy means for firms to signal their value and it follows that they have to support high costs when issuing debt and selling bonds to the public. They will try to compensate for a lack of information on their projects, a poor disclosure policy and the incertain procedure of issue by more sophisticated characteristics of the securities. This will make the organization of a secondary market of sufficient size, depth, resilience and liquidity more difficult in order to ensure a succesful placement of the securities among investors. Without a very solid professional experience of investment banks and security dealers, rating agencies, market makers, delivery and settlement systems, global custodians etc., there are no real chances for developing a performing bond market. The same is true for the public debt, as long as the very basic instruments of a reliable and secure market do not exist.

Anyway, the growth of the public debt might be the starting point of a genuine securities market. Treasury bonds and bills are risk-free; they may present fiscal privileges. Moreover, the budget deficit of the state provides a regular source of securities. Experience and professional ability may grow rapidly, and the premises of consistent organization might soon appear. In the case of an equilibrium or surplus of the budget, the public debt might still grow as long as, for instance, the government buys back the bad debts endangering the soundness of the balance sheets of banks and firms and swaps them for new long term bonds issued with its public guarantee. This would probably represent the best way to forgive this embarrassing debt, providing a means of getting rid of it at a cost that would progressivly be spread over several years and mutualized across the different sectors of the whole economy.

The growth of the public debt is a necessary condition for implementing open market operations. Indeed it is a much better support for repurchase and reverse repurchase agreements, or pension operations in the interbank or money market than bonds issued by the Central Bank itself (as in Poland for instance). There are many flaws in that method since a conflict might arise at any moment. The Central Bank would suffer from selling or buying back bonds in the market at a lower or higher price than the issue price, causing deliberate changes in the value of its debt.

If it is too costly to develop simultaneously the two components of the capital market, a sequencing process must be chosen. Priority goes undoubtedly to the equity market and banks should be capitalized first. Then a public debt market could be started, while firms benefiting from bank loans or/and participations could signal their value to the market and try to sell their newly issued debt. Very little chance of success could be granted to a reverse order of sequencing trying to develop first a securities market without the assistance of well capitalized banks.

1.3 Efficiency of financial intermediation

The new theory of financial intermediation, as surveyed for instance by Lewis (1991) and Chant (1992), suggests its superiority over market solutions for solving the asymmetries of information and the uncertainty of liquidity production problems that arise in the financial process.

Lenders have a natural tendency to assess the investment projects of firms to the extent that they want to select the best combination of risk and expected return for the assets they will include in their portfolio. Now, it is generally admitted that the cost is too high if individual investors try to get more information than the one that is publicly displayed when new bonds are issued in the securities market. It is also costly for savers to observe the behaviour of borrowers and to check if firms really invest the funds in the right project and meet their contractual obligations in servicing their debt. Financial intermediaries complete that task more efficiently than individual savers as they receive a delegated monitoring function (Diamond, 1984) from them.

Specialization in this activity lowers the monitoring cost and is beneficial to both savers and intermediaries.

As is well established, another factor of efficiency associated with financial intermediaries is their ability to realize economies of scale and scope. The amount of borrowed resources from a great number of individual savers is large enough to authorize a thorough diversification of assets among a variety of projects which differ by types of firm, activity, geographical location and maturity. As a consequence, financial intermediaries can offer a higher return and a lower risk on their portfolio than individual investors. At the same time, intermediaries can offer a lower credit cost to borrowers, particularly to those firms whose size is too small, and reputation or rating too low for them to be allowed to enter the capital market.

The advantage of borrowing from an intermediary is obvious for a firm. First, it can save its capital for longer and more attractive investments than simply financing its current borrowing needs. Second, a bank loan can be used as a financial signal to the market which enables the firm to display its projects and to reveal its real creditworthiness. The firm can take a clear and credible commitment to service its debt while its willingness to accept bank monitoring is publicly announced. Under these circumstances, access to the capital market should be made easier and less costly than for a firm of identical size and characteristics but whose creditworthiness remains unrevealed to the market.

The firm will benefit in engaging in a long term relationship with one or several intermediaries. This link will be enhanced when the firm accepts to invest in part its own capital or when it deposits securities as a collateral for guaranteeing, at least partially, new demands for loans. On the contrary, it should be clearly understood by the firm that the intermediary can suddenly terminate a credit contract and withdraw or ration its supply of funds, when the firm does not reimburse its loan according to the terms of the contract.

An extra protection can be drawn from a steady and close link between a firm and an intermediary. A great number of shareholders makes it difficult to monitor the managers of a firm so that its performance may decline without the knowledge of the owners. The firm may then become an easy opportunity for an agressive take over attempt. If, on the contrary, the firm can rely upon the assistance of its usual partners in the credit market, it can borrow enough resources to discard the threat. Shareholders may also conclude an agreement with the suppliers of credit in order to make their own interests to coincide with those of the firm, by using the influence that intermediaries can have on the management. Many interesting solutions to agency problems can be provided by financial intermediaries. An extreme case of integration, often referred to, is the presence of bank representatives in the board of direction of a large number of firms in Germany.

1.4 Banks and other intermediaries

A financial intermediary transforms illiquid assets (loans) into liquid assets (deposits). It performs two parallel functions, namely a production of information function and an insurance of liquidity function. A great variety of intermediaries play these roles : saving associations, insurance companies, credit unions, investment funds, pension funds etc, including commercial banks.

Banks are special since a fraction of their liabilities are accepted in transactions as means of payment. Observation of payments made by their depositors gives the banks an informational advantage such that they can select potential borrowers among their depositors and finance their projects by granting them new loans. Banks are unique, because they are the only intermediary which can offer simultaneously to their depositors such a menu of joint services : information, insurance, liquidity and payment services.

A potential instability threatens the bank permanently. The bank can maintain its activity and survive only if its resources are not withdrawn by its depositors. Now, in order to keep deposits in its balance sheet, the bank must guarantee that it will convert them at sight into currency or transfer them to any other intermediary at a fixed rate. If this specific clause did not exist, demand deposits would not be accepted as immediate means of settlement or perfectly liquid assets. As a consequence, unexpected and important withdrawals of deposits from the bank jeopardize its survival.

A variety of assets enter the portfolio offered against more liquid claims to depositors. Some are short-term and risk free notes or bills with constant nominal value. Other assets are more risky, such as loans or long term bonds or equities. The deposits backing portfolios composed of riskless assets are themselves free of capital risk; their value only depends on the amount of transactions completed and on the value accrued interest. However, the banks creditors may prefer to hold deposits backed by risky portfolios; the value of their account must then fluctuate not only as a function of withdrawals and new deposits but also as a consequence of changes in the market value of this portfolio. In case of a decrease in the value of assets, the value of deposits must also decline and the bank can no longer keep its promise to convert at fixed rate deposits for currency. These depreciated deposits are now *de facto* inconvertible. Perhaps the bank prefers to maintain an illusory fixed value of deposits in nominal terms but the subsequent losses affect its results. This will lead to an exhaustion of capital and to an insolvency position of the bank. If no compensating measures are adopted, the bank will go bankrupt.

One can imagine a separation of the two functions of financial intermediation on the one hand, and of servicing means of payment on the other hand. Different institutions can complete these different roles. For instance, certain investment or merchant banks use their own capital to invest in equities or buy bonds from other firms and they prefer not to grant loans to those firms. On the opposite, some other intermediaries specialize in issuing credit cards or banks'cheque guarantee cards and they earn commissions they prefer not to invest in assets portfolios. This sort of solution is workable to a certain extent only.

Mutual funds or unit trusts are designed partly to solve these problems. The basic idea is that they value and redeem deposits according to the current market value of their portfolio, no matter whether it is worth more or less than face value. As long as there is no obligation to price and payout deposits on a fixed-priced basis, the risk of loss must be taken by the shareholder. There is no incentive to join in the line since no first come-first served rule applies and there should be no run.

Indeed, mutual funds should be kept apart from transaction services in order to preserve the security of the payment system. As is now well established, the separation between mutual funds and deposits did not survive attempts by funds to enter the liquidity market and, for instance in the U.S. and other countries they succeeded in creating money market-deposit accounts or similar formulaes.

In any case, banks are the most important intermediaries for managing the clearing and settlement needs in the transaction process. They are responsible for the continuity and the efficiency of the payment system, and what might be considered as a by-product of the services they offer to the public is, on the contrary, a fundamental function they assume. Moreover, in servicing transactions (by processing cheques, book-keeping and recording of settlements, clearing various instruments of payment etc.), banks generate external effects for the whole economy. A failure would create damages to solvent institutions and shocks of this sort might result in serious consequences to the real sector.

It is generally admitted that the presence of externalities justifies a control of banks by a public regulator. This is a reason why banks receive a privileged protection against the risk of running short of liquidity. They also benefit from an implicit insurance since a lender of last resort would help them by providing a loan of unlimited amount but at a penalty rate if necessary. Of course, this assistance is, in principle, reserved to solvent institutions which accept the rules and regulations edicted by the banking authorities.

The existence and functioning of this safety net gives the banks a supplementary advantage over the capital market and with respect to non bank financial intermediaries. It is possible for them to charge a lower price to their customers for the liquidity risk associated to any loan offer they decide to extend.

2. THE STRUCTURE OF THE BANKING INDUSTRY

The optimum degree of competition in the banking industry has long been a matter of controversy. The reconstruction of competitive financial systems in the transition economies of CEE offers an unexpected new opportunity to the advocates of the free banking principle, whereas legal restrictions prevail in the whole world today. It is reported that some experts (George Selgin, for instance is often quoted) urge the recently elected representatives of Ukraine to issue a new currency unit (the *khrivna*) and organize a competitive system of issue by various private banks, rather than concentrate it in the hands of a public monopoly. Although this position has little chance of being adopted by most governments, at least in its most radical formulation, some lessons can be drawn from history. In organizing a modern banking industry, governements must avoid building artificial barriers, enacting useless restrictions and introducing costly distortions like so many countries did in the past. Actually, choices are rather constrained in CEE countries, because the banking sectors of the Economic and Monetary Union in Western Europe and of the other OECD countries are very close competitors.

2.1 Free banking or legal restrictions ?

Originally, the free banking doctrine in its strong version, rejects legal tender currency whose issue would be monopolised by a public Central Bank (Dowd, 1989). Banks are allowed to issue any liabilities they want, particularly notes convertible in gold, or, at least, in other banks' notes if the economy is no longer ruled by the gold standard. In order to persuade the public to hold the outstanding amount of notes and deposits, the bank has to refrain from issuing liabilities in excess. Otherwise, in case of an excess supply of one bank's liabilities over their demand, they simply will be returned to the bank for redemption. The need to maintain convertibility leads banks to avoid over issue. As a consequence, banks might be forced to hold 100% reserves against their liabilities to prevent illiquidity. Usually however, fractional reserves are sufficient if the bank has acquired a solid reputation and has a moderate issue policy.

It is very difficult to imagine how a free banking system could work if there exists a legal tender money, if currency is inconvertible in gold and if people prefer to use deposits in much larger proportions than notes to settle their transactions. Private monies are now dominated by legal currency and the quantity of unborrowed reserves that banks can hold is largely exogeneous to their issuing policy. It depends on the variations in the sources of the monetary base, namely foreign exchange operations, extended credit to the Treasury and open market transactions of the Central Bank.

The main task of a bank consists in choosing a level of the interest rate served on deposits that guarantees a stable market share or a fixed proportion of depositors. Having determined the size of its balance sheet, the bank maximizes its profit (or utility) in investing in a diversified portfolio of assets. Holding fractional reserves is sufficient to insure liquidity to depositors as long as their consumption needs are not affected by unanticipated shocks. In case of an unexpected run, banks would be unable to redeem deposits and that is the reason why the Central Bank has to behave as a lender of last resort. According to the classical argument of externalities, a supervision of banks must be organized, implying legal restrictions to the banking sector.

2.2 Regulatory constraints to banking activity

As soon as free banking is restricted, the government enforces more or less restrictive rules concerning the statute of banks and the entry of firms in the industry of banking.

Banks have a legal statute, whether a charter, or an agreement, or an affiliation, or a registration on an official list etc. The authorization of entering the banking business must be formally given by a legal regulator. This gives the authorities latitude to check conformity of the by-laws of the company running the bank, the level of capital owned by the bank, the moral reputation of its managers etc. The bank is allowed to practice a precise and limited number of registered operations, while others are forbidden. Rules are imposed concerning compulsory reserves that banks must hold with the Central Bank, namely their rate, period of reference, date of constitution, and the penalties incurred in case of infraction.

Prudential ratios may also be defined; for instance, a risk distribution ratio limits to a certain proportion of the capital the total risks concentrated on a single borrower. A liquidity ratio leads the bank to match its short-term liabilities by at least an equivalent amount of liquid assets. A ratio of permanent resources, acting as a mismatch ratio, compels banks to finance a given percentage of their fixed and long-term assets by means of long-term liabilities. Strict limits may also be imposed concerning any equity participation that a financial intermediary may hold in non-banking companies.

It should be acknowledged that these restrictions imposed to the banks give them in return substantial privileges, for instance, in many countries, a right to borrow freely from the Central Bank (as in France), or, at least, a certain maximum amount (as in Germany), or under specified circumstances (as in the United States), at the current discount rate. In most cases, banks are also placed under the protection of a deposit insurance system ruled by a government institution. Moreover, the Central Bank is entitled to discriminate against those financial intermediaries which would not meet all the legal restrictions, and as a regulatory authority it has the power of suspending, or closing, existing banks as soon as they are suspected of fraud and to refuse affiliation of new candidates to entry in the industry.

In a growing banking sector, strong pressure can arise as competition for getting market shares increases. If regulators want this emulation to improve the efficiency of the industry, they have to liberalize conditions of application for new candidates and lower barriers to entry. The case of Poland is illustrative of this situation with its burgeoning creation of dozens of new banks in a few months. Indeed, most of these institutions will never reach a sufficient size to be able to survive. Concentration will develop, resulting in mergers and acquisitions throughout the industry.

The entry of foreign banks into the national banking sector is of particular importance. It might well be justified to adopt, at least for a while, the infant industry argument to develop a protection against a risk of destructive competition. Of course, this kind of protection will not be acclaimed by proponents of market mechanisms. However, a transition process should be managed as long as a consistent organization of the domestic sector has not emerged, this for reasons of safety and soundness.

2.3 Entry in the banking industry

A foreign bank willing to enter the domestic banking industry has a choice between several strategies. Three examples follow.

(i) First, it can open a branch or subsidiary in the local market. If the home country welcomes this opening, that is if the new bank conforms to all necessary legal restraints, it can then build relationships and enter into the set of transactions best done locally. Entry is very costly but it may give access to high risk and return investment opportunities to the extent that some customers are unsatisfied with the financial services offered by local banks. This will result in an increased welfare if, for example, the new entrant owns proprietary technology or financial techniques that enable it to perform banking functions more efficiently. On the opposite, some local banks, unable to withstand increased competition, will go bust and exit the market, which causes the goodwill built up by these exiting banks to be lost (Montgomery, 1991).

(ii) Second, the foreign bank may obtain an identical result with a lower cost of entry in taking over an existing local bank. It enables the bank to lend to and borrow from local intermediaries and customers already linked by a long-term relationship. To the extent that the bank has a market power in the local deposit market, which gives it access to a supply of cheap funds, and that lending in a locality is more efficiently done, for monitoring reasons, by locally based intermediaries, the new entrant can benefit from a comparative advantage.

(iii) Third, a foreign bank can offer its financial services at a distance, that is from its original location abroad. The market for banking services is here supposed fully integrated and competitive. Comparative advantage, in that case, will depend either on relative factor endowments or on differences in production costs. This kind of cross-border activities of financial intermediaries depends on the absence of market power or externalities. In some cases, that of wholesale banking, for instance, imperfect competition might be economically justified and banking services will be concentrated in large firms dealing with many customers, both domestic and foreign. It would be the case if there are significant increasing returns to scale that can be exploited.

The net welfare gains or losses to opening a country's financial markets to foreign banks depend on the extent to which the location of financial intermediaries is of relevant interest. Some banking services markets may be internationally segmented while others are completely integrated. As long as integration is a reality, the case for government protection is rather weak and domestic banks should welcome foreign banks and accept their superiority in offering specialized services, such as financial engineering, mergers and acquisitions methods, international issuing, or syndication of loans, and other investment banking activities. On the contrary, there might be a case for protection when local factors dominate in customers' relationships, whether in the deposit or the loan markets.

2.4 Separation of banking functions

In certain industrial countries like the U.S. and Japan, regulators have for long separated banking activities between distinct types of intermediaries. Initially, this sort of segregation was rather strict. As time went by, numerous financial innovations and new practices were authorized, leading to a certain extent, to greater globalization by offering financial services under one single roof. Some other countries never adopted similar constraints and promoted a model of universal bank which was most popular in Western Europe for instance. But there seems to be circumstances where some "Chinese walls" are necessary in order to avoid disorderly and malfunctioning intermediaries. What has been learned from experience and are there some lessons to be suggested to CEE countries ?

Nobody would seriously advocate a separation of banks on a geographical basis today. Prohibition of interstate branching enacted by the McFadden Act (1927) in the U.S. has in fact been unanimously criticized. Indeed, it has been an important element of an antitrust legislation but today, there are, to be certain, more efficient means of preventing firms from acquiring an excessive market power in a given industry. It has been proved, by contrast, that restraining the possibility of extending loans to a limited area increases the exposition of banks to credit risks. Over the years, many bank failures in rural regions of the United States can be explained, at times, by bad weather conditions ruining a given production. A similar result has been observed in the case of banks having portfolios that are excessively concentrated on speculative investments---commercial real estate, for instance. Diversification should be the key-word and separation of activities on a locational or sectoral basis should definitly be removed. It is not quite clear, however, whether the new sovereign states, which were federally linked in the former Soviet Union, will allow their national banks to create branches or subsidiaries throughout the region. It should be emphasized that, in certain areas, banks which could not reach a sufficient size might be hindered by an excessive specialization or concentration of their deposits, or investments, or both.

Separation of commerce and banking has been a long tradition in the United States. Continental Western Europe never adopted such restrictions as those edicted for instance by the Bank Holding Company Act (1956) and Douglas Amendment. On the contrary, great efforts have recently been devoted to creating big financial conglomerates, both at the domestic and at the intra-EEC levels, for instance between banks and insurance companies --- the so-called *bancassurance* or *Allfinanz* schemes. A somewhat similar case can be made of U.S. financial supermarkets that include banks. As is often argued (e.g. Litan, 1987), two categories of potential economies of scope could be realized. Firms may realize internal economies of scope through joint production and marketing of complementary financial services (banking, insurance, securities and real estate, for instance), whereas consumers may realize external economies of scope through joint consumption of these services. Whether these economies are easy to identify and exploit is a difficult and unsolved question. If no clear gain can be assessed, perhaps a careful attitude would consist in avoiding confusion between different types of activities. After all, a banker has not exactly the same type of occupation as an insurer.

The segregation of banking institutions from the securities industry, and vice versa, is still quite an issue in the U.S. and in Japan. The Glass-Steagall Act (1933) and other banking laws in the U.S., article 65 of the Japanese Securities and Exchange Act (1948) have established similar regimes in both countries for comparable reasons. First, there is a potential conflict of interest between the banking activity and the securities industry. It occurs when, for instance, a bank offers a loan to an underwriting client to avert a default on bonds or enhance the management credibility in the capital market. In that case, the bank sacrifices the depositor's interests to protect investors in corporate bonds, despite the fact that protection of depositors should naturally be a major concern of the bank (Benston, 1990). Such conflicts of interest still exist and one cannot be sure that repealing the old restrictions would eliminate them.

A second reason justifying separation is that banks should not participate in risky securities business (But the same argument could be put forth concerning the loan business --- which is actually a risky investment. Taking risk is inherent to banking after all. A third point relates to the elimination of monopolies and enforcement of an antitrust legislation. And finally, as financial services become internationally integrated, some effort in harmonization, or at least, coordination among major countries might be undertaken, particularly in view of the future course of EMU.

Unless CEE countries adopt a universal banking scheme, a feasible solution consists in allowing commercial banks and securities firms to establish an investment bank subsidiary that can engage in all areas of the securities industry, such as underwriting corporate bonds, corporate equity and trust services. Alternatively, both types of firms could create subsidiaries that can participate in a particular area of banking or the securities activity. These solutions are probably superior to the universal banking firm for solving the conflict of interest problem and they might be recommended to transition economies in Europe.

Due to the great variety of financial intermediaries operating in a special business, such as mortgage credit, consumer finance, portfolio investment, payment services etc., legal provisions are required in order to limit increases in systemic risks or investor risk facing individual depositors. Recent developments prove that regulation of non bank financial intermediaries has often been much more flexible and looser than for banks themselves. Deregulation has too easily been accepted, or even encouraged, for Savings and Loan Associations in the U.S. resulting in the present collapse. Heavy problems linked to over-indebtness of many households in Britain may be traced back in part to a systematic extension of variable interest rate lending procedures adopted by building societies in the early 1980s. Many similar problems arising in various specialized sectors of financial intermediation and affecting most of industrial countries prove that no satisfactory solution has been found yet. The next section will examine some features of prudential control addressing these problems.

2.5 Towards a "focused universal bank" ?

After the Second World War, many countries have adopted a set of regulations which, unlike the German universal bank scheme, favoured a high degree of specialization. For instance, the banking laws of 1941 and 1945 in France distinguished banks according to several criteria: the main distinction between *banques de dépôts* and *banques d'affaires* was supplemented by taking into account either the average maturity of loans (*banques de crédit à moyen et long terme*), or the field of economic activity (*crédit agricole, crédit maritime* etc). The Banking Act of 1984 introduced more uniformity in the banking sector by referring to a general concept of *établissement de crédit*, already defined under the broad notion of "credit institution" under the European Directive adopted in 1977. Anyway since 1984, all credit institutions are subject to a unique set of regulations and to the same supervisory institutions (de Boissieu, 1990). The complementary trends of financial deregulation and prudential re-regulation have also been underway for years in the U.K. (Hall, 1991), and, indeed, in most of the financially developed world. A certain common tendency toward a universal banking model, more or less similar to the German scheme, can be identified in the EC context.

The second Banking Directive enacting the "home country rule" stipulates that if a bank (or, rather, a credit institution) is allowed to operate by the regulatory authorities in any EC country, then it will be allowed in every EC country. One can then anticipate that in the near future, this principle will be extended to Central European countries associated with the EC.

Traditional banking was a rather narrow and simple business of intermediating funds between savers and borrowers and providing transaction services. It has now evolved into a broader and more complicated business including a host of new savings and investment products and financial offbalance sheet services. Banks have now to supply efficient, flexible and professional services to their customers at competitive prices, to market them adequately, and deliver them conveniently. Successful achievement of these strategies will require reliable and safe operations, a flexibility to offer products that fit new markets and changing customer needs, and an innovating ability in product development, marketing and delivery.

There is a high cost associated with this sort of universal banking strategies and most of credit institutions will seek to exploit specialization niches where they have a comparative advantage resulting, for instance, from an innovating product or financial expertise. Unfortunately, niches are hardly temporary abodes of profit opportunities to the extent that innovations in financial services are impossible to protect from competitors. Registered trade marks do not apply in the banking business.

Sooner or later, newly created banks in the transition economies will have to reveal their market value when barriers to entry are removed under international pressure. By that time, they will have to display a positive spread between their stock price value and their net accounting value as it represents the only proof of solvency. As always, the market mechanism will require that each monetary unit invested in a banking business be valued at par or at a premium. Otherwise, losses and failure will follow rapidly. A bank cannot survive unless its return on equity is at least equal to the cost of capital. Maintaining this fragile equilibrium is indeed a difficult task.

3. BANKING POLICY

Banking policy is the natural complement to classical monetary policy for the regulation and control of the financial system. Monetary policy contributes to macro economic adjustment whereas banking policy is justified by systemic risks. Its objective is to promote a safe and sound banking system through a more or less restrictive combination of incentives and controls.

When a banking system has not yet completely matured, regulators have to design a consistent system of rules and controls which will not replicate errors made elsewhere. The final section of the present paper selects four issues of interest to the economies in transition.

3.1 Prohibition of interest payments on demand deposits

As means of payment generally accepted in transactions, demand deposits generate an important non pecuniary flow of services which lowers information, transaction and liquidity costs. Demand deposits are available on request. Their nominal value is known with absolute certainty as their capital value is constant. They have a fixed exchange rate against legal currency which is guaranteed by banks. These special characteristics of demand deposits may justify that banks do not offer interest payments on these accounts. This non-payment might be seen as a compensation for the cost that the bank is bearing for managing these deposits.

A few industrialized countries still prohibit interest payments on demand deposits, as the U.S. or France. Some others authorize banks to pay a rate exogeneously fixed by regulatory institutions. This rate may have a unique value or may fluctuate within predetermined limits. Quite often, the deposit rate has a low absolute value (e.g. 1,5 - 2%), not even indexed to the rate of inflation. Finally, other countries have entirely deregulated deposit rates and do not discriminate against demand deposits since the rates served on savings accounts, time deposits, certificates of deposits etc. are set by a market mechanism. Each bank resource has its cost : there is no such thing as free liquidity.

Prohibiting interest payments on demand deposits has benefits and costs. The most obvious result for banks is that they borrow freely from depositors, and this increases their interest margin. If banks have, to some degree, a monopoly power and use a mark-up to fix their lending rate, the level and the whole term structure of interest rates can be lower than they would be in a competitive market.

True, depositors do not perceive interest revenues on their checking accounts; they do not pay either for cheques they write nor for the book-keeping services offered freely by banks. Using cheques as means of payment becomes more popular and increases the number of bank customers. Banks can use the profits for increasing their network of branches over a greater area or the whole country. This effort results in an increased diversification of depositors and potential borrowers, a factor of safeness for the banking sector as a whole.

In fact, when a regulation sets fixed interest rate on demand deposits, it creates a rent for commercial banks. Surprisingly enough, no part of this rent accrues to the regulatory authorities themselves (Chiappori, 1991). This rent differs from the interest margin, or spread, between the deposit and the lending rates which is a normal part of bank profit. The rent is equal to the difference between the real cost associated with using demand deposits as resources, and their opportunity cost, that is their borrowing cost in the market. This surplus, levied at the expense of depositors and regulators, benefits only banks. Thus, they receive a net income transfer.

Distortions follow. As the operating cost of cheques and the real price of payments services is not charged to depositors, the number of cheques grows excessively, implying costly investments in computerizing the processing of cheques. Similarly, banks compete to increase the number of their customers, attracting even more low income households whose returns to the banks are weak to the extent that they consume few high value added services. There appears a tendency to over-banking and an excessive growth in the use of costly means of payments. Besides, banks use their rent to cross-subsidy an artificial reduction in lending rates in order to attract new depositors.

Prohibition of interest payments on deposits leads banks to multiply channels for attracting off-balance sheet resources. They create undertakings for collective investment in securities, such as mutual funds, open-end unit trusts etc., in order to attract high income depositors, while they pay nearly the same rate as on the money or the bonds markets. Indeed, there is an interest rate risk on the shares sold to the public for which banks declare unresponsible. This may lead to some embarrassing misunderstanding between banks and their customers in case of capital losses, to say the least.

This analysis tends to suggest that a strict regulation of demand deposits is unnecessary and may cause damages to the financial system. The risk of an excessive growth in mutual funds in response to prohibition of interests on demand deposits is not the least inconvenience. Complete deregulation of interests paid on demand deposits is not a better solution either if it creates a destructive competition between banks in an immature payments system. A fairly good solution might consist in setting exogeneously a positive and low interest rate on demand deposits. This would create a fixed point or a nominal anchor to the whole term structure of interest rates, a stabilizing factor for the value of the currency and the safety of the payments system.

3.2 Evaluating bank assets

The slow development of the securities market in economies in transition raises specific problems related to the valuation of bank instruments. There is little case for using securities as collateral to bank loans. Discounting bills of exchange is a completely unknown procedure in most of these countries. Off-balance sheet commitments such as acceptances, endorsements, standby letters of credit, back-up lines for commercial paper etc. are unfrequently used or hindered by an inadequate legal framework. Credit can only be extended by very simple and risky techniques such as overdrafts or pure consumption loans. The sole valuable claims that banks posess are mortgages or rights over physical assets of the firm that should be sold in case of default.

Bank portfolios also include stocks. Banks often engage in joint ventures with firms or they acquire as a lasting investment parts of their capital. Such stocks and shares are often unlisted in the stock exchange and very difficult to value and trade.

Banks register these assets in their balance sheet at their accounting value, that is their nominal acquisition cost. In case of non performing loans or default in debt servicing, attempts to adjust the reported values of loans for changes in credit quality are problematic. Banks have no other possibility than to constitute a loan-loss provision or supplementary reserves in the results account. A similar procedure should be applied when the value of the shares and stocks decline.

However, provisions are a rather crude way of handling bank risks. They compensate losses partially when the borrowers fail. Managers, investors, and regulators would prefer a more accurate indicator of changes in the value of assets included in the bank's portfolio. What is really needed is a measure of changes in values due to changes in interest rates, increases in asset prices or reductions in the price of liabilities, which would be available before the asset or liability affected is disposed of (Benston, 1990. a). In short, banks would certainly prefer to have assets and liabilities of firms stated in terms of economic market values.

The issue is of importance since banks have a crucial role to play in the process of privatisation of public firms. As outlined by Brainard (1991), at the heart of the problems of reforms lie the balance sheet losses of firms that neither banks, nor governments want to push into bankruptcy, since banks fear the impact on their own results, and the government the effect on its budget. Of course, these losses have to be assessed before some solution can be imagined to solve the problem.

Adoption of generally accepted accounting principles by firms and banks would hardly represent a first step in the evaluation process, since these principles rely on historical and not market values. Strict rules have to be enforced for avoiding manipulations of book values and incomes recorded in balance sheets of firms or banks. For instance, a portfolio manager can choose to recognize the price of an asset used in a trading transaction according to the earlier or later prices paid for asset sold by adopting first-in, first-out (FIFO), or last-in, first-out (LIFO) inventory pricing. A bank can hold securities designated as long-term investments that have decreased in value at the price paid originally for them, while selling securities that have appreciated, with the gain recorded as income rather than capital gain for tax reasons.

Despite the general agreement among economists that historical cost accounting is not justified for measuring the value of assets and liabilities of firms and banks, market-value accounting is rarely used in practice, even in industrialized countries today. Why is it so ?

First, banks specialize in assets that do not trade in markets, particularly loans, uneasy or even impossible to mark to market. Second, banks also hold a substantial proportion of their portfolio in off-balance sheet commitments which usually do not trade in markets either. It must be admitted that models suggesting that these assets might be valued as if they were traded are rather experimental and far from being popular among bankers.

Another reason explaining reluctancy to market accounting principles is the implicit conflict existing between revealing the real value of the bank and securing financial services offered to the economy. For example, a firm has to finance its working capital and its treasurer needs fixed nominal values. When a treasurer concludes a repurchase agreement with a bank, what he needs is funding and he is not interested in realizing capital gains on collateralized securities. Random prices, due to changes in market interest rates, would kill the necessary safety inherent in treasury's transactions. Besides, capital gains would imply an extra tax adding to the usual interest revenue tax.

Prudential regulation is trying to cope with this kind of problem. Following EC accounting directives, the French Committee for Banking Regulation, in its 90-01 Regulation, has recently defined three categories of bank portfolios according to the length of intended holding period, namely: a trading portfolio, a placement portfolio and an investment portfolio. Assets included in the trading portfolio are marked to market; those held for a longer term, but sold before they mature, are subject to provision in case of potential capital loss but capital gains are not registered, in application of the "principle of prudence"; and finally, securities held till they mature are priced at their nominal value.

Typically, these principles are more realistic to enforce than market accounting rules in many current cases. A market economy, particularly in the financial services industry, should never be mixed up with gambling.

3.3 Minimum capital requirement

Requiring a minimum ratio of capital to assets should solve two contradictory issues. If fixed too high, it represents a barrier to entry for the banking industry. Then, the quantity of bank loans available might be unable to finance a growing economy. When, on the contrary, the value of the ratio is too low, its role can be nil as it fails to provide an incentive to the owners and managers of the banking firm to self-regulate and limit its risk exposure.

An opposite and paradoxical point of view is however defended by theorists (Kahane, 1977, Koehn and Santomero, 1980) who argue that rising the capital-asset ratio leads banks to take more risks, and not less, on their investment portfolio. In order to maintain an unchanged return to the shareholders, managers choose high yield-high risk investments. Imposing a capital requirement to banks would induce an inefficiency and increase systemic risk.

This result was criticized (Furlong and Keeley, 1989; Keeley and Furlong, 1990) on the ground that the reference model, a mean-variance theory of portfolio choice, is inadequate in the case of bank behaviour. Indeed, when bankrupcy occurs, the distribution of perceived returns fails to follow a normal law; it is truncated. In that case, a regulation aiming at limiting the financial leverage by a higher capital requirement, succeeds in reducing the total risk facing the banking firm and fails to increase the portfolio risk.

Basically, anyhow, the situation looks like a bet or an option whose result is maximization of an expected gain under financial distress conditions (Ronn and Verma, 1986; Furlong, 1988). The equity value of a banking firm may be considered as a call option on the value of its assets. Debtholders (depositors) can be thought of as effectively owning the assets of the bank and giving the stockholders the option to buy the assets back at maturity. At that date, the value of the net worth (the option) would equal the difference between the value of the assets and the face value of the liabilities if that difference were positive, and zero otherwise. The exercise price of the option is equal to the bank's debt at maturity, and the option would be exercised if the net of worth of the bank were positive, that is if the value of assets were greater than that of liabilities. In the opposite case, the stockholders would not exercise the option and would allow the depositors to keep the assets. The debtholders are then left with a value of the assets insufficient to cover their claims (deposits) on the bank.

The stockholders do not hesitate to withdraw from the bank to the extent that depositors are supposed to be insured against their loss by a public organization. It is not easy under these circumstances, to identify whether it is the minimum capital ratio or the deposit insurance mechanism that is responsible for this unpleasant result. As a matter of fact, the two mechanisms are intricately linked together in this typical moral hazard situation.

A safe and sound banking sector would include a better capital requirement regulation that would not interfere, if possible, with an automatic deposit insurance scheme. The Cooke ratio or the EC solvency ratio may, in part, achieve that objective. It must be noted however that only default risks are addressed by this regulation whereas interest rate and exchange rate risks are not. The ratio tries to weight the relative riskiness of the different types of assets, although the criteria used (type of borrower and regional location) are rather crude.

If the new banks created in Central and Eastern Europe have to be subject some day to the Cooke or the EC ratio, it will be difficult for them to reach rapidly the required rate of 8%. They should try anyway to increase their actual capital-to-asset ratio because their international credibility depends on its value. Issuing bonds or notes in the international market, receiving a rating from a foreign agency, engaging in cross-border interbank transactions etc., are privileges restricted to well capitalized banks. Needless to say how their situation in this respect is important since the cost of their borrowings depends on their rating.

An interesting feature of the EC solvency ratio must be outlined. It might ease the banks endeavours to raise the required amount of capital, although they still have a long way to go to meet the 8% target. Despite their qualification as supplementary capital, provisions can be diverted from the operating results and included in the second tier of the capital standard. This could give the banks an incentive to adopt as early as possible a very cautious stance and take the opportunity of favourable tax treatment to raise their provisions for their non-performing loans.

The risk-based capital standard also includes, in the second tier, hybrid debt-equity instruments and subordinated debt. This latter instrument may amount to no more than 50 percent of tier-one capital, which is formed mainly of equity capital and disclosed reserves. Subordinated debt receives a better fiscal treatment than equity capital since interest paid is deductible from the tax base. It results that subordinated debt is less costly than core capital. Furthermore, it is easier fot the bank to maintain a constant return to shareholders since the minimum proportion of tier-one capital is only 4 percent. Consequently, the bank might be able to reduce the aggregate risk of its investment portfolio.

Creditors holding subordinated debt instruments have a better position, in case of bankruptcy, than shareholders. Subordinated debt absorbs losses only in the event of liquidation. Debtholders of these instruments thereby have an incentive to prevent bankruptcy more actively than shareholders. Moreover, unlike deposits, their claims are not insured. Finally, one could expect that monitoring of banks by debt-holders will be reinforced.

3.4 Efficiency of the safety net

As mentioned earlier, the most serious difficulties arise from moral hazard. The connections between deposit insurance and minimum capital requirement give a good illustration of these problems. In order to analyze them, we shall begin by explaining the flaws of most deposit insurance systems; then we shall proceed to the connected subject of how the regulating authorities intervene in this matter.

A frequently expressed concern is that a deposit insurance mechanism, in which the premium paid by the bank is independent from the aggregate risk of the asset portfolio, creates a moral hazard problem. The motivation for the creation of such systems is the traditional one of protecting "small" depositors and reducing the incentive for a bank run. However, this last objective is unlikely to be met as deposits are only insured up to a certain amount or proportion of their value. For this reason, the deposit insurance system is enhanced by lender of last resort facilities. The level of monitoring by depositors and debtholders is therefore likely to be small. Monitoring finally rests on the shoulders of bank supervisors. Shareholders receive insufficient incentives and they often tend to reduce the volume of the funds they invest as capital in the bank.

Insurance covers only the deposits on which the required premium has been paid. In case of a bankruptcy, other depositors should not receive any compensation at all for their loss. However, the regulators are reluctant to adopt immediately the ultimate solution consisting in closing the bank and organizing its liquidation. The first reason for such an attitude is that regulators have practically no means of knowing in advance whether a bank is merely illiquid or really insolvent. The efficiency of the supervisory process in detecting impending failures can be seriously questioned. A second explanation lies in the fear that shareholders of the bank will complain in case of an early intervention of the regulators, while the bank possibly meets transitory difficulties. The third reason is that closing a bank can trouble the regular course of payments, and might, by contagion, trigger other banks failures.

These reasons explain why the supervisory authorities prefer bailout rather than closure of banks in order to keep them in business. The Central Bank, acting as a lender of last resort, will extend a loan to a bank that is not yet obviously insolvent, possibly on the ground that, given a chance, the bank will recover. If the bank's situation is deeply troubled, regulators will try to find a merger partner, while allowing it to keep afloat. Such partners, however, are difficult to find. It suffices for them to wait until the condition of a troubled bank deteriorates to the point where it is taken over by the insurance institution. The price as which the bank can be bought is then much lower.

When the regulators bail out the creditors of a troubled bank, there is no way for them to escape protecting all depositors, including uninsured creditors, from loss. If the current receipts from the premia paid by banks are insufficient to cover current insurance fund expenditures, then the deposit insurance institution commits the taxpayer to pay the difference. This commitment is strictly equivalent to a subsidy granted to the shareholders and the managers of the bank for them to increase their risk-taking.

Deposit insurance can thus produce the systemic instability that it is supposed to prevent. Attempts to protect safety and preserve public confidence in the banking system by preventing failure of large banks --- "too big to fail" --- and by protecting creditors from incurring losses create new distortions. Protecting against failure in this way promotes inequities, prevents the market from discriminating between large and sound banks and those which take on excessive risk and increase aggregate risk to the banking and payment system.

Many projects have been proposed to reduce the risk of a systemic run while increasing the incentives for bank monitoring by depositors. One can think of an ex post penalty imposed on all current and former depositors, preventing strategies to escape the losses incurred in a bank failure. Various formulae of removing most of the subsidy offered by deposit insurance are presently discussed, but none has proved yet able to reach an optimum. An interesting mechanism is suggested by the French Banking Law of 1984 which proposes, under the supervision of the Central Bank, that other banks co-insure the depositors of a troubled bank. More precisely, according to a concept of "market solidarity" (article 52), banks (all of them or just a subset of banks closely linked to the troubled bank) are requested to help the bank whose failure would be detrimental to the financial center reputation (in 1988, a rescue along these lines was organized in favor of Al Saudi Bank in Paris).

Anyway, the efficiency of any single part of a safety net --- whether a deposit insurance scheme, or a minimum capital requirement, or even a lender of last resort facility --- can be questioned on the ground that none of them can solve the basic moral hazard problem underlying the banking activity. This is the reason why a resilient safety net must closely associate several parts working together on a complementary basis. Undoubtedly, a deposit-insurance is, by no means, the best incentive one can imagine for preventing a bank manager to take more risk, but it can alleviate the task incumbing to the lender of last resort in case of bank distress. Similarly, a minimum capital requirement may prove harmful, under certain circumstances. But when it suffers from temporary liquidity problems, a bank will certainly prefer to borrow freely, even at a higher rate, from the Central Bank, rather than spend its own-funds or sell assets from its portfolio. Finally, what really matters, as far as moral hazard and efficiency of the safety net are concerned, is that the whole package, rather than each of its components, particularly deposit-insurance and capital adequacy requirements, should have a satisfactory risk-related element.

One key for building up an efficient safety net consists in avoiding the replacement of market discipline by discretionary intervention by regulators. A set of automatic rules might prove useful. One might imagine, for instance, that the supervisory authorities should be compelled to take strong action against any bank whose capital falls below a certain predetermined rate. Indeed, such a procedure could lead to closing troubled banks prematurely under certain circumstances. Again, it also would imply that regulators are able to assess the genuine value of capital, that is its market value rather than its accounting value. This is a very important point. If capital is not measured according to market values (remember how difficult it is for non-traded loans), economically insolvent institutions will be allowed to continue operating despite their considerable incentives to take excessive risks.

CONCLUSION

Economies in transition from a centrally planned to a market adjustment mechanism represent a fragile environment. In the financial structure, much more underdeveloped than the industrial sector, systemic risk is permanently present. This is so because the financial services industry and the banking sector will not easily find their equilibrium, considering the number of intermediaries and the conditions of entry. Failures will continue until this equilibrium is defined.

The rules of the game in the banking sector imply that a high capital requirement is essential to safe and sound banking. Capital provides a cushion against losses. More important, the incentives of the bank owners must be compatible with the depositors' interest in bank safety. There must be a monitoring mechanism enabling the regulators to be sure that the capital is real. Such a system requires market value reporting of assets and liabilities. These reports must be examined *in situ* and carefully verified. The regulators must be able to promptly take action before net worth is too low, either by forcing owners to recapitalize the bank with new funds, or by taking over the bank. One must realize that these principles must be firmly enforced, which means that the financial system must be preserved from complete deregulation in a market economy.

REFERENCES

Benston G.J. (1990a), "Market-Value Accounting by Banks : Benefits, Costs and Incentives", in G.G. Kaufman, ed., *Restructuring the American Financial System,* Boston, Kluwer, 35-55.

Benston G.J. (1990b), *The Separation of Commercial and Investment Banking. The Glass-Steagall Act Revisited and Reconsidered,* London, Macmillan, in association with the City University Business School.

Berger A.N., K.K. King and J.M. O'Brien (1991), "The Limitations of Market Value Accounting and a More Realistic Alternative", *Journal of Banking and Finance,* vol. 15, n° 4-5, September, 753-783.

Bernanke B.S. (1983), "Non-Monetary Effects of the Financial Crisis in the Propagation of the Great Depression", *American Economic Review,* vol. 73, June, 257-276.

de Boissieu C., ed. (1990), *Banking in France,* London, Routledge.

Brainard L. (1991), "Reform in Eastern Europe: Creating a Capital Market", Federal Reserve Bank of Kansas City, *Economic Review,* January-February, 49-58.

Calvo G.A. and J.A. Frenkel (1991), "From Centrally Planned to Market Economy - The Road from CPE to PCPE", IMF *Staff Papers,* vol. 38, n° 2, June, 268-299.

Calvo G.A. and J.A. Frenkel (1991), "Credit Markets, Credibility and Economic Transformation", *Journal of Economic Perspectives,* vol. 5, n° 4, Fall, 139-148.

Campbell T.S. and W.A. Kracaw (1980), "Information Production, Market Signalling and the Theory of Financial Intermediation", *Journal of Finance,* vol. 35, September, 863-882.

Capie F.H. and G.E. Wood (1990), "Financial Structure in a Changing Regulatory Environment : Europe after 1992", in *Game Plans for the '90s,* Proceedings of the 26 th Annual Conference on Bank Structure and Competition, Federal Reserve Bank of Chicago, 562-608.

Chant J. (1987), *Regulation of Financial Institutions - A Functional Analysis,* Bank of Canada, Technical Report 45.

Chiappori P.A. (1991), "Non Rémunération des Dépôts à Vue : Quelques Eléments Théoriques", *Revue Française d'Economie,* vol. 6, n° 3, Eté, 39-60.

Corbett J. and C. Mayer (1991), "Financial Reform in Eastern Europe : Progress with the Wrong Model", *Oxford Review of Economic Policy,* vol. 7, n° 4, Winter, 57-75.

De Cecco M. (1989), "Alternative Modes of Financial Organization", in Ch. Kessides *et al.,* eds, *Financial Reform in Socialist Economics,* Washington D.C., The World Bank, 196-204.

Diamond D.W. (1984), "Financial Intermediation and Delegated Monitoring", *Review of Economic Studies,* vol. 51, July, 393-414.

Dowd K. (1989), *The State and the Monetary System,* Hemel Hempstead, Philip Allan.

Fama E.F. (1980), "Banking in the Theory of Finance", *Journal of Monetary Economics,* vol. 6, January, 39-57.

Fama E.F. (1985), "What's Different About Banks ?", *Journal of Monetary Economics,* vol. 15, January, 29-39.

Furlong F. (1988), "Changes in Bank Risk-Taking", Federal Reserve Bank of San Francisco, *Economic Review,* Spring, n° 2.

Furlong F. and M. Keeley (1989), " Capital Regulation and Bank-Risk-Taking : A Note", *Journal of Banking and Finance,* vol. 13, 883-891.

Gennotte G. and D.H. Pyle (1991), "Capital Controls and Bank Risk", *Journal of Banking and Finance,* vol. 15, n° 4-5, September, 805-824.

Hall M.J.B. (1991), "Financial Regulation in the U.K. : Deregulation or Reregulation ?", in C.J. Green and D.T. Llewellyn, eds, *Surveys in Monetary Economics,* vol. 2, *Financial Markets and Institutions,* Oxford, Basil Blackwell for the Money Study Group, 166-209.

Kahane Y. (1977), "Capital Adequacy and the Regulation of Financial Intermediaries", *Journal of Banking and Finance,* vol. 1, 207-218.

Keeley M. and F. Furlong (1990), "A Reexamination of Mean-Variance Analysis of Bank Capital Regulation", *Journal of Banking and Finance,* vol. 14, 69-84.

Kessides C., T. King, M. Nuti and C. Sokil, eds (1989), *Financial Reform in Socialist Economies,* Washington, D.C., The World Bank, EDI Seminar Series.

Koehn M. and A. Santomero (1980), "Regulation of Bank Capital and Portfolio Risk", *Journal of Finance,* vol. 35, n° 5, December, 1235-1250.

Kornai J. (1990), *The Road to a Free Economy, Shifting from a Socialist System : The Example of Hungary,* New-York, W.W. Norton and Company.

Leland H.E. and D.H. Pyle (1977), "Informational Asymmetries, Financial Structure and Financial Intermediation", *Journal of Finance,* vol. 32, May, 371-387.

Lewis M.K. (1991), "Theory and Practice of the Banking Firm", in C.J. Green and D.T. Llewellyn, eds, *Surveys in Monetary Economics,* vol. 2, *Financial Markets and Institutions,* Oxford, Basil Blackwell for the Money Study Group, 116-165.

Litan R.E. (1987), *What Should Banks Do ?* Washington, D.C., The Brookings Institution.

Montgomery J.D. (1991), "Market Segmentation and 1992 : Toward a Theory of Trade in Financial Services", Board of Governors of the Federal Reserve System, *International Finance Discussion Papers,* n° 394, April.

Ronn E.I. and A.K. Verma (1986), "Pricing Risk-Adjusted Deposit Insurance : An Option Based Model", *Journal of Finance,* vol. 41, September.

Saunders A. and I. Walter (1991), "Reconfiguration of Banking and Capital Markets in Eastern Europe Banking and Financial Markets", *Journal of International Securities Markets,* Fall.

Selgin G. (1988), *The Theory of Free Banking - Money Supply Under Competitive Note Issue,* New-York, Rowman and Littlefield.

Szöke M. (1991), "Some Aspects of Building up New Financial Structures : Reflections About the Hungarian Way", in R. O'Brien and S. Hewin, eds, *Finance and the International Economy,* 4, The Amex Bank Review Prize Essays, Oxford University Press, 24-38.

CHAPTER 7

PRIVATISATION AND SMALL BUSINESS FINANCING: LESSONS FROM THE UK AND GERMANY*

Andy Mullineux

INTRODUCTION

This chapter briefly reviews the UK privatisation programme and the performance of the German privatisation agency (the Treuhandanstalt), the function of which is to restructure of the economy of the former German Democratic Republic. It is observed that the restructuring of the 'New Federal States' (NFS) of the Federal Republic of Germany involves not only the costly restructuring and privatisation of the former state sector enterprises, but also the provision of loan guarantees (by development and other banks and the 'Treuhand') to small and medium sized enterprises (SMEs). Financial and other arrangements supporting the SME sector in the UK and Germany are briefly discussed and compared.[1] In comparing and contrasting the privatisation programmes and SME policies of the UK and Germany, lessons are drawn for the UK and for the Central and Eastern European (CEE) countries.

1) THE UK PRIVATISATION PROGRAMME (1979 TO DATE)

The UK programme was initiated following the election of the first Thatcher government in 1979 and was still underway over a decade later. Its future hung on the General Election to be held on 9 April 1992. The Conservatives, now led by John Major, intended to continue with the programme and further privatisations are currently being prepared. The Labour government did not intend to proceed with the remaining planned larger privatisations (such as

---

* The author wishes to thank the Anglo-German Foundation for funding the study and for the support and encouragement provided by its staff.

[1] For a fuller discussion see the April 1991 Anglo-German Foundation Report by Graham Bannock and Horst Albach entitled: *Small Business Policy in Europe*

British Rail) and had raised the possibility of re-nationalising some of the 'natural monopolies' but were not firmly committed to doing so.

In 1979 the nationalised industries in the UK accounted for approximately 10% of Gross Domestic Product and employed 1.5 million people. Their performance, in terms of criteria such as return on capital employed, productivity, and level of customer satisfaction, had been disappointing. Because their borrowing was underwritten by the state they directly and indirectly added to the Public Sector Borrowing Requirement (PSBR). As a corollary, despite the advantage of having access to cheap finance, they suffered periodically from financial restraints; particularly when the growth of the PSBR had to be curbed for macroeconomic policy reasons. This made the task of the management, especially in the sphere of long-term investment planning, more difficult. Successive governments had attempted to improve on the performance of the nationalised industries and firms by introducing surrogate market pressures, particularly on the management, with little success.

Through privatisation, the post 1979 Conservative government decided to replace surrogate market pressures with real ones. It aimed to bring about an improvement in efficiency and to reduce the PSBR; a goal to which it was committed via its Medium Term Financial Strategy (MTFS) introduced in March 1980. Privatisation reduces the PSBR to the extent that it reduces state funding of the nationalised sector and raises revenue in the form of proceeds from the sale of nationalised companies. The revenue is counted as negative expenditure in the UK and, therefore, helps to reduce government expenditure, another goal of the original MTFS.

The goal of the privatisation programme has never been revenue maximisation from sales. As noted, a key goal was to raise efficiency. This could be achieved as a result of releasing management from budgeting uncertainty and 'state interference' in areas where the previously nationalised industry had been providing 'social services' using cross-subsidisation; and by providing employees, especially management, with clearer objectives and greater rewards for success. The privatised firms, because they could no longer rely on state backed funding, had to subject themselves to capital market discipline. In a number of cases 'natural monopolies' were privatised with the result that they were not exposed to rigorous competition in their product markets at the regional or national level (eg. gas, telecommunications and electricity). Regulatory bodies, therefore, had to be established to monitor their activities, particularly their pricing policies. This seems to be an expensive and unsatisfactory result and the public has yet to be convinced that it has improved the quality of service provided. As a result, the government has been considering opening such industries up to outside competition; by connecting the UK to European (and Russian) gas supplies, for example. This would appear to be viable solution in the case of some 'natural monopolies', but it is less easy to see how opening up to outside competition would help to improve the efficiency in others (eg the British Rail network).

The other key objective of the UK privatisation programme was to encourage wider share ownership and this policy ran parallel with the policy of increasing home ownership with the overall goal of creating a 'property-owning democracy'. To the extent that the number of private share owners trebled to over 5 million (24% of the adult population), the programme achieved success. In addition 90% of employees become shareholders in their companies on privatisation. To the extent that employee share ownership leads to increased worker productivity and improved management, it should contribute to the goal of improved efficiency. Such issues are the subject of intense debate however.

It is also to be noted that a significant proportion of the original buyers of privatisation stocks were 'stags' seeking capital gains who consequently sell their stocks fairly soon after the privatisation. To widen share ownership, priority in the allocation of shares is normally given to small investors. The pricing of the shares is set below the revenue maximising one in order to attract small investors (and 'stags') to achieve the goal of wider share ownership and incentives are given to encourage long term shareholding. Nevertheless, in the post 1979 period the proportion of all shares held by the institutional investors (pension funds, insurance companies, and unit and investment trusts) has grown inexorably. The appetite of these investors is such that there is usually a healthy demand for the stocks the 'stags' wish to sell and the capital gain made by the 'stags' indicates that if small investors were not given priority, a higher price could have been raised for the privatisation stock. This has of course lead to allegations that the 'family silver' has been sold for a song. Whilst this is clearly an overstatement, it is evident that revenue maximisation has not been the prime goal of the UK privatisation programme.

1.1 Mechanics of the UK Privatisation Programme and the Role of the Banks

Privatisation is a relatively complex process and each case has its own peculiarities. A small number of basic methods of privatisation can, however, be identified. The preceding discussion related to privatisation by public flotation on the stock exchange. This is the approach normally associated, and successfully pioneered, by the UK programme and the one that has spawned similar programmes in other countries. Not all UK privatisations have been of this form, however. Others have entailed: trade sales, where a company is sold to a single firm or a consortium; placings with groups of investors; and management and/or employee buy-outs (MBOs).

Before sale, the company, and the shares to be offered, must be valued. Professional advisors, normally merchant or investment banks but sometimes accountancy firms in smaller privatisations, are retained, by the government and by the company to be privatised, for this purpose. In addition other merchant and/or investment banks and accountancy firms are retained to advise on other financial aspect of the sale. In the case of flotation, specialist brokers are retained to oversee the sale of shares and 'receiving banks' (usually one or more of the large commercial (clearing) banks) are retained to distribute shares to small investors, register share ownership, and provide custodian services. Finally, a group of banks 'underwrite' the share issues. These normally consists of UK merchant banks, who have a traditional role in the 'acceptance business', and foreign, particularly US, investment banks.

2) THE ECONOMIC RECONSTRUCTION OF THE FORMER GERMAN DEMOCRATIC REPUBLIC (GDR)

German Economic and Monetary Unification (GEMU, 1 July 1990) and Political Unification (3 October 1990) brought five new states (Länder) with a population of 16 million into the Federal Republic of Germany (FRG), henceforth referred to as Germany in this report. The industrial and agricultural sectors in the new Federal States (NFS) were almost entirely state owned and so was much of the land and housing. The service sector was underdeveloped relative to that of the former FRG (West Germany) and accounted for a much smaller proportion of employment than typical in OECD countries, but there was some private ownership in this and the handicraft sector. The dominant industrial sector was organised into large conglomerates (Combinats) working with a capital stock that was, in the main, obsolete and rundown and agriculture had been collectivised. The workforce was well educated and trained, but not quite to the high West German standards. Labour productivity was, however, less than a third of West German levels because of the poor capital stock, inefficient management, and 'hidden' unemployment.

The scope of the restructuring task therefore dwarfed that undertaken by the UK, which had sought to tackle the problems of a nationalised sector accounting for 10% of GDP and employing 1.5 million people. The UK programme has involved the privatisation of about 50% of the nationalised sector over a decade or so to date. The Germans had to consider how to deal with a nationalised sector that employed virtually the whole of the working population in the NFS. A problem which also had major political and regional ramifications given the threat of large scale migration.

An independent state backed agency, the Treuhandanstalt ('Treuhand') was established to oversee the restructuring of the nationalised sector. It was capitalised by the state and took over about 8000 industrial companies and over 20,000 small businesses (mainly shops, cafes and restaurants) as well as agricultural and other land and property and assumed the debts of the nationalised sector. These debts were converted upon EMU at a rate of two Ost marks to one Deutsche mark. The state bank's branches and non-central banking operations were quickly sold to the leading (West) German commercial banks, Deutsche (approx 2/3) and Dresdner (approx 1/3) who, along with Commerzbank, the other major commercial banks, rapidly developed branch networks in the NFS. The savings and cooperative banks of the former GDR were linked to the West German savings and Cooperative banks, which are organised on a regional basis with central institutions in Western Germany. The commercial banking debts were underwritten by the state budget and the Treuhand was entrusted with the task of untangling the outstanding debts to banks. Consequently, a viable banking system, unencumbered with past bad and doubtful debts, was rapidly introduced at a very early stage, enabling the restructuring to proceed.

The Treuhand is required to privatise, as quickly as possible, the entire nationalised sector in the NFS, subject to certain constraints. These relate to employment and investment. As a result, it does not necessarily seek to maximise the purchase price and instead prefers to sell to firms whose business plans include maintaining reasonable employment levels and commitments to future investments. The objective is to create viable firms and an efficient economic structure and to negotiate a (socially) optimal purchase price. The Treuhand not only absorbs debts, usually through a discount on the sale price, but also absorbs costs relating to pollution control, again via price discounts, since it also aims to promote improvement of the environment in the NFS.

As in the UK, methods of privatisation vary from direct sales to flotations. Direct sales, often involving auctions, are particularly appropriate for small businesses and in this way the 20,000 or so small businesses referred to above were disposed of. Some large industrial plants have been sold in this way too. One of the main difficulties in the early stages of the programme was a welter of, often conflicting, claims for restitution by people disposed by the 'Nazi's' during the 2nd World War or the 'Communists' subsequently. Legislation has since been passed which allows the Treuhand to give priority to purchasers whose business plans they prefer. If this is not the former owner, then the latter can make a claim for compensation through the appropriate channels (not the Treuhand).

By November 1991, the Treuhand had privatised 5,000 industrial companies but still had 6,200 to sell, including many of the larger ones. The original 8000 industrial companies (which included a number of large combines) had, via restructuring, been broken up into over 10,000 units. Management 'buyouts' and 'buyins' were being encouraged and 808 had been executed. It is expected that 70% of the remaining firms will be sold and 30% will be liquidated. 815 companies had been closed down or liquidated by November 1991. Overseas investment had been disappointing, accounting for 233 of the enterprises sold.

Most of the purchases were, therefore, made by German entrepreneurs and companies. Despite its efforts on the employment front, the official rate of unemployment had risen to double West German levels. The Treuhand's expenditure on restructuring had exceeded the proceeds from privatisation. In 1991 revenue had been DM 18bn and the deficit was DM 21bn. In 1992 the figures were DM 12bn and DM 31.5 bn. The Treuhand's financial deficit is covered by medium term loans from the state via the Unity Fund and it has been allowed to raise working capital by issuing commercial bills since August 1991.

The work of the Treuhand is, therefore, far from complete and plenty of restructuring and privatisation remains to be done. Clearly, whilst firms are being restructured ready for privatisation, they need finance. The Treuhand offers generous liquidity credit guarantees to encourage the commercial, savings and cooperative banks to provide loans. This was intended to be a temporary arrangement but it is proving difficult to wean the banks off the guarantees in the light of the high risks involved in the current uncertain environment and exposes the Treuhand to further substantial losses. The liquidity credits were originally intended to bridge bottlenecks and speed modernisation but are now being used to offset losses and to continue paying wages in some firms which remain overmanned, implicitly adding to the costs of the social support programme. In 1992 the Treuhand intends to cease to make guarantees generally available. Instead guarantees will be contingent on the firms' business plans and financial prospects.

Largely due to the rise in unemployment, the Treuhand has never been popular in the NFS, where it is widely believed that the agency is acting primarily in the interests of the large West German firms, but criticism has also mounted in Western Germany. The major Economic Research Institutions and the 'five wise men' have argued that privatisation and restructuring should be separated. The opposition SPD party, in contrast, would like to see the Treuhand pursuing a more active industrial policy. Others see an injection of equity and investment capital as the answer. The influential trade union IG-Metall would like to see the Treuhand become an industrial holding company devoted to employment preservation and medium term restructuring. It seems unlikely that privatisation and restructuring can be entirely separated and, as will be argued later when discussing lessons for the CEE countries. There is a logic in having a privatisation agency that uses the proceeds from privatisation to ameliorate the social disruption that result from the restructuring process. It also seems likely that the hardest part of the task has yet to be done and that the Treuhand may become, defacto, a medium term holding company of the sort advocated by IG-Metall.

The problem of financing the firms being restructured by the Treuhand without extending generous guarantees remains. The Treuhand plans to tackle this problem, whilst also reducing the cost of privatisation and speeding up the process, by enroling the services of Participation Corporations (PCs), which are a German species of venture capital funds. The aim is to ask the major banks (which have set up PC subsidiaries) to buy companies (or groups of companies) from the Treuhand and to restructure and then re-sell them, if possible via the stock exchange. Some experimentation has already taken place. The groups of companies usually consist of a mix of good, which can be sold quickly, not so good, which will need help with restructuring, and bad, which may well have to be closed down or liquidated, at least in part.

It is too early to gauge the extent to which such proposals will contribute to accelerating the restructuring and privatisation process but it seems likely that the German universal banks are more likely to participate via Pcs than to build up equity stakes on their own books and large loan exposures. Hitherto, however, the 'participations' have mainly been in small and medium sized companies (SMEs). The aim has been to widen the capital base of such companies which, as private companies, have no access to the stock exchange. The Pcs can, however, get listings on stock exchanges and can therefore tap equity finance to fund the expansion of SMEs. The Pcs also provide expert support to the management of SMEs, helping to improve their performance. It is clear, therefore, that Pcs cannot expect to play a major role in the larger privatisations and their role as providers of equity capital may be more appropriate once the newly privatised companies have matured a bit. The larger companies will remain a problem and the dominant party of the coalition government has recently attached greater emphasis to the restructuring role of the Treuhand and to the possibility of 'nationalising' (sic) 10 to 15 companies of major regional and sectoral significance in the NFS! The 'nationalised' companies would be part-owned by the FRG and part- owned by the new Länder and by municipalities.

A key component of the postwar industrial success of West Germany has been the 'Mittelstand'. This consists of the small and medium sized enterprises (SMEs) which are organised as private (in the sense that they do not issue shares which are traded on stock exchanges) companies. The Treuhand naturally regards the creation of a thriving SME sector as a key component of the restructuring process in the NFS. This accounts for the rapid privatisation of the 20,000 or so SMEs it took control of. The hope is that the SMEs will take on workers laid off as part of the process of restructuring companies. Given that the service sector in the NFS is underdeveloped, there is certainly plenty of scope for expansion in the SME sector, but demand for services also depends on income, and wage levels, despite considerable catching up in 1991, remain significantly below those prevailing in the Western Länder. In Western Germany, the Mittlestand is an important provider of components and inputs to industry. Hence, if the industrial sector in the NFS declines too quickly, the development of this sector will be inhibited by lack of demand; from industry and from its former employees who join the ranks of the unemployed and suffer a fall in income.

3) SMALL AND MEDIUM SIZED ENTERPRISE (SME) FINANCE AND SUPPORT IN GERMANY AND THE UK

3.1 The Situation in the UK: Short-Termism and the Case for a National Investment Bank

In the UK, it has long been recognised that there was a gap in the provision of finance to SMEs. It has also been alleged that there is a shortage of long and medium term loan finance. The 1931 Macmillan Committee Report on the UK financial system led (eventually) to the establishment in 1945 of two institutions, the Industrial and Commerce and Finance Corporation (ICFC), to provide long term loans to SMEs, and the Finance Corporation for Industry (FCI), to provide larger medium to long term loans. These institutions were part-owned by the major UK clearing banks and part-owned by the Bank of England. They were merged in the early 1980s to become Finance For Industry (FFI) and later evolved into Investors in Industry, which eventually adopted the logo 3i. Its main business is now venture capitalism, which since the mid 80s has mainly involved the funding of management buyouts and ins, rather than the provision of 'seed corn' capital for business start-ups. Because of its increasing overlap with the business of the major UK clearing banks and their subsidiaries, and the banks need to boost their capital ratios, 3i is to be floated on the stock exchange in the next year or so.

The 1980 Wilson Report on the UK financial system, and particularly the 1979 interim report, indicated that a gap in the provision of finance for SMEs still existed. It expressed less concern about the lack of provision of long and medium term finance to larger firms, given the high level of development of the capital markets in the UK, and rejected proposals for the establishment of a National Investment Bank. The establishment of such an institution has long been supported by the Labour party in the UK and was supported by a substantial dissenting minority in the appendices to the Wilson Report. Instead, the Wilson Report advocated measures to increase the access of SMEs to the capital markets. Many of these proposals were indeed adopted in the 1980s, including: the establishment of the Unlisted Securities Market (USM), and, for a short period in the Post 1986 Big Bang era, the Third Market, with less demanding reporting requirements than for a full stock exchange listing; and the introduction of the Business Expansion Scheme (BES). The latter aimed to stimulate equity investment in medium sized companies, whose shares are not listed on the stock exchange, through the provision of tax relief to individual investors or via an approved Business Expansion System Fund. More generally, Personal Equity Plans (Peps) have been introduced giving tax relief on investments in 'listed' companies. BES Funds for property and housing related investments were soon permitted and became the prime focus of the Scheme, which, it was announced in the March 1992 Budget, is to be withdrawn at the end of 1993.

Additionally, a Small Business Loan Guarantee Scheme (LGS) was introduced in 1981. The government initially guaranteed 80% of loans extended by the 'clearing banks' to borrowers whose projects exceeded the banks' risk tolerance limit, or who could not provide adequate security or collateral. The government charged a 3% premium (over 'normal' lending rates) on the guaranteed part of the loan (2.4% to borrowers with a 80% guarantee) to discourage exploitation of the scheme. Fairly low ceilings were set (currently £100,000) on the maximum size of the loan. The repayment period varied between two and seven years and no security was required. The scheme proved popular initially but one in three participating firms failed. The rules were tightened in 1984, at the end of the initial three year pilot period. The maximum guaranteed proportion of loans was reduced to 70% and the premium was raised to 5% (3.5% net on a 70% guaranteed loan) and the popularity of the programme diminished dramatically (from guaranteeing 400 loans a month to approximately 45). In 1986 the minister responsible for small businesses persuaded the Treasury to think again and, as a result, the premium was halved, but the 70% guarantee level was retained. Acceptances subsequently increased but remained (at about 90 a month) well below those for the original scheme. The failure rate, until the recession of the early 1990s at least, was reduced to about one in four, however. In the North West region of the UK, survey responses indicated that bankers believed that, of all the projects covered by the scheme with which they were involved, only about 5% would have had risks below the banks' risk the tolerance levels and would therefore have been supported by the banks without guarantees. The alternative to expensive guaranteed loans for SMEs is equity based finance through the BES or through venture capital funds. Venture capitalists tolerate more risk than banks but at a price in terms of cost of capital and reduced control. Venture funds proliferated in the UK in the 1980s but, like the LGS, are not as widely used by SMEs as had been expected.

It is clear that SMEs do need access to equity like capital to fund investment. They also need ready access to working capital and an efficient clearing and bill settlement system, so that they do not suffer from cash flow problems. There remains a view in the UK that medium to long term loan finance at fixed rates is more useful to SMEs, especially in their early stages, than equity like capital, and that subsidised lending and more generous provision of guarantees is needed to stimulate the growth of this sector. In the UK the LGS has proved expensive because the banks pass the cost of the government guarantee charge onto the borrower and consequently it is not as widely used as it might be. Further, in the recession of the early 1990s, record failures were recorded amongst SMEs. This was in part due to the absence of a prompt bill settlement system. The larger firms seem to have simply withheld payments from smaller firms to improve their own cash flow, with disastrous consequences. Bills are paid much more promptly in Germany, for example. The commercial banks also came in for considerable criticism for allegedly aggravating the situation in 1991. They were accused of not reducing interest rates to SMEs in line with the fall in the base rate. The banks were probably, and understandably, raising lending margins to cover for the increasing risks that they were facing as a result of the record business failure rate, and to help cover their mounting bad and doubtful debt provisions. They did, however, also impose additional charges (without notice), withdraw overdraft facilities and decline to renew loans. The net result has been that the banks were instructed (by the monetary authorities) to introduce codes of conduct for business clients. They have, however, also become more cautious about taking on new lending to SMEs and supporting start-ups.

In the UK, advocates a National Investment Bank (NIB) commonly point to France, Japan and Germany as examples of countries where such an institution appears to have played a key role. A related problem, to the shortage of long and medium term finance which is alleged to afflict the 'Anglo-Saxon' countries (particularly the UK and the US) is short-termism. It is argued that the business sector is forced by its financiers to adopt a short-term perspective. Institutional investors are particularly important in these countries, as noted above, and demand high and growing dividend payments to maintain their performance in a competitive savings market. This forces public ('quoted') companies to concentrate on short-term profitability so that they can maintain dividend payment growth, often at the expense of investment, and even, at least in 1990, in a recession. There has been some evidence of a reduction in dividend payments in the US and the UK in 1991, even amongst banks. Another way in which short-termism is induced is through the use, via mergers and acquisition (M&A), of the stock exchange as a market incorporate control. Corporate governance is exerted via threat of takeover and, it is argued, to prevent takeover, the institutional investors must be discouraged from selling shares to hostile bidders by maintaining dividend payments and concentrating on short-term profits. The institutional investors claim that they do not concentrate on short term issues when appraising the merits of a bid by a potential new management.

To some, the solution to short-termism lies in improving the system of corporate governance in the UK by reducing its reliance on the hostile takeover threat and encouraging closer associations between institutional investors, and possibly banks, and the corporate sector. This could be done by establishing a state backed National Investment Fund (NIF), rather than a NIB, which the institutions, and perhaps banks, would be encouraged (perhaps via tax incentives) to participate in The NIF could then supply equity and loan finance for investment and business start-up purposes.

Opponents of the NIB and NIF-type proposals feel that an active industrial (and regional) policy will lead to inefficiency because there will be a temptation to sponsor particular companies and sectors whilst the market should be left to allocate finance. They council that, if there is a case for encouraging investment relative to consumption, then the tax system should be used and general investment and depreciation allowances should be made available, for example, leaving the market to pick the winners. The market in the case of the SMEs, consists largely of clearing bank managers, often specialising in small business lending, and venture capital fund managers. For larger firms it is much wider and encompasses not just the domestic money and capital markets, but also the Euromarkets. To the extent that bank managers and venture capitalists develop lending strategies that target markets, rather than concentrate on narrow balance sheet criteria, they too are involved in 'picking winners'. It is not clear that they are particularly adept at doing so and there may be a case, often made by advocates of a NIB for the UK, for concentrating expertise in this area in institutions that provide loan guarantees, as in Germany.

Proposers of closer involvement of institutional investors in corporate governance often have in mind the German model of universal banking. This not only combines commercial banking with securities business, but also entails banks holding participations in non-financial firms substantial enough to enable, with the help of proxy voting on behalf of clients who deposit shares with them, to wield considerable influence (often reinforced by their executive board members' membership of supervisory boards) on corporate clients. Not only can they exert influence but they gain additional access to information that makes them more willing to commit loanable funds for longer terms and, in so doing, to foster 'long-termism'.

In the UK it is not the banks but the institutional investors that hold the large equity participations in public companies. Bank finance, typically in the form of working capital (ie overdrafts or short-term loans) is separated from equity finance. The solution, therefore, appears to be: either to encourage institutional investors in the UK and the US to become involved in corporate governance, or to allow banks to build up equity stakes in their corporate clients. This is currently not permitted in the US. It is allowed in the UK but has been discouraged by the Bank of England. In Germany, and in other universal banking countries, eg Switzerland, equity participations were often initially built up as a result of debt for equity swaps to assist ailing clients. In the recession of the early 1990s there have been a few swaps in the UK, but the clearing banks involved have declared that this should not be seen as the beginning of the conversion of UK banks into German-style universal banks.

It is also worth noting that the influence of German banks over their clients is probably exaggerated. The banks have been encouraged to reduce their participations by the anti-trust bodies in recent years and tax efficiency implies that holdings of about 10% are optional. This level is rarely exceeded and smaller stakes are more common. This is because article 12 of the banking law requires banks to limit the sum of their investment in fixed assets (total participations and equity securities) to the amount of their regulatory capital, participations being defined as holdings exceeding 10% of outstanding capital in this case. EC banking regulations (applying with effect from 1993) will also limit banks' industrial holdings by requiring: that their sum does not exceed 15% of a bank's capital; and that the sum of non-financial holdings is limited to 60% of a bank's capital. German banks would currently have little difficulty in abiding by these rules. In 1976, the ten largest banks held 1.32% of the nominal capital of all joint-stock companies, whilst in 1989 they held only 0.57% and the number of participations had been reduced substantially as well. Further, the influence of the supervisory boards on company management is often also exaggerated.

3.2 SME Finance in Germany

Not only does Germany have state-backed development banks but it also has: a network of loan guarantee banks; investment and depreciation allowances; government financed assistance for establishing data bases and providing information, training and consultancy to SMEs; generous expert credit guarantees; and a system of Chambers of Commerce at home and abroad that makes the British Chambers of Commerce look like poor relations. To assist with the economic reconstruction of the NFS, these facilities have been martialled, supplemented, and targeted: on infrastructural and environmental programmes, and on the promotion of SMEs in particular.

The contrast with what is available in the UK (although the contribution of the regional Development Agencies, particularly the Welsh Development Agency should not be belittled) is stark. Through the banking sector various programmes of funding and guarantees are provided. The normal route is for an SME is to approach its bank with a business proposal, which the bank then vets and, if it approves, submits it for consideration by one of the three development banks overseeing the disbursement of funds from the various programmes outlined below. The banks are therefore closely involved in the process and there is no need for the development bank to develop its own branch network. The provision of funds through the various programmes also has a catalytic role; reducing the risks faced by the banks themselves and encouraging them to lend to SMEs more readily than they might otherwise have done, if they would have lent at all.

The major promotion programmes for SMEs are the Equity Capital Assistance Program (ECAP); European Recovery Program (ERP) Loans for Establishing or Investing in Business in the NFS; the Small and Medium-Sized Business Program of the Kreditanstalt fur Wiederaufbau (Reconstruction Loan Corporation, KfW); and various loan guarantee programmes. The characteristics of the loans vary. They often require security or collateral (unless guarantees can be obtained through the guarantee programmes), carry favourable, and often fixed (at least for an initial period) interest rates, and have medium to long term (up to 20 years) repayment periods with up to 5 year grace periods. In some cases, when the applicant is ineligible for guarantees, the bank will impose its own security or collateral requirements.

The promotion programmes for SMEs, along with other infrastuctural and environmental investment programmes are administered by the KfW the Bonn-based Deutsche Ausgleichsbank (German Equalisation Bank). The KfW was set up in 1948 to manage ERP funds for the postwar reconstruction of Germany and is owned by the Federal (85%) and Lander governments. It has continued to operate as a development bank and finances most of its operations, of which its ILP programme for SMEs has been most important, by raising funds on the capital markets, where it carries a top grade triple A credit rating. From time to time it also receives funds for disbursement from the government; such as those supplied out of the Unity Fund for the current ERP programmes for SMEs, environmental protection and municipal infrastructural investment. Such funds currently account for about a quarter of its lending. The other two development banks also receive funds from the government for disbursement and are currently being used to help with the reconstruction of the NFS.

The state owned Deutsche Ausgleichsbank (DtA) advances, via banks (as explained above), loans to the SMEs. ERP loans for establishing in businesses and for environmental protection in the NFS are disbursed primarily by the the DtA. The KfW's own Small and Medium-Sized Business Program is bond financed. Funds are also supplied for the modernisation and restructuring of firms still under the Treuhand's control. Loan-guarantees are available to enterprises that lack adequate collateral. They are supplied via specialised guarantee banks, and the Treuarbeit AG, which handles Federal deficiency guarantees for loans for major (non-Treuhand) investment projects and operating capital, and does not, therefore, deal with SMEs. The guarantees are backed by Federal and Länder government and augmented to support long term investment loans in the NFS which are intended to assist the start-up, expansion, conversion and rationalisation of SMEs.

Credit guarantee associations or 'guarantee banks' were established in the 1950s as self-help facilities for SMEs lacking the securities to raise a loan. In the early 1990's, there were 20 guarantee banks operating in the Western Länder. The KfW sponsored their development with concessionary loans. It has strongly supported the establishment of 5 guarantee banks in the NFS under the leadership of the Joint Committee of the Federal Credit Guarantee Association. As in the case of the BI, guarantee banks normally guarantee up to 80% of a loan, with the lender retaining the risk on the remaining 20%. The new 'guarantee banks' in the NFS are, however, being given special support until they can develop into self-help organisations. Under current regulations, the Federal government covers 80% of the new guarantee banks' default risks with a back-up guarantee. In addition they receive ERP loans from the KfW on concessionary terms (interest rate 1% pa for 15 years with 5 initial grace years). The ERP funds also cover 10% of the amount guaranteed against default and the guarantee bank, therefore, has to bear a risk of 10%. The new guarantee banks commenced business in early 1991.

The European Investment Bank (EIB), which supports infrastructural investment and regional development in the EC member states, naturally also regards the NFS as a priority area and provides loans and guarantees accordingly. Its priorities include infrastructural improvement, protection and improvement of the environment, and promoting SMEs. It can therefore complement the activities of the German development banks, which have similar priorities.

As mentioned above, there is all sorts of additional support, from Chambers of Commerce and the Federal government, for new enterprises in the NFS, including: allowances for training, consultancy, development of information systems etc; and investment and depreciation tax allowances. The provision of export credit guarantees at concessionary rates, primarily via the agency Hermes, ran into difficulties in early 1992. A factor aggravating the problems of companies (particularly in the industrial sector) in the NFS was the collapse of trade with the Central and Eastern European (including the erstwhile USSR) countries. It was hoped that generous export guarantees would rekindle some of this trade but, following the disintegration of the Soviet Union and its replacement by the Commonwealth of Independent States (CIS), the credit risk resulting arising from Hermes' exposure to Russia increased and the agency had to curtail its activities sharply.

Apart from supporting the development of SMEs directly, funds have been made available to support rapid infrastructural development, housing modernisation and repair, and environmental improvement and pollution control. These are mainly disbursed by the KfW to local authorities and municipalities in the form of concessionary loans. It is increasingly being accepted that infrastructural investment, due to its beneficial externalities, helps stimulate private sector investment. In the case of the NFS, it is hoped that an increasing proportion of this will come from overseas as the business and living environments improve and the proximity of the NFS to the new markets in the CEE countries (including Western CIS states) is fully appreciated.

4) LESSONS FOR THE CENTRAL AND EASTERN EUROPEAN(CEE) COUNTRIES

In early 1990, some of the CEE countries wholeheartedly embarked on economic reform programmes which were designed to transform their economies from centrally planned to 'market' economies. The central European countries (Poland, The Czech and Slovak Federal Republic (CSFR), and Hungary) have made most progress to date. At least some of the CIS states are about to embark on similar reform programmes. Russia made a start in January 1992 by liberalising prices and replacing turnover tax with Value Added Tax (VAT), which is a tax paid at source of production and passed on to purchasers of goods.

In the aforementioned countries, which were linked through the Council for Mutual Economic Assistance (CMEA, also known as COMECON) trading block, which had been based on the transferable Rouble, rather than an internationally convertible currency, the initial scope of the reform programmes was similar. Post 1989, this trading block disintegrated with the effect that traditional export markets were all but lost. The problem for the non-Soviet CEE countries was exacerbated when (in 1991) the USSR began to charge for oil and gas (on which they are heavily dependent for energy) at market, rather than the hitherto subsidised, rates, and to demand payment in international currencies. Similar problem will be experienced by former soviet states, especially oil and gas importers, unless they can secure mutually acceptable trade agreements through the CIS. The currently planned introduction of separate state currencies and abandonment of the Rouble may well exacerbate frictions.

The NFS, in contrast, now have access to alternative energy supplies from the west and can rapidly reduce their usage of the 'brown coal' which has caused so much environmental damage. They also have numerous other advantages over the CEE countries. As noted above, there has been a massive burst of infrastructural and environmental investment funded, not without complaint, by taxpayers (mainly in the Western Länder, but also elsewhere in the EC) and by increased government borrowing (and therefore by future tax payers, including those in the NFS). The CEE governments have not merged with a larger 'rich uncle' state and are not yet members of the EC. Being adopted by a 'rich uncle' had other major benefits too. The business infrastructure (banks, accountants, legal and regulatory systems, telecommunications etc) could also be introduced relatively quickly along with: a democratic institutional structure supported by a tax system; and a social 'safety net', to provide welfare support to those that become unemployed and to provide pensions for the aged.

Following EMU, the inhabitants of the NFS also had a convertible international currency and could be allowed to buy consumer goods immediately from well stocked shops with little regard to implications for the balance of trade. Finally, and perhaps most importantly for rapid economic reconstruction, the NFS had access to a pool of private capital in the Western Länder and western management skill and 'technical know-how' and entrepreneurship backed by a banking system geared to sponsoring and serving the needs of SMEs. Further, EMU and adoption of a credible central bank (the Bundesbank) committed to maintaining the value of the Duetsche mark protected the savings of the populous of the NFS (and the Western Länder) against the hyper-inflation that has occurred (at least briefly) following price liberation in the CEE countries. Savings levels in the NFS remain high and are often held in low interest accounts, providing the banks with a cheap new source of finance to fund their (largely guaranteed) lending in the NFS.

It is all very different in the CEE countries. Not only do they have run down physical infrastructures but the business, especially the banking and wider financial, infrastructure, must be virtually built from scratch and largely using internally generated funds whose value has been eroded substantially following the 'price adjustment'. The extent to which they can attract overseas funds, especially from the private sector, is also circumscribed, compared to the NFS, by greater political risk and general uncertainty about business prospects. Additionally, the potential for state funding of development is limited by the need to pursue macroeconomic stabilisation programmes (and therefore to limit the budget deficit) to secure access to funding from international agencies and markets. State revenue was previously derived primarily from 'state enterprises' but this source of revenue is disappearing as the enterprises are 'commercialised' and privatised. An alternative tax collection system takes quite some time to establish and stabilisation often means curtailing government expenditure as a consequence. This too is difficult because restructuring, as in the NFS, naturally leads to unemployment and increased government transfer payments through the 'social safety net', which is necessary for humanitarian reasons and to secure political support for the reform programme and discourage migration. On solution to this problem, and one being actively pursued in the NFS, is to encourage SMEs to take up the employment slack and become the engines of the economy. The problem is that there is no supporting infrastructure (or funds) and little tradition of SMEs, especially in the industrial sector, in the CEEs.

One potential source of revenue in CEE countries is the privatisation agency. A decision has to be made at an early stage in the reform programme as to whether this agency is to concentrate solely on revenue maximising privatisation or whether it is really an economic reconstruction agency with social, regional and perhaps industrial, policy responsibilities, like the Treuhand. As noted above, the Treuhand runs at a loss. A revenue maximising privatisation agency would clearly make a substantial profit, but social, regional, environmental, and, possibly other, industrial costs would simply fall on the state budget instead. Revenue maximisation would also lead to a substantial drain on domestic wealth (accumulated past savings) which have already been decimated by the inflation following price liberalisation in these countries. Revenue maximisation may, therefore, imply slow privatisation, especially as the pool of new domestic savings will be relatively (compared to the size of the stock of companies to be privatised) small. If quick privatisation is required, then revenue must be foregone and the price set accordingly. Lower prices will attract more foreign interest as well, and decisions must be taken about the perspicacity of 'selling the family silver' to foreigners. Quick privatisation will, of course, also absorb a larger proportion of private sector wealth and savings flows. As a result, fewer funds will be available for sponsoring SMEs through bank lending of private sector deposits. In other words, due to financial constraints, there is likely to be a trade-off between the speed of privatisation and the development of a thriving SME sector.

The problem of developing the SME sector is also compounded by lack of a supportive banking sector able to provide working capital, investment loans, and a payments and settlements system. In the CEE countries, the major banks have yet to be privatised and lack risk-appraisal and other skills. Further, they are saddled with bad and doubtful debts extended to the former socialist enterprises and badly need a capital injection to allow them to function effectively. The cost of recapitalising the banks would logically fall on the privatisation agency; as part of the cost of restructuring firms prior to privatisation and at the cost of reducing privatisation revenue. Otherwise, a direct state budget allocation would have to be made to cover it. This would create yet another expense at a time when cutbacks are required and has been afforded a low priority. The lack of action on this issue appears to be a major mistake in the reconstruction programmes hitherto adopted by the CEE countries and stands in marked contrast to the programmes for the NFS, which quickly dealt with the bank debts. Germany, of course, had the added advantage of being able to transfer a highly efficient banking system geared to the needs of the SMEs. In addition, the larger privatised firms in the NFS will have access to the capital markets based in Frankfurt, whilst privatisation in the CEE countries is handicapped by the underdevelopment of their capital markets. This makes UK-style large-scale privatisations through stock exchange flotation virtually impossible. Because of this, and out of consideration for financial constraints and equity, the privatisation agencies in the CEE countries have adopted a mixture of privatisation methods and do not aim for revenue maximisation.

Small privatisations usually proceed by direct sales, as do some medium and large privatisations, including those involving foreign purchasers. In the central European countries, small privatisations were undertaken as quickly as possible, subject to resolution of restitution and compensation issues. For medium sized privatisations, the alternative option of 'spontaneous privatisation', originated by the management, and perhaps supported by the workers, has been used. These are effectively management buy-outs. They are not uncontroversial because they allow the 'nomenklatura' to retain control of companies. Most of the planned medium and large scale privatisations in Poland and the CSFR will use the 'voucher system'. Hungary, in contrast, is persevering with direct sales and stock exchange flotations in Budapest and Vienna.

Under the 'voucher system', the vouchers are distributed to the general public, which can use them (at the cost of about a weeks wages in the CSFR per voucher book) to 'buy' shares. A proportion of the shares are also allocated to workers and reserved for sales to overseas investors. In Poland, the shares are to be held by state holding companies and the vouchers can be used effectively to 'buy' shares in these companies. This seems to be a relatively sensible arrangement in the medium term and should provide the public with the protection of diversified portfolios. In the CSFR, investment funds were set up at the end of 1991 by large banks, enterprise managers, and individual entrepreneurs. They are marketing their alleged investment expertise to encourage citizens (confused by the complexity of the privatisation process) to deposit their voucher books with the funds which will then use them to develop portfolios of privatisation stock and have promised to pay a handsome (tenfold in many cases) dividend in a years time. The schemes are described by some privatisation officials as a hoax, but they have stimulated a flood of registrations for voucher books. Legislation to control the activities of the funds is expected to be presented to parliament in the Spring of 1992. In the mean time the privatisation officials cannot see how the funds can honour their promises and fear that public support for the privatisation programme will be damaged as a result. Further, they fear that the funds will have to be liquidated after a year and will then cause a stock price collapse, which will also damage the attractiveness of shareholding in the future by highlighting its riskiness. The Polish solution seems to be the better one, but in Poland, following the October 1991 government elections and the subsequent political uncertainty, the large privatisation programme stalled, at least temporarily.

As noted, the Hungarian authorities are persevering (with some success) with direct sales to domestic and foreign investors and flotations whilst the voucher based programmes in Poland and the CSFR appear to be facing difficulties. In principle, the 'voucher system' should allow faster privatisation but the hare does not always win the race and Hungary also has a longer tradition of SMEs, having started its reforms, howbeit gradually, much earlier. As far as 'fairness' is concerned, voucher distribution appears to have advantages, but the shares procured through the voucher lottery may not be particularly beneficial. Dividend receipts from many privatised companies may not be substantial in the early years and stock prices could well fall, as they did after the early Polish privatisations, leading to capital losses. It might be better to sell to keen investors and to distribute any proceeds to the public via temporary tax reductions. It may well be, of course, that fully costed privatisation programmes (involving restructuring, employment support, and investment subsidies etc) yield no profit and in fact makes losses, like the one being conducted by the Treuhand.

5) CONCLUSIONS

With respect to the UK, it is concluded that the government would be well advised to appraise the adequacy of current support for small and medium sized enterprises (SMEs) provided via the Loan Guarantee Scheme; especially in the light of the decision in the March 1992 Budget to withdraw the Business Expansion scheme with effect from the end of 1993.

With respect to the Central and Eastern European (CEE) countries, it seems unlikely that a fully costed privatisation programme, which includes provision for social costs and transfers associated with the unemployment generated by restructuring, will raise revenue for the budget; especially if it is executed quickly. Further, privatisation through sales of assets, rather than (virtually) free distribution using vouchers, will absorb savings that might otherwise have been lent (via banks) to stimulate and nurture the SME sector that is vital to the future prospects of the CEE countries.

A crucial difference between the former German Democratic Republic (GDR) and the CEE countries is that the Federal Republic of Germany (FRG) could afford to underwrite the bad and doubtful debts of the former state bank of the former GDR whilst the well capitalised banks from the Western Länder of the FRG took over its commercial banking operations. The CEE governments, in contrast, have been under pressure to reduce their budget deficits and have been unable to recapitalise and modernise their banks at a stroke. Until the banks are recapitalised and have learnt modern risk appraisal and other techniques, however, they cannot be expected to allocate capital efficiently. But this is what they must do if these economies are to thrive post central planning.

CHAPTER 8

PRIVATISATION AND FINANCIAL STRUCTURE IN EASTERN AND CENTRAL EUROPEAN (ECE) COUNTRIES*

Andy Mullineux

1) INTRODUCTION

The conversion of ECE countries from 'state capitalist' (centrally planned or 'Communist') to 'market capitalist' (but in reality 'mixed' or 'social market') economies entails a change in the method allocating capital. Under state capitalism: a 'mono banking' system was in operation (Garvy, 1975, 1977); interest charges were used mainly to recover costs and did not respond to the supply and demand for loanable funds or reflect credit and other risks (Wilczynski, 1978); and working and investment capital was allocated through the 'monobanking system' in accordance with the state plan.

In reality the 'monobanking' system had more than one bank. Typically there was: a state bank, which combined central and commercial banking functions as well as functions associated with ministries of finance in OECD countries; one or more, often sectorally (eg agriculture) oriented, investment banks, which undertook mainly project lending; a savings bank, which provided rudimentary banking services to the public and channelled savings into the state budget; and a foreign trade bank. There was considerable variation among ECE countries and 'reforms' or restructuring had taken place in most countries in the 1960s (Garvy, 1975; Mullineux, 1987. ch. 4.2) but they were marginal in effect. Yugoslavia had deviated most from the 'monobanking' model in its pursuit of 'decentralised socialism' under President Tito.

Prior to the momentous events at the end of 1989, attempts to reform the banking system were already underway in most ECE countries. China had in fact shown the way by creating a 'two-tier' banking system in 1984. The central bank, the Peoples Bank of China, divested itself of commercial banking

---

* The author gratefully acknowledges the support of the Anglo-German Foundation and the EC(ACE) programme for funding trips (to East Germany (Chemnitz, Dresden) and Poland (Lodz, Warsaw), respectively) to enable him to conduct interviews that provided background material for this paper.

functions, which were taken over by the Bank of China and its 'sister banks' in order to concentrate on its central banking functions (Mullineux, 1987, ch. 4). In the mid to late 1980s Hungary, Bulgaria and USSR followed suit, with some variations (Mullineux, 1987, ch. 4). Hungary, for example, encouraged joint ventures with foreign banks at an early stage and state 'socialist' enterprises' were allocated to banks less strictly in accordance to their sectoral origin than in Bulgaria. In the USSR a number of cooperative banks sprung up very quickly.

The basic idea in each country was the same, however. State sector companies would initially be allocated to one of a number of state commercial banks, which would be their main or lead bank and would be created out of already existing banks, including the state bank, which typically had a branch network. The commercial banks were expected to begin to develop commercial lending practices, so that there would be less reliance on the Plan to allocate capital after the reforms, and to charge interest rates accordingly. After a learning process, the state companies would be free to move their accounts and the banks would be forced to compete for business. In some countries, the investment bank became a commercial bank and in others it was converted into a development bank, so that it could offer subsidised loans and serve as an agent of industrial, regional and social policy.

Prior to these reforms, interest rates had come to be used increasingly as a means of trying to improve the performance of state firms. Penal rates were, for example, charged to enterprises that needed to borrow in excess of their allocation of credit under the plan, especially if they had failed to hit targets. This had, however, stimulated a significant growth in interfirm credits. The reforms can be seen as an attempt to impose hard(er) budget constraints on firms by reducing their access to state funding and forcing them to raise funds on a more commercial basis. The growth of interfirm credits was a means of avoiding the new restraints. At the end of 1989, attempts to reform state capitalism were dramatically abandoned in the ECE countries and have either been abandoned, or are likely to be abandoned soon, in most of the erstwhile member states of the USSR.

2) CREATING A MARKET ECONOMY

To create 'market' capitalism, it is necessary to reintroduce private property and to construct a legal system to support it and to introduce limited liability and bankruptcy laws, so that entrepreneurship can be fostered. It is also necessary to create a financial sector which allocates capital more efficiently than the state proved capable of doing, since, if it can't, then public support will be lost. It should be noted that 'market' capitalism is not necessarily synonymous with 'democracy'. South Korea and Chile are often quoted as counter examples. Further, democracy may impose political constraints on the transformation process which might not be present under more autocratic regimes.

As noted above, the transformation from state to market capitalism entails putting in place an alternative (to the plan) method of allocating capital. In OECD countries, financial markets and intermediaries, basically banks and capital (securities) markets and supporting institutions, including institutional investors (pension funds and insurance companies), channel funds from surplus units or agents (households, firms etc) to deficit units (including the state). At the beginning of the 1990s the ECE countries and the 'Soviet' states had heavily bank oriented (Rybczynski, 1986) financial systems with no capital market to speak off. Some government and corporate bonds had been issued but the secondary market was virtually non-existent. The recently created state commercial banks were still at a very low level on their learning curves with regard to risk appraisal and portfolio management skills and interest rates were still largely controlled. Further, they were burdened with bad debts and seriously undercapitalised. The banks were, therefore, in no position to take over, from the planning agency, the responsibility for allocating capital. Before they could do so, a substantial investment in human capital and financial restructuring was required.

The problem is that, in practise, a substantial and immediate injection of human capital will not be possible and a, perhaps fairly lengthy, period of learning by doing and training will be required.[1] Additionally, the cost of restructuring will be high, since the accumulated past debts of all state companies must be dealt with, and can't take place until sufficient revenue has been raised. This is not easily resolved either, since hitherto government expenditure has been largely financed from the 'profits' of state companies and a new tax system has to be devised to replace it. This is taking longer than expected.

Once the legal framework, financial infrastructure (including auditing and accounting services, as well as banks and other intermediaries) and tax system are in place, the transformation can proceed in earnest. In practice the transformation has begun before the legal, financial and fiscal infrastructure have been fully constructed and are working efficiently. Nevertheless, success requires that the basic infrastructural needs are attended to at an early stage and it is not clear that this has been the case in the financial sphere. Relatively little has been done to restructure the 'two-tier' banking system. It was not until October 1991 that the first ECE country, the CSFR (Czech and Slovak Federal Republic), announced its intention to establish a bank restructuring fund.

---

[1] ECE countries are receiving help with staff-training from the EC (PHARE) programme and the World Bank (IBRD) is supporting a 'twinning' arrangement between nine Polish state banks and Western European banks.

Transformation also entails structural reform, including privatisation, and price (including interest rate) liberalisation. Given that, prior to the transformation, inflation was repressed and savings exceeded desired levels because of lack consumption opportunities (the 'monetary overhang'), and the government and state firms were not subject to 'hard' budget constraints (Kornai, 1980), there was a need to introduce a stabilisation policy in the early stages of the transformation. It is sometimes argued that stabilisation should proceed structural reform (especially privatisation), since reform will be easier once uncertainty has been reduced through stabilisation. It is, however, difficult to see how stabilisation can be achieved without structural reform; which is necessary to harden budget constraints and introduce a mechanism for corporate governance.

A key structural reform is price liberalisation and removal of subsidies. This creates inflation, or releases repressed inflation, as the excess, ('forced') savings ('monetary overhang') are reduced. In times of high uncertainty, such as those prevailing in the transforming ECE countries, some of the 'monetary overhang' is likely to be retained as 'precautionary balances', but the remainder of the excess savings will be spent, fuelling inflation. The only way to stop this is to instigate a 'monetary reform' to effectively confiscate forced savings. This is likely to be a politically suicidal measure in an emerging democracy and was not executed in the ECE countries.[2] A burst of inflation, therefore, seems to be an unavoidable part of the adjustment process, and should be accepted. Policy makers should, however, try to stop the burst of inflation, and the accompanying real wage adjustment, developing into a wage-price spiral. This too may be difficult for an emerging democracy to achieve. The key to preventing the emergence of such a spiral is the introduction of 'hard budget constraints': on the government; and on state and privatised firms.

To impose a hard budget constraint on the government, it is necessary to deny it access to funding from the central bank and the wider banking sector. The central bank must not be permitted simply to print money to allow the state sector to pay wage bills, as has been effectively happening in Yugoslavia and the USSR in recent years. This could be achieved by revising the constitution of the central bank to forbid it from undertaking lending to fund state budget deficits, as proposed in connection with the establishment of European Communities (EC) central bank. To make this possible, the central and State governments must establish alternative sources of funding. This will require the establishment of a bond market and the introduction of a new tax system.

---

2 It remains a possibility in the former states of the Soviet Union, although the partial reform in 1991, when large denomination rouble notes were recalled by the Gosbank, was extremely unpopular.

To impose hard budget constraints on state and privatised firms, excessive reliance on interfirm credit[3] must be eliminated and banks should be induced to advance only profitable (to them) loans. Even in OECD countries, however, this is not easily achieved (Mullineux, 1991). It requires the central bank to cease granting banks ready access to its 'discount window'; but this is difficult because it is hard to see how large state banks can be allowed to fail[4] at such an early stage in the transformation, and thus a moral hazard problem is created. The banks, therefore, need to be re-regulated as soon as possible in order to curb the moral hazard problem, perhaps by introducing risk-related capital adequacy or deposit insurance requirements. We will return to this point later.

Before risk-related capital adequacy requirements can be introduced, however, the banks must be restructured and, at least partially, privatised. Some privatisation seems necessary: to reduce the cost of recapitalising the banks; and to force them to bear the consequences of having to raise new capital at market prices if the aggregate risk in their portfolio rises. Further, to ensure that state firms can no longer rely on banks, or the Treasury, to provide funds on demand, they too must be 'marketised'[5] or privatised. Fully privatised firms can be forced into bankruptcy. This reduces the liability of the state, leaving it with a residual and essentially political, responsibility for 'marketised' state firms. It also allows commercial banks to terminate commitments in a way that they were unable to in the past and in a way that they might find it more difficult to do when dealing with 'marketised' state firms in an adverse political climate.

Privatisation can only work, however, if the privatised firms can finance their activities. Consideration also needs to be given to how the remaining state firms, which are expected (Hare and Grosfield, 1991) to account for over half the assets of three of the ECE countries (CSFR, Hungary and Poland)in 1993, (three years into their transition programmes), are to be financed. Clearly, privatised and marketised state firms will need access to bank finance. The domestic capital markets are unlikely to provide a significant alternative source of finance since they can be expected to take time to grow to maturity in the light of experiences in OECD countries and in other developing countries. Domestic banks can, therefore, be expected to remain the key financial intermediaries in the short to medium term (Brainard, 1990; Dehesa, 1991). The

---

3 Interfirm credit naturally arises in 'market economies', but excessive use of it results in disintermediation of credit and therefore dilutes the effectiveness of monetary policy. It also allows more efficient state sector firms to cross-subsidise and support less efficient ones.

4 The Vnesheconombank of the former USSR may be an exception, but it is not involved in lending to firms and its foreign debt servicing activities can easily be taken over by the Russian foreign trade bank (Rosvneshtorgbank) or the central bank.

5 'Marketised' here is used to mean subjection to market pressures. This entails more than 'commercialisation', which is usually taken to mean changing the legal structure of state firms by converting them to (initially 100% state-owned) 'joint-stock' companies.

banks are however burdened with bad debts, need to be recapitalised and lack credit risk appraisal expertise. This is a serious constraint, and suggests that overambitious privatisation programmes will run into difficulties. There are also overall financial constraints on the process. These will be discussed in the section after next.

3) LESSONS FROM EAST GERMANY

At the outset, it is instructive to note how different it all is for the former German Democratic Republic (GDR) (Fels and Schnabel, 1991). The legal system and financial infrastructure were already in place in the Federal Republic of Germany (FRG), to which it was appended, and the overall financial constraint on the process was much weaker. The FRG has been able to make massive transfers which have been funded by increased taxation and by borrowing from the capital markets, which were already established, as was the tax system. The Treuhandandstalt was established to take over, restructure, and privatise the former GDR state-owned enterprises.

Despite the advantage of having a legal system in place, a well capitalized banking sector, and an established capital market, privatisation has proved more difficult than expected and has taken longer. It has recently been accepted that some of the firms privatised in the early stages were underpriced and that the prices should be renegotiated, indicating the dangers of undue haste. Despite having an established auditing and accounting system, it was difficult to value firms on the basis of the meagre information available in the early stages. Valuation has become easier as the firms have traded, and therefore generated information, under the watchful eye of the 'Treuhand'. Valuation will clearly be at least as difficult in the ECE countries, again suggesting that a cautious approach to privatisation should be adopted.

As has been the case in the ECE countries (Hare and Grosfield, 1991; Dehesa, 1991), 'small privatisations', of shops and small businesses etc, took place at an early stage. This was clearly sensible in the former GDR because the supporting financial infrastructure was rapidly introduced. The West German banks in particular were quick to establish branches in the Eastern Lander. Without similar access to banks experienced in dealing with small and medium sized enterprises (SMEs)[6], it seems likely that there will be a considerable incidence of 'failure to thrive' amongst SMEs privatised in the ECE countries.

By July 1991, one year after German economic and monetary union (Gemu) and nine months after political union, it was already apparent that the

---

[6] See Chapter 7 for an account of the subsidised loans and loan guarantees available, via the banking system, to SMEs in Germany.

transformation of the Eastern Lander was in reality facing financial constraints. A tax increase had been announced and public opinion polls showed an unwillingness amongst Western Germans to accept any reduction their projected living standards, as required by the transfer payments to the Eastern Lander. Further, central and state government departments seemed unwilling to cut their expenditures and the Bundesbank was repeatedly warning about the consequences of the rising government borrowing requirement, and excessive wage increases: in the West, as attempts were made to maintain real income growth; and in the East, as attempts were made to reduce differentials with the West. Inflation and interest rates rose as a consequence and the Bundesbank threatened to keep on raising interest rates until the inflationary pressures subsided. To reinforce this message, interest rates were again raised in December 1991.

Transformation in the former GDR has proved very costly. The costs include the provision of a 'social safety net' to ameliorate the effects of the unemployment resulting from the restructuring of industry and commerce in the Eastern Lander. These costs were contained in the first year or so as the Treuhand required many of the firms under its control to maintain employment levels. The job protection agreements ended on July 30, 1991, however. As the firms are restructured, to convert them into attractive privatisation prospects, they can be expected to shed substantial amounts of labour. The more so after a year of substantial wage increases which have far outstripped productivity growth, and have reduced the differential with their Western German counterparts.

In such a politically charged environment, and with considerable uncertainty about business prospects, the banks have had to have the loans they advance guaranteed by the Treuhand. The latter had hoped that, as more information about the firms under its management became available, and after some restructuring, the banks could be weaned of the guarantees. This too has proved more difficult than anticipated, possibly due to lack of competition for banking business in the Eastern Lander. The big German commercial banks that have recently returned to the Eastern Lander were not fully competing with each other in the early stages. They were preoccupied with establishing their new branch networks. Some of these branches previously belonged to the state bank. Additionally, they faced less competition from savings, cooperative and other banks than they do in the Western Lander. The lack of competition notwithstanding, it is likely that the lending in the Eastern Lander would carry a substantial, and perhaps prohibitive for fledging enterprises, risk premium if guarantees were discontinued too soon.[7]

---

[7] See Chapter 7 for further discussion.

The Treuhand has also absorbed the bad debts of firms, which has accumulated through the interfirm credit system, and of the former state banks, which, as noted above, had their networks sold to the large German commercial banks, Deutsche and Dresdner (which were required to retain and retrain the staff). Perhaps not surprisingly, the Treuhand's expenditure net of privatisation revenue has exceeded its budget and it applied for increased funding in the Autumn of 1991. Restructuring and privatisation has proved to be costly, even for Germany.

4) PRIVATISATION: HOW TO PROCEED?

Privatisation, price liberalisation and financial sector reform are the key elements of the structural reform required in the transition from state to market capitalism, at least for a closed economy. Matters are, of course, more complicated when countries don't exist in isolation but instead trade with each other. Then the issue of currency convertibility comes to the fore. In this paper such issues will be ignored[8] and the interrelationship between privatisation and financial sector reform will be focused upon.

There has been much discussion about the appropriate method of privatisation[9]. The main options, of which there are numerous variations, are transferring ownership of state assets directly to the public (the 'vouchers' system) or selling the assets to the public or to foreigners (sales). Hungary has opted primarily for sales and the CSFR and Poland have opted to use both sales and vouchers. The privatisation of small and medium sized, especially service sector, firms ('small' privatisations) was well underway in all three countries in 1990 with auctions being commonly used. The privatisation of large state enterprises ('large' privatisations), in Poland the CSFR involves both sales (including sales to foreigners but with some restrictions) and the distribution of vouchers, which will be used to buy shares either directly in privatised firms or via holding companies (Poland). These 'large' privatisation programmes ('mass privatisations') have not proceeded as rapidly as originally hoped. In the Autumn of 1991, for example, the CSFR announced a schedule for the first block of large privatisations. Previous large privatisations had either been spontaneous or the result of keen foreign interest (eg Volkswagen's partnership with Skoda). Spontaneous privatisations arise when the management of a state firm present plans for privatisation. Many of these have subsequently proved controversial as the management has effectively used inside information to buy at a price which undervalues the assets. Spontaneous privatisations are now

---

8 Fry and Nuti (1991) provide a useful review of convertability and exchange rate issues.
9 See references in Dehasa (1991) and Hare and Grosfield (1991).

vetted by the privatisation agencies or ministries that have been established in the CSFR, Poland and Hungary.

In the medium term, even if the currently ambitious privatisation programmes succeed, a sizeable state sector will continue to exist, and, some firms, 'utilities' for example, may be retained in the state sector. How these firms are to be managed and financed needs to be considered too.[10]

The voucher system is often recommended for mass privatisation because it is seen as equitable and egalitarian and it facilitates rapid privatisation (Blanchard et al, 1991; Dehesa, 1991). It is, of course, also populist. Many people in the former GDR thought that this would have been the correct solution too and feel that the Treuhand's 'sales' solution is unfair. This is because they feel that they, as members of the public, owned the state's assets and that the state accumulated the assets by forcing them to consume less than they desired and perhaps by expropriating surplus value. This may be so, but such a view confuses socialism with state capitalism; under which the state is effectively acting in its own interest and the 'nomenklatura' can be regarded as part of the state system. In this view, voucher issuance may be seen as a means of dispossessing the 'nomenklatura', however.

Before privatisation can commence, the problem of dealing with claims for restitution by dispossessed former owners of property needs to be dealt with. Germany initially opted for restitution of property whilst Hungary opted for compensation. The advantage of compensation is that privatisation can proceed more quickly. In response to problems in dealing with restitution claims, however, Germany passed an investment promotion Bill in March 1991. This increases the number of exceptions to restitution and gives priority to new investors (Fels and Schnabel, 1991).

Distribution of ownership via vouchers may not turn out to be egalitarian after all and could backfire on governments using such systems to enhance popularity. Through this lottery, for that is what it effectively is given the information deficiencies, some people will end up with valuable shares and others with virtually valueless ones. The privatised stocks on the Hungarian and Polish exchanges have performed badly to date, it should be noted. Sales do have the advantage of raising revenue, but at the risk that the nomenklatura (who prospered under state capitalism and have the most private wealth) and foreigners will end up holding most of the shares. This may be the natural outcome since the nomenklatura are the only group with managerial experience. Even under the voucher system, if shares can be sold on a secondary market, the nomenklatura may end up as the largest holders. In this case, however, they would transfer wealth to the sellers of shares rather than to the privatisation agency. Politically, however, it is clear that constraints must be placed on the

---

10 See Hare and Revesz (1991) for further discussion.

sales process to ensure that foreigners and the nomenklatura are not seen to be taking over the ECE countries. This may account for the mix of vouchers and sales with restraints on foreign participation in the CSFR and Poland. It should be noted that in Poland the vouchers cannot be exchanged directly for shares in privatised companies. Instead, they can be used to 'buy' shares in state run (western expert managed) investment funds, ensuring that the public buys into a diversified portfolio. The lottery is therefore a modified one. In the CSFR, investment funds have sprung up spontaneously and are causing concern to the authorities in the absense of regulation.[11]

It seems likely, however, that the most equitable and egalitarian approach is to distribute the net revenue (if there is any) from privatisation to the public via tax cuts or waivers. Sales, however, imply slower privatisation than the use of vouchers. The case for quick privatisation is largely political (Dehasa, 1991). It is seen as a way of creating a property owning middle class as quickly as possible, and as a means of avoiding a feared lapse back into state capitalism. If it is felt necessary to secure public participation, concentration on privatisation of state owned dwellings and employed share ownership schemes (ESOPS) may be preferable (Fels and Schnabel, 1991). Rapid privatisation has, however, come up against logistical and political constraints. As mentioned earlier, spontaneous privatisation allowed many unpopular get rich quick deals, often involving former nomenklatura, which have since come to light. There is, therefore, a need to control the process via a state privatisation agency, even if this adds a layer of bureaucracy. The need to avoid future mistakes and ensure that the legal and other prerequisites are in place has also led the currently ambitious programmes in the CSFR, Hungary and Poland to fall behind schedule. Politically, the 'window of opportunity' for rapid mass privatisation may already have passed and more measured, and economically costed, programmes should be designed. This should take full account of the financial constraints. The transformation is not costless, as the experience of Germany attests. A full cost benefit analysis is required.

5) FINANCIAL CONSTRAINTS

Apart from the political constraints, there are financial constraints. The assets to be privatised represent accumulated past savings (or wealth). If they are sold to the public they absorb current savings flows. To the extent that current savings exceed desired levels and there is a dearth of attractive savings instruments (ie there is a 'monetary overhang')[12], then sales may contribute to

---

[11] See Chapter 7 for further discussion.

[12] The high inflation in the early stages of the transition eliminated the 'monetary overhang' in most ECE countries and probably also had negative wealth effects.

stabilisation. But current savings levels are not sufficient to absorb the currently planned sales of large tranches of assets without driving prices down. To avoid this privatisation we must proceed at a slower pace or sales to foreigners must be significant or some of the assets must be given to the public. There are political constraints on the scale of sales to foreigners and anyway their interest cannot be relied upon (Debs, Shapiro and Taylor, 1991). Sales to foreigners would clearly provide a useful additional source of revenue for the privatisation agency however. Sales might also induce the return of flight capital, although the significance of this is likely to be small compared to the Latin American countries, for example, due to non-convertibility under state capitalism.[13]

In the early stages, the revenue raised through sales may be needed by the government to replace income previously derived from firms,and to finance the transition, at least until corporate and income tax systems and a government bond market is established. It should be noted, however, that sales will attract funds that might otherwise have been invested: in the bond market and might therefore inhibit its development; or, via banks, in SMEs, discouraging the growth of this important sector.

5.1 The Privatisation Agency

One possible solution would be to set up a state privatisation agency which is broader in scope than the existing agencies in the CSFR, Poland and Hungary, or even the Treuhand. Its responsibilities might include:

1) recapitalisation of the banks;
2) restructuring firms financially and organisationally;
3) restitution and compensation;
4) guaranteeing bank loans, and administering venture capital funds;
5) setting up state holding companies to manage firms requiring long term restructuring;
6) monitoring the activities of 'utilities'.

The agency should be funded out of privatisation proceeds. If the experience of the Treuhand is any guide, a sizeable surplus is unlikely in the early years and a deficit is a distinct possibility. If a surplus is (eventually) generated, it should be transferred to the government and used to help fund the provision of a 'safety net', to cope with the effects of unemployment, and retraining schemes; both of which can be regarded as part of the restructuring process.

Because of the lack of available expertise, it is likely, at least initially to be advantageous to concentrate these activities in a single agency. As this

[13] Although in 1992 the Russian government's tax on export earnings (to create a hard currency fund to stabilise the rouble) created an incentive for exporters not to repatriate their earnings.

constraint relaxes, various activities could be hived off to separate agencies. A state holding company could, for example, manage firms requiring long term restructuring and another agency could monitor 'utilities'.

Venture capital funds could alternatively be overseen by a development bank, which could also provide loan guarantees. They have been included in the list of functions of the privatisation agency because such an agency must not loose sight of its ultimate goal (the creation a thriving market economy) and concentrate entirely on methods of privatisation and their execution.

In the OECD countries it has increasingly been recognised that a thriving SME sector is a key to rapid growth. This has certainly been the case in FRG (Fels and Schnaber, 1991) and provides strong support for executing 'small' privatisations as quickly as possible, the risk of the nomenklatura establishing themselves as the petit bourgeoisie notwithstanding. Regardless of the latter risk, small privatisations seem to have been genuinely popular. Small privatisations by auction will absorb some savings and help to establish the SME sector. The continued growth and prospects of this sector, however, requires access to bank loans and funds to sponsor new ventures and expansion. Banks in the west are notoriously bad at providing start-up capital and, as a result, in many countries specialist government agencies have been established to provide loan guarantees, refinancing support to banks, and subsidised loans.

In the ECE countries, the banks, faced with such an uncertain environment, have enough risks to worry about without getting involved in lending to small businesses and providing start-up capital. Loan guarantees (as in Germany) and a state-backed venture capital fund, therefore, appear to be called for. Because they are an integral part of the overall restructuring process and privatisation by sales absorbs some of the savings which might potentially have been lent to SMEs, loan guarantees and venture capital funding should be financed using privatisation proceeds.

5.2 Restructuring Banks and the Wider Financial Sector

A key function of the privatisation agency should be the restructuring and refinancing of banks. Until banks have had the bad debts removed from their books and have been recapitalised, it is impossible to proceed successfully with privatisation (small or large) because the privatised firms must have access to finance to survive and thrive. The restructuring of firms, including those that remain in the state sector, helps the banks by making their clients more viable. It seems sensible to privatise banks at a relatively early stage, so that they face the consequences of their actions and begin to impose hard(er) budget constraints on their clients. Before this can be done, their bad debts must be replaced with viable assets and they need a capital injection to increase their capacity to lend to an appropriate level to support the transforming economy. The costs naturally fall to the privatisation agency, which should perhaps set up a subsidiary: to work out bad loans and absorb the costs of write-offs, where these prove sensible or necessary; and to oversee the recapitalisation of banks. Bad debts could perhaps be replaced by government backed assets such as bonds (Brainard, 1990).

One reason that an increased supply of bank credit will be required is that over-reliance of interfirm credit should be discouraged: to increase the effectiveness of monetary policy and reduce inefficient cross-subsidisation in the state sector. In the recession of the early 1990s in the UK 'cash-flow' problems were a major cause of business failures and there have been suggestions that a legal requirement to pay invoices within a required period might be appropriate. This solution to the problem is adopted in a number of EC countries and could usefully be adopted by the ECE countries, where the establishment of an efficient clearing and payments system is also crucial for SMEs.

In many developing countries, such as Nigeria money and capital markets have developed following the issue of Treasury bills and bonds by the government. Equity markets developed later with the encouragement of the central bank (Central Bank of Nigeria, 1979; Mullineux, 1987). The development of money markets is particularly important for promoting the efficient allocation of resources by the banking sector because banks with surplus funds need to be able to place them, via an interbank market, with banks that are short of funds. This is particularly important in ECE countries, where state savings banks used to channel their surplus directly into the budget for disbursement via the state bank. They are likely to continue to have a surplus, even after the creation of a 'two-tier' banking system, whilst the commercial banks remain starved of funds.

The issuance of Treasury bills not only helps to provide the government with working capital but also sets a benchmark rate for the wholesale money markets and thereby helps to sponsor the development of an interbank market and should be instigated as soon as possible. Demand for Treasury bills can be assured by imposing liquid reserve requirements on banks for prudential and monetary control purposes. Restructuring banks, by replacing bad debts with bonds, may also encourage the development of secondary bond market as banks learn to manage their assets and liabilities more actively. With regard to developing an equity market, the banks could be encouraged, perhaps via inducements, to help by engaging in debt for equity swaps.[14]

It is through such financial restructuring of their clients that the equity participations of many European commercial ('universal') banks developed

---

14 Exchanging the debts of their corporate clients for equity participations.

(Mullineux, 1987). It has been argued (Corbett and Mayer, 1991) that monitoring by banks, and therefore corporate governance, is improved if banks not only extend collateralised loans but also have equity exposure to their clients, as in Japan and Germany for example. Monitoring is likely to be a problem in the newly privatised sector of the ECE countries, especially in the absence of well established auditing procedures. To the extent that vouchers lead to more dispersed share ownership (than sales) they make the monitoring problem worse.

The Polish investment funds could potentially play a monitoring role. In some OECD countries, particularly the more capital (less bank) oriented countries such as the US and the UK, institutional investors (pension funds and insurance companies) hold the majority of shares and have been more actively involved in corporate governance in the early 1990s. Whether this is a special feature of the recession in the US and the UK in that period is yet to be seen, but it is unlikely that institutional investors will be key players in the ECE countries in the near future. If banks are to be the key monitors of business performance, then the central banks or bank supervisory agencies must monitor the monitors carefully by establishing a suitable supervisory regime, a point to which will be returned to later.

Before proceeding to a summary and more specific proposals it should be re-emphasised that the government will face a funding problem as privatised and 'marketised' firms can no longer be relied upon to provide the bulk of government revenue. A tax system and a bond market must be established at the same time as the banking sector is being reformed, and before mass privatisation is embarked upon. Also, hard(er) budget constraints must be imposed upon the government and firms, whether they remain in the state sector or not. Privatisation is part of the answer, but the bulk of the large firms will remain in the state sector in the short to medium term and must be 'marketised' by cutting off their access to central bank money.

To conclude this section, it should be noted that the Treuhand wields considerable leverage over banks because of the credit guarantees it provides. By providing such guarantees the ECE privatisation agencies would be able to do the same. The problem of weaning the banks off the support is difficult enough in Germany, however, and could be more so in the ECE countries.

SUMMARY AND CONCLUSIONS

Financial sector reform is a key element in the transition from state to market capitalism and yet it has received relatively little attention. It is fundamental because the transformation entails the establishment of a new means of allocating capital. Additionally, stabilisation requires the imposition of hard(er) budget constraints on firms and the government (see also Chapter 2) and a credible stabilisation programme is needed to reduce uncertainty, stimulate internal investment flows and attract foreign investment. Further, the restructuring of the manufacturing and services sectors requires: financial support during the 'marketisation', financial restructuring and privatisation process; infrastructural investment, for which foreign and domestic capital must be raised; and finance for privatised firms and the firms that are to remain in the state sector, but which should not rely on budgetary finance in the interests of stabilisation.

It is difficult to see how the transition can proceed successfully in the absence of an adequate financial infrastructure: to facilitate restructuring; to nurture privatised firms; and to sponsor new enterprises through the provision of venture capital. Partnerships with foreign capitalists may also be relevant in this connection. The nature of the required financial infrastructure may depend on the chosen method of privatisation. Voucher distribution emphasises the importance of capital markets for secondary trading and may require the establishment of investment funds, as in Poland. Post privatisation, however, firms will need access to finance to supply working and investment capital. Mass sales of state assets clearly require the establishment of primary capital markets, although investors, particularly the foreign ones, would clearly be encouraged if they could exit by selling shares on a secondary market. Substantial blocks of shares might, however, be issued to banks, via debt for equity swaps perhaps, and to pension funds. Shares could also be sold on foreign stock exchanges.[15] In the Autumn of 1991 the Treuhand began to encourage banks to take over, rationalise and sell groups of Eastern German companies as a means of speeding up the privatisation programme.

The underdeveloped nature of the existing financial sector and the need refinance banks, along with the overall financial and political constraints discussed above, seem to indicate that the ECE countries should proceed more slowly than currently planned with mass privatisation. Even if it were politically feasible to sell sizeable chunks of state assets to foreigners, they are unlikely to have the appetite.[16] The state run sector, despite the currently ambitious privatisation programmes, will remain large and hard(er) budget constraints must be imposed to ensure fiscal discipline. As was the case with the Treuhand, in order to reduce social costs and political tension in the early phases, the privatisation agency or ministry may, however, be expected to pursue unemployment limiting objectives. The costs of achieving them should, if possible, be taken out of the privatisation proceeds, rather than the state budget. There seems to be a strong case for minimising disruption by pursuing

---

15 Some Hungarian shares are quoted in both the Budapest and Vienna.

16 Although Hungary had reasonable success in attracting foreign capital in 1991 as it proceeded with its relatively measured privatisation programme.

slow and partial privatisation, in the manner of Italy and France (and recently proposed in Argentina), of the large state sector employers. Joint ventures between the state and foreign investors can be viewed as a form of partial privatisation and have been used with some success (particularly in Hungary) to attract foreign investment. Emphasis should be placed on creating a thriving SMEs sector through rapid small privatisation and ample provision of venture capital, perhaps through the privatisation agency. Loan guarantees will also be necessary to encourage the banks to lend in this high risk sector.

Banks must be restructured and refinanced at an early stage and given ample funding to allow them to train their employees in risk appraisal and modern banking skills. They will remain the key financial institutions for the foreseeable future. To accelerate the learning process joint ventures (Hungary) and twinning (Poland) with western banks should be encouraged. Joint ventures will of course also bring in new capital. The banks' bad debts must be replaced with viable assets and new capital must be provided (Brainard, 1990).

Interest rates should however be liberalised and an interbank market should be developed as soon as possible to facilitate the efficient allocation of capital (Mckinnon, 1973, Shaw, 1973). A positive real rate of interest will also boost private saving, which, as far as possible, should be channelled into new enterprises, rather than collected by the state through privatisation sales, and discourage capital flight.

The privatisation agency, by providing loan guarantees, would, like the Treuhand, have leverage to support its corporate governance/monitoring function. Also, if restructuring of firms involved debt for equity swaps with banks, their monitoring role would be enhanced. Many of the ECE countries aspire to EC membership and the 2nd 'Banking' Directive (European Commission, Dec. 1989) limits bank shareholding. Since membership is probably some way off, the banks could be allowed to exceed this limit in the medium term, whilst alternative institutional shareholders, such as insurance companies and pension funds, become established. The state is, however, as elsewhere in Europe, likely to remain the major supplier of pensions for some time. The insurance market could all too easily become dominated by the major European companies. There may be a case for some infant industry protection here. Also, elsewhere in Europe (eg. Germany) domestic insurance institutions are commonly required to hold a certain proportion of government bonds in their portfolios. This too will have to be phased out as a result of EC directives in the run up to '1992'. In the ECE countries, however, there may, be a case for requiring insurance companies to hold a certain proportion of government bonds in their portfolios whilst the bond market is being established. Such a development, along with tax reform, is a matter of urgency if the state is to be cut off from central bank funding as a means of stabilising the economy. With regard to corporate governance, voucher distribution is problematic whereas, under slow sales, monitoring can be shared between the privatisation agency, the bank, the investment funds, and the emerging institutional investors. The universal banking model seems appropriate from a governance perspective. Also, under universal banking, the banks could underwrite capital issues and act as brokers, reducing the need to develop specialised institutions to support the capital market.

The small business cash-flow and interfirm credit problems could be dealt with relatively easily by imposing legal requirements to issue invoices and for them to be paid within, say, three months. The banks could also provide an electronic invoicing and payments service similar to these recently developed in some EC countries. The results would be: improved monetary policy effectiveness; greater financial discipline and reduced cross-subsidisation in the state sector; more transparency in firms financial positions, facilitating monitoring and reducing lending risks; and, probably, fewer small business failures due to 'cash flow' problems. Calvo and Coricelli (1991) have argued that restricted access to the lender of last resort will increase credit risks and this will lead to a voluntary reduction in inter-enterprise credit. They cite the case of Poland to support their proposition. Even if this is correct, small firms may need legal backing to help them get prompt payment from larger firms.

A bank regulatory and supervisory system would need to be established to contain moral hazard problems, reduce systemic banking risks and, thereby, increase the authorities' ability: to impose effective monetary restraint; and to impose hard(er) budget constraints on firms and the government. Given that the ECE countries aspire to EC membership, it seems likely the emerging EC regulatory and supervisory framework[17] will be adopted. Not only does the 2nd EC 'Banking' Directive allow universal banking, but it also permits Allfinanz and bancassurance, which is the combination of banking and insurance business. This too might be allowed in the ECE countries if strong financial institutions, capable of competing with giants from the EC, are to be established.

The central bank should be encouraged to sponsor the development of a money market, by issuing Treasury bills: to provide the government with working capital, and to provide a benchmark rate for corporate and bank bills. It should also sponsor the development of a government bond market, which would provide benchmark rates for other securities help to and satisfy the state's longer term financial needs.

As regards the establishment of an interbank market, which is important for the efficient allocation of bank credit, this is perhaps best done by establishing what might be termed a super clearing house. This could provide money transmission and clearing services, including: central clearing by adjusting bank

---

[17] See Mullineux (1992a).

accounts held with the clearing house in line with net end of day deficits or surpluses; and the aforementioned invoice issuing and payment service. It could also provide a market or brokering service through which banks with surplus funds could lend to banks with insufficient funds. This would also reduce reliance on the central bank's discount window.

Whilst competition in the banking sector is likely to be beneficial to consumers of banking services, failures of large banks cannot be allowed and so big banks will enjoy state backing de facto. The resulting moral hazard problem will have to be dealt with through regulation. Some sort of risk related bank insurance package (Chapter 2) seems appropriate and considerable central bank intervention can be expected in the early stages as central banks try to impose monetary restraint whilst maintaining financial stability and avoiding 'credit crunches' (Mullineux, 1992). Competitive pressure will have to be assured, in line with the rest of the state sector, by allowing open access to foreign firms and learning can be accelerated by encouraging joint ventures. This of course leads us back to the open economy reality and the issue of how and when to introduce currency convertibility, which we have largely ignored in order to focus attention on financial sector reform.

In connection with the structure outlined in the diagram below, the following points should be noted. In line with the proposed European Monetary Union arrangements, the central bank would be independent of the Finance Ministry with respect to monetary, and possibly exchange rate, policy.

The Finance Ministry should initially concentrate on balancing the budget until access to bond markets allows a deficit to be financed and should widen the tax base as soon as possible to ensure that it no longer needs to borrow from the central bank or other banks.

The central bank should concentrate on establishing a viable financial sector. Financial stability must be established to allow the monetary brakes to be applied in connection with the macroeconomic stabilisation programme. Also, a 'credit crunch', resulting from over cautious lending, should be avoided by providing loan guarantees. These are best provided out of tax revenue or privatisation proceeds (via the privatisation agency or a development bank) and not by the central bank; which needs to eliminate commercial bank reliance on its lending.

Suggested Financial Sector Structure

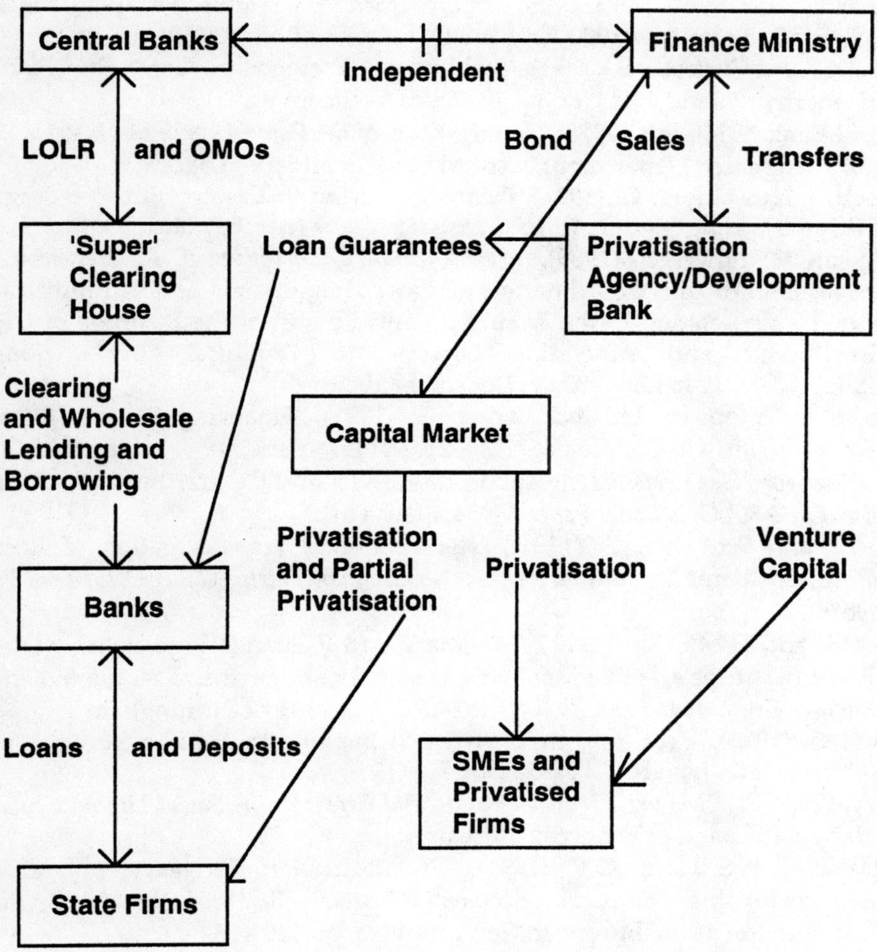

REFERENCES

Blanchard, O., Dornbusch, R., Krugman, P., Layard, R. and Summers, L. (1991), '*Reform in Eastern Europe*' Cambridge, Mass: MIT Press.

Brainard, L.J. (1990), 'Reform in Eastern Europe: Creating a Capital Market'. MAEX Bank Review 1990 First Prize Essay, London: AMEX

Calvo, G. and Caricelli, F. (1991), 'Stabilizing a Previously - Centrally - Planned Economy: Poland 1990', *Economic Policy* forthcoming

Central Bank of Nigeria (1979) '*Twenty Years of the Central Bank in Nigeria: 1959-1979*', Research Department, Central Bank of Nigeria, Lagos

Corbett, J. and Mayer, C. (1991) 'Financial Reform in Eastern Europe: Progress with the Wrong Model', *CEPR Discussion Paper No 603,* London

European Commission (1989), *Second Council Directive of 15 December*, 89 /646/EEC on the Coordination of Laws, Regulations and Administrative Provisions Relating to the Taking up and Pursuit of the Business of Credit Institutions and Amending Directive 77/780/EEC Official Journal Reference: OJ No L386/32. 30 December 1989

Debs, R.A., Shapriro, H. and Taylor, C. (1991), 'Financing Eastern Europe', *Group of Thirty (G.30) Study Group Report,* New York

de La Dehesa, G. (1991) 'Privatisation in Eastern and Central Europe', *Group of Thirty (G.30) Occasional Paper No 34,* New York

Fels, G. and Schnabel, C. (1991), 'The Economic Transformation of Eastern Germany: Some Preliminary Lessons', *Group of Thirty (G.30) Occasional Paper No 36,* New York

Fry, M.J. and D.M. Nuti (1991), 'Monetary and Exchange Rate Policies During Eastern Europe's Transition: Some Lessons from Further East'. *International Finance Group Paper No: IFGWP - 91-15,* University of Birmingham

Garvy, G. (1975), 'Post Reform Changes in Banking in Eastern Europe', Bana Nazionale de Lavaro, 28 (115), pp 370-386

Garvy, G. (1977), '*Money, Financial Flows, and Credit in the Soviet Union,* Chicago: National Bureau of Economic Research

Grosfield, I and Hare, G.P. (1991), 'Privatisation in Hungary, Poland and Czechoslovakia' *European Economy,* Special Edition No 2, Brussels: Commission of the European Communities, pp 129-156

Hare, P.G. and Revesz, T. (1991) 'Hungary's Transition to a Market Economy in The case against a "Big Bank"', *Economic Policy,* forthcoming

Kornai (1980) '*Economics of Shortage*', 2 volumes, Amsterdam: North Holland

McKinnon, R.I. (1973) '*Money and Capital in Economic Development*', Washington: Brookings Institute

McKinnon, R.I. (1991) 'Financial Control in the Transition to a Market Economy', *Journal of Economic Perspectives*, forthcoming

Mullineux, A.W. (1987), '*International Banking and Financial Systems*', London: Graham & Trotman

Mullineux, A.W. (1991) 'Bank Regulation, Financial Fragility and Monetary Control in the 1990s' *Business and Economics Review*, Summer, pp 29-36

Mullineux, A.W. (1992) '*European Banking*', Oxford: Basil Blackwell.

Rybcynski, T.M. (1986), 'The UK Financial System in Transition', *National Westminster Bank Quarterly Review*, November pp 26-42

Shaw, E.S. (1973), '*Financial Deepening in Economic Development*', New York: Oxford University Press.

Wilcynski, J. (1978) *Comparative Monetary Economics*, London: Macmillan

CHAPTER 9

THE TRANSITION PROGRAM OF THE POLISH BANKING SYSTEM

Jaroslaw Bauc, Boguslaw Grabowski and Andrzej Raczko

1. INTRODUCTION

At the end of 1989, after more than forty years of central planning and about a decade of trying to reform the economic system within a "socialist" framework, the Polish economy was almost in chaos. Production was decreasing very quickly. Cooperative links among state-owned enterprises began to fall apart. Partially freed prices for food rose quickly and the inflation rate reached more than 30% per month, in the last quarter of 1989. Despite this, shortages were increasing and queues growing longer. The official exchange rate was subject to devaluation almost each week and the black market exchange rate skyrocketed reaching a level which was not to be reached again by the convertible zloty untill August 1992. Foreign currencies and especially the US dollar played the role of means of payments in rapidly growing sectors of the internal market and also among state-owned firms. More then 80% of household savings were denominated in foreign currencies. The balance of payments was deteriorating and the huge foreign debt (about 40 billion $ US) was not serviced. Because of huge subsidies and social spending the budget deficit reached at the end of August 1989 almost 30% of GDP.

Under such circumstances the newly elected Solidarity led government embarked on a reform program which aimed to stabilize and restructure Polish economy through its transformation into a market economy. The Balcerowicz Plan combined the elements of institutional reform: price liberalization, internal convertibility of zloty, foreign trade liberalization and a privatization program with a typical stabilization program: restrictive fiscal and monetary policy, devaluation and wage control. The plan was introduced in January 1990.

Monetary control seems to have played the most important role in this plan since inflation was assumed to be the most serious problem of the Polish economy in the short run. As far as the financial system is concerned the problem emerged of what should have been the role of the banking system reform during this period of macroeconomic disequilibrium with structural disturbances. On the one hand, reform of the financial system was form the basis for more effective monetary control, credit allocation and saving encouragement. On the other hand however, macroeconomic stability supported by the structural reform of the economic system required successful reform of the financial system. Interest rate liberalization, for instance, is the key instrument for the efficient credit allocation and strengthening propensity to saving. But the effective functioning of the interest rate mechanism requires the interest rate sensitivity of all agents acting in the credit market.

The government seemed to choose the gradual approach in the reform program of the banking system. The successive steps in the program were subject to mutual interdependence of reform sequencing, a macroeconomic situation and progress in structural reforms implemented in the real sector of the economy. Therefore, at the initial stage of the Polish transition program, the existing banking law was in force.

The law was introduced in January 1989. Before that date the Polish banking system functioned as a typical system for the centrally planned economy. In such an economy where both volume and structure of production, cooperation links, technical methods of production and allocation of productive factors were determined by an obligatory central plan formulated in real terms, the banking system seemed to be redundant. In reality, because of the existence of, at least, "accounting" money, a small (but significant in Polish agriculture) private sector, and wages paid in money a banking system of a special sort turned out to be necessary. The monopolistic Narodowy Bank Polski and its network of regional branches was created. In addition there were three more specialized banks which provided services to foreign trade, agricultural producers and handled private savings.

The banking law which was introduced at the beginning of 1989 was designed for the so called "Program of Economic marketization". The most important element of this banking bill were as follows:

- from the structure of The Polish National Bank (NBP) nine new commercial banks were separated; it was done on the basis of its previous local branches,
- the local and functional monopoly were broken up; firms could choose the bank and their mutual relations were not subject to administrative control,
- the Head Office of NBP became the Central Bank whose President was appointed by the President of the Republic of Poland.

In reality these solutions were not observed and practised. For instance the Central Bank could still impose (informally) the level of the interest rate, determine the allocation of preferential credits or directly determine the sum of the credit. Although the President of the Central Bank was formally independent of the government, as a member of the communist party he was obliged to follow economic policy prescribed by the Politbiuro. At the same time the Presidents of commercial banks were appointed by the NBP's President.

2. THE BANKING SYSTEM AND THE BALCEROWICZ PLAN

Only the political changes (Autumn 1989) and elaboration of the stabilization program altered the attitude toward the Banking system. The Balcerowicz Plan supported the system with some significant measures:

- preferential credits were no longer in use;
- the interest rate of previously granted preferential credits was sharply increased;
- the state budget could not be financed by the central bank credit.

As the control of inflation was the main goal of the Balcerowicz stabilization programme priority was given to these elements of the financial sector reform which are strictly connected with the monetary management. As it was already mentioned the 1989 banking law introduced the two-tier system. But beginning January 1990 commercial banks did not have to transmit information and instructions from the Central Planner. For the first time they faced market conditions and were forced to negotiate with firms. The main problem inherited from the former practice was whether they would be able to resist the demand for credits and, if they could carry out the policy of expensive credit.

The government for various reasons was convinced that banks would not pass this exam. First of all the banks were suspected of running a policy of soft credit constraints in respect state-firms. Personal connections among the banks management and firms directors could outweigh market signals. In other words, instead of economic indicators, the common interest of the group of managers could be the main criterion of credit allocation.

That is why the authorities decided to exercise direct control upon the credit supply and postponed deeper reforms of the banking sector. NBP simply assigned individual banks credit limits. At the same time the central bank intervened in setting interest rates so that they were positive in real terms but not excessive. The credit supply control seemed to be an attempt at moral hazard elimination. In this case, moral hazard arises when a borrower can go bankrupt, in which event the lender gets back only a portion and possibly none of the loan. This could occur if the interest rate were set at the equilibrium level. In other words, banks were suspected of prolonging bad debts and to grant their credits independently of any efficiency criteria. As a result the increasing value of bad debts could threaten the stability of the whole financial system.

The creators of the reform programme were aware that the inherited banking system did not fit the requirements of the market economy. Therefore, though the Central Bank did not give up administrative control over commercial banks, the significance of indirect instruments in monetary management has been growing and new institutional solutions in financial system were introduced.

New elements concerned four spheres:

- changes within NBP, its position and functions,
- rules of bank creation, functioning and supervision,
- rules of the money market operation,
- changes in technical equipment, organizational and accounting system bringing Polish banks closer to European standards.

3. MONETARY MANAGEMENT

For more effective and market-type control of the money supply traditional central bank instruments were introduced. In 1989 refinancing credit was the main source of money channelled to the banking system. It accounted for about 65% of the value of credit granted to economic agents. Such a situation discouraged commercial banks seeking new deposits and became an obstacle to the emergence of an interbank money market.

In 1990 the NBP undertook some measures to change the size and conditions of refinancing. The so-called basic refinancing credit was reduced to 50% of its level at the end of 1989. At the same time agreement with commercial banks was made, that the whole amount of the refinancing credit will be repaid in six annual instalments, till 1995. So this simple form of credit for banks will not be provided after that time.

According to new rules of credit provision, 40% of the credit limit is put on the current account while its remaining part is recorded as an off balance sheet item. This is the, so called reserve refinancing credit which can be used at the bank's request.

From the beginning of 1990 the interest rate differentials between the basic refinancing credit and refinancing credit for preferential purposes (agriculture and food processing) were eliminated.

Though the significance of rediscount credit increased a little in 1990, it was still very limited. An interfirm credit, not supported with bills of exchange was still preferred among enterprises.

The new form of central bank credit allocation, which was introduced in 1990 was the Lombard credit. It is lent to a bank on collateral of securities issued by treasury, central bank and some big banks. The list of these securities is published by the central bank. That kind of credit can also be granted on collateral of bills of exchange received for rediscounting. The maturity time of securities cannot be longer then three months. Obviously the sum of this credit has to be lower than the value of securities. For treasury and central bank securities it is equal to 90%. For securities issued by other banks and bills of exchange the credit cannot exceed 75%.

It is assumed that as far as the market for securities develops the Lombard credit will become the main source of money given to commercial banks by the central bank. This would be in line with continuous reduction of credit limits allowed in operation of the refinancing credit system. So far its role has turned out to be insignificant.

It is also intended for the central bank to control the money supply through the open market operations. But this form of monetary control has not been developed yet. Because of this, mandatory reserves are still one of the most important money stock control tools. The appearance of NBP bills did not changed this situation. According to banking law the highest level of mandatory reserves is 30% and 50% of the reserves can be kept in bank's vaults in cash form. Because of the excess liquidity of the Polish economy in 1990 (due to the sharp increase in foreign exchange reserves) NBP had to increase ratio of mandatory reserves to its limit (30%) and as a result it has been increasingly ineffective. Such a very high rate combined with the practised rule that reserves produce no income makes the spread between interest rate on credit and interest rate on deposits very high. In the future, when the lower interest rate on credit will be important requirement for investment expansion, and the high interest rate on deposits will be required to boost the propensity to savings, observes will become an increasingly inferior method of money stock control.

It is worth mentioning that neither restrictions put on refinancing and Lombard credit, nor setting the obligatory reserve ratio exhausted the ways of controlling credit supply provided by the state commercial banks. Direct credit limits were still used as the main tool of credit policy.

4. THE CENTRAL BANK

Experiences during the introduction of the stabilization program exerted decisive impact upon the concept of the central bank in Poland. According to this concept the central bank should use all necessary tools for the control of the money supply and commercial banks supervision.

The new solutions were designed not only to eliminate excessive expansion of the commercial banks sector but to eliminate the supply of money wastes resulting from budgetary or/and political pressure exerted on the central bank. To implement these solutions two questions had to be solved. First, the budget deficit was not allowed to be financed by the NBP credit. Second, the position of the NBP management within the structure of economic management should be clarifieded.

As far as the latter is concerned the most important points from the 1989 banking law were confirmed. The President of NBP remained responsible for the monetary policy and independent of the government. He is appointed by the president of the Republic of Poland and approved by the parliament for 6 years. The NBP President submits a report and the projection of the monetary policy. At the same time his position in the framework of the central bank seems to be unquestionable. He practically decides official stand on important issues, appoints vice-presidents, the members of the management and finally he is not obliged to conform to the opinion of the management.

The transformation of former NBP into the real central bank required some changes in its structure and functions. It was decided that new NBP would consist of 5 basic departments: foreign, treasury and money-issue, operation, economic and supervision and till the end of 1991 it would abandon some activities inherited from the central planning period like account service for several thousand economic agents. Similarly the services offered to other banks should be separate and entrusted to other institutions. For instance inter bank clearing should be performed by the independent Clearing House. On the other hand NBP should create departments responsible for economic analysis, forecasting etc.

The central bank domination manifests not only in the credit control sphere but also in the field of banking supervision and licensing of new banks.

The law concerning licensing of new banks distinctly favours an increase in the number of banks. This is due to the following reasons. First of all, the amount and structure of existing state commercial banks does not correspond to requirements of a market economy. Secondly, initial experiences of state enterprise privatization has shown this to be a very slow process. Therefore the creation of new banks is supposed to fill a gap in the system of state commercial banks and to strengthen the competition among banks. For that reason every new bank can practically provide all banking services it wants to.

5. BANK SUPERVISION SYSTEM AND NEW TECHNICAL SOLUTIONS

Bank supervision in a fully state-owned banking system was limited to checks that the banks complied with credit allocation directives and foreign exchange regulations. It exhibited the problem of lack of competition and efficiency. The financial soundness of banks and protection of the depositor/consumer were much neglected. In other words it had very little to do with the system of banking supervision in mature market economies. The realization of the restructuring program however showed distinctly the urgent need for establishing supervisory system. The two tier banking system introduced in January 1989 when the National Bank of Poland (NBP) was divided into the central bank and 9 commercial banks could not function properly without some kind of supervisory system. This need was also confirmed by other post-communist countries in the conference of "Bank Supervisors of Central and East Europe" held in Budapest in March 1991. Underdevelopment of the banking system, as well as the whole economy, and the awareness that without an appropriate supervisory system it is impossible to build a modern market economy, created two tendencies. On the one hand, one may observe the temptation for a quick fix to immediately adopt modern standards of bank supervision. On the other, hand proper sequencing of measures to be taken was clearly necessary. It seems that the reality of the current of the Polish bank supervision resembles a compromise in this regard. A modern market based supervisory system involving rather a sophisticated and established framework of laws, banking structures and networks, well trained people with good banking skills and long market practice.

There was a discussion on who should exercise and be responsible for the supervisory system, from three viewpoints: the decentralized system, a centralized one and a system stating a mixture of them; the centralized version was adopted. The legislation of January 1989 which initiated the supervisory system (Banking Law and the bill on NBP) put the responsibility for a prudential bank supervision on NBP. "The organization of the supervisory system and the way of performing its tasks are determined by the President of NBP" (Act on NBP, art.47/3). The second part of the discussion concerned the way the supervision should be exercised. Three models were considered: the British example where the system relies upon the prudential reports and their evaluation, the German model based on functioning of independent auditing and consulting firms; and finally the American system with its own investigation teams. Events showed that under the best of circumstances it would take at least 5 years to train a good team of on-site bank examiners. They must be able to examine according to generally accepted accounting principles but in the framework of clear banking laws. None of these existed for establishing the basis for a supervision system in Poland. It also turned out impossible to rely exclusively on consulting firms due to financial problems. Finally the lack of qualified staff implied rejection of a pure off-site model. Consequently the solution chosen for Polish supervision model consist of elements from all three models with a priority given to off-site approach.

LICENSING

In the framework of NBP The Department of Organization and Information is responsible for the licensing of new banks. The law in this respect is unclear and relates to the following bills: Banking Law (I,89) and Act on NBP (I,89) with several changes, Trade Code (1934), Cooperative Law (1982), Foreign Exchange Law (II,1989). The rules of establishing a new bank consist then of a mixture of regulations taken from quite different economic systems. As a result the requirements, in order not to contradict all these bills, must be very general and vague i.e.:

- 70 bln zl. (or $6 ml for a foreign bank) of own capital and other means required to run such a kind of activity;
- proper premises;
- an appropriate staff;
- three year plan;
- one year to start the activity.

INFORMATION INFLOW

An efficient supervisory system should ensure the institutions being supervised conform to the established rules of game. Initially (in 1989) banks were obliged to submit monthly prudential reports on: profitability, the structure of assets and liabilities and dispersion of payments terms. Since 1990 the list has been to supplemented to include:

- concentration of assets; credit granted for one unit cannot exceed 15%, and it cannot be greater than 10% of bank's own funds,
- riskiness of assets; the classification of assets bearing risk have been introduced; according to this there are 5 categories of assets of different types of risk: 0% for cash, claims on governments and central banks of OECD, up to 30% on claims for public sector agents, 20% for other governments and central banks, 50% for credits on collateral of real estates and 100% or more for other

claims; it is assumed that the capital adequacy of 8% according to capital adequacy guidelines by the Basle Committee (July, 1988) will have been reached by all Polish banks by January 1993,

- liquidity; in order to maintain day to day operational ability some requirements on liquid assets have been set; the lack of automation, underdeveloped branch network and the lack of banking habits result in over-reliance on cash for transactions; depending upon the relation of different kind of liquid assets to total short term liabilities the cash-flow ratio equals from 10% to 50%.

So far on-site supervision has only been used sporadically. However it is assumed that a full investigation should be applied every year for every bank; it will also encompass assets and liability management and the evaluation of bank management as a whole.

6. SUPERVISORY SYSTEM IMPLICATIONS

The basic objectives of the bank supervision namely the protection, safety and soundness of the banking system, small depositors protection, reduction of systemic risks etc. also have to be associated with encouraging competition, efficiency and the privatisation process. These two sets of objectives contradict each other. Therefore in the process of deep restructuring too much "freedom" might threaten the stability of the economy. On the other hand overly restrictive requirements of the supervisory system will probably damage competition and perpetuate the current structure of the banking system. The implications of the latter problem are already well recognized. For the former problem, negative side-effects may be described in the form of monetary and budgetary implications.

The banking system has the power to create money. If the resources through lending to inefficient enterprises are channelled to those which are unable to generate an appropriate supply it will result in inflationary pressure. The reality seems to confirm this hypothesis. State banks often automatically roll-over credits to state sector. Enterprise losses substance for the bank losses which in the framework of the state sector represents a sort of a fiscal credit.

It is worth stressing that so far the banking supervision has not been able to control whether banks watch carefully all the above mentioned categories. Polish banks still do not pay attention enough to rules imposed by the system of banking supervision. This does not mean that the supervision system does not realize other irregularities. Banks generally do not ignore what the supervision system recommends but they usually put it off as a result of the lack of proper penalties.

The basic set of banking system transformations described above should be supplemented with some technical measures which can be used to measure the success of economic reforms. First of all the whole system of accounting will have to be rebuilt. The current one is still deeply rooted in the tradition of the centrally planned economy. The new system has been elaborated with the cooperation of the IMF, the French Central Bank (the accountancy of commercial banks) and The Austrian Central Bank (the accountancy of the central bank) of unified classification of assets, liabilities and liquidity has been introduced. The plan prepared for the commercial banks makes it possible to manage assets and liabilities while the one prepared for the central bank guarantees monetary policy and banking supervision. The decision concerning the creation of the clearing house has also been taken. This will be associated with a compatible information system.

All these transformations reveal difficulties resulting from the lack of well trained people in the banking sphere. That is why some other measure have been undertaken to train and prepare new staff for this kind of job (Banking School, Banking Courses in Poland and abroad, more attractive financial conditions etc.).

The first two years of Polish reforms show how difficult is the transformation process and prove that this process should be continue longer.

CHAPTER 10

BANKS, PRIVATISATION AND RESTRUCTURING IN POLAND

Andy Mullineux

1) THE FIRST PHASE

In January 1990, after nearly a decade of trying to improve the performance of its heavily indebted centrally planned economy, the Polish government embarked on a programme which aimed to transform it into a 'market economy'. The Balcerowicz Plan combined widespread ('Big Bang') price liberalisation with an IMF approved monetary and fiscal stabilisation programme, zloty devaluation and internal convertibility, wage controls, and an ambitious privatisation programme. It was introduced following a period of quasi-hyperinflation in 1989, which had virtually eliminated the 'monetary overhang' and had, therefore, made the introduction of a monetary reform programme unnecessary.

With hindsight the removal, via inflation, of the 'monetary overhang' may have been unfortunate. The meaning of the term 'monetary overhang' is not easy to pin down concretely and its magnitude is, by its nature, difficult to quantify. Broadly, it relates to monetary balances held in excess of desired levels and it is closely related to 'forced savings', which in turn are related to 'repressed consumption'. The latter is a common feature of centrally planned economies and results when prices of consumer goods are held below market clearing levels whilst supply of consumer goods is restricted, often because a high priority is given by the authorities to producing military goods and supporting a large military sector i.e. guns rather than butter. Its existence, along with 'repressed inflation' is manifested by the differential between state shops' and the higher 'black market' prices of goods. The corollary of repressed consumption is 'forced savings', i.e. saving at a rate exceeding that which would voluntarily prevail if goods were readily available at subsidised prices. It is, of course, virtually impossible to gauge what the savings rate would be if prices were liberalised. It should be noted, however, that also contributing to the reduction of any remaining monetary overhang were the high nominal (40-50%) interest rates on zlotty savings deposits in 1990. This not only encouraged some savings (although real interest rates remained negative) but also provided an incentive, along with the absense of devaluation in 1990, to convert dollar denominated savings, which were substantial but attracted low (3-4%) nominal interest rates, into zlotty savings depotis.

Over time a considerable amount of 'forced saving' can take place in centrally planned economies but it is not clear what proportion of accumulated past saving is voluntary and what proportion is 'forced'. Prior to the reform of the monobanking system (which was typical in centrally planned economies) the accumulated past saving (or wealth) was largely held as cash or as deposits with the state savings bank. This was because there were few alternative financial or non-financial assets available to the public. The portion of wealth that exceeds the desired level is likely to be spent on consumer goods, when they become available, and is dubbed the 'monetary overhang'. Its size may, however, be dependent on the level of price subsidy. The lower the subsidy, the less the overhang. Price liberalisation is, therefore, likely to reduce the overhang via both this 'substitution' effect and also as a result of a negative wealth effect. As prices rise, real wealth, unless it is price index-linked (which is not the case in the former centrally planned economies) will be reduced. The price increases will also reduce the real value of (non-indexed) debts.

Whilst the households were the largest creditors, the largest debtors were the 'state-enterprises'. These were financed, in accordance with the central-plan, with funds supplied from the state budget via the state bank; which combined central and 'commercial' banking activities. The term 'monobanking' system has been used to describe this arrangement. In reality there were typically other banks. In Poland, for example, there was: a state bank specialising in lending to the agricultural sector; over one thousand five hundred agricultural cooperative banks, which specialised in lending to the non-collectivised agricultural sector (which accounted for about 80% of agriculture); a bank for international settlements (Bank Handlowy); a bank handling dollar accounts for the public (Bank Polska Kasa Opieki (PeKaO)); and, most importantly, a state savings bank. In other 'mono-banking' systems, the state bank sometimes provided mainly working capital, whilst a separate (investment) bank provided finance for investments, especially large scale ones, and there was no specialised agricultural bank (eg the USSR). The budget was in turn financed predominantly by levies on the 'profits' (more strictly the revenue or turnover) of the state-enterprises. The state (and investment) banks' lending capacity was enhanced by the recycling of the money deposited with state savings banks, whose ability to lend to the public (for consumer durable and house purchases, for example) was severely circumscribed. The 'monetary overhang', therefore, helped to provide a cheap source of finance for working capital and investment purposes to the extent that savings exceeded desired levels, the government did not have to pay competitive interest rates to attract savings and discourage consumption.

The disadvantage of eliminating the overhang via inflation, rather than monetary reform, is that more than just the overhang might be eliminated. It seems likely that the extent to which monetary wealth was reduced during the 1989 quasi-hyperinflation exceeded that necessary to eliminate the overhang, some of which might have disappeared anyway had prices been liberalised (subsidies removed) earlier, via a sort of substitution effect between consumption and saving. The corollary of this is that the aggregate debt of the state-enterprise sector was also reduced significantly. It is often argued that a comprehensive monetary reform, in which old currency (as well as savings balances) are exchanged for a new currency at an adverse exchange rate and debts are written down, eliminates the inflationary risk. Poland missed the opportunity of using monetary reform, but it seems unlikely that a fledgling democracy would be able to blatantly (rather than covertly via inflation) reduce household monetary wealth to help reduce the state-enterprise sector debt. Not surprisingly, the February 1991 partial monetary reform in the USSR, which involved the effective confiscation of the largest denomination notes, proved to be extremely unpopular. Nevertheless, inflation is a blunt instrument and is difficult to keep under control. Given that it is difficult to decide how much of household wealth represents monetary overhang and given that this wealth provides a major source of enterprise finance, it might have been sensible to force (or to induce via attractive interest rates) the households to purchase medium to long term government bonds to raise funds for the restructuring process. The funds could have been used: to finance a state pension and unemployment scheme (i.e. to provide a social 'safety-net'); to finance the activities of the state privatisation agency (Ministry for Ownership Changes); to recapitalise the commercial banks (see below) and perhaps also to launch a state run development bank. Finally, it is worth noting that the increased uncertainty engendered by the economic restructuring process has probably increased the level of voluntary (precautionary) saving and this has led to a natural reduction in the 'monetary overhang'.

When Finance Minister Balcerowicz introduced his plan in January 1990, however, the 'overhang' had already been largely eliminated, as explained above, and stabilization was the priority following the 1989 hyperinflation. The stabilization programme subsequently inflicted heavy social costs. Two years later, state sector industrial output had fallen by 35-40% and, in 1991, unemployment doubled to reach 11.4%, GDP fell by 8-10% and investment fell by 8%. Inflation, however, had been reigned back to 60% per annum and there had been some restructuring. In 1990, there had been a rapid 'small' privatisation programme in which the bulk of the trade and retailing sectors had been privatised, largely by auction and buy-outs. Output of the private sector rose by nearly 50% in 1991, whilst output of the state sector declined by about 20%. At the end of 1991 the non-agricultural private sector accounted for about

25% of the work force, the state sector employed 62% and the balance worked in the co-operative sector. Agriculture was 80% privatised and had never been forcibly collectivised. The planned mass privatisation programme had not been launched, however, and none of the medium to large scale industrial 'firms' had been shut-down. This was despite the fact that nearly 40% of approximately 8,500 state 'enterprises' were estimated to be running at a loss, were unwilling to pay taxes, were building up debts with other state enterprises and banks, and were selling assets and laying off workers to keep afloat. There had been a few 'large' privatisations in 1991, but the share prices of these companies, quoted on the stock exchange created in 1991, had declined as the recession induced by stabilisation and restructuring deepened.

1991 also saw the budget and balance of payments swing from surplus to deficit. In 1991 exports had increased by 18% (in dollar terms) whilst imports had risen by 72%; having been boosted by the rise in soviet oil prices following its decision to price oil at market prices and in dollars, rather than the transferable rouble. The disappointing growth of exports was partly a result of the difficulty in gaining access to and developing alternative markets in the EC, as well as Hungary and the Czech and Slovak Federal Republic (CSFR), to replace lost markets (especially in the erstwhile USSR) following the collapse of the Council for Mutual Economic Assistance (CMEA, COMECON). The trade agreement concluded by Poland (and Hungary and the CSFR) with the EC in 1991 should improve export prospects.

The deterioration of the budget surplus was particularly worrying because it led the IMF to suspend disbursements in September 1991. This in turn made it likely that the World Bank would follow suit at some stage and raised the spectre that the 50% staged official debt write-off agreed with foreign governments in 1991, conditional on abiding by targets agreed with the IMF, would be stalled. The decline in the surplus was partly a result of a relaxation of the restrictive wage policy in the state sector during the lengthy presidential and parliamentary election campaign in 1991, but was primarily due to the restructuring recession. This led to a substantial increase in social 'safety net' expenditure, as unemployment and the number of pensioners increased rapidly, and to a decline in tax revenue from the state 'enterprise' sector. Prior to 1990, more than 85% of state budget revenue had come from 'profits taxes' and the government failed to rapidly introduce an alternative tax collection system. Further, tax evasion and avoidance is reckoned to be widespread and substantial.

The widening deficit raised the risk of a return to accelerating inflation, because it was feared that the central bank, the National Bank of Poland, would begin to 'monetise' the government budget deficit again; even though it had been made independent under the new banking law and was supposedly not allowed to finance government deficits. In addition, the uncertainty surrounding 1991 elections caused the mass privatisation programme to be put on hold. The restructuring recession, however, also made the programme more difficult to execute and led the privatisation ministry to reduce the list of enterprises to be privatised via the 'voucher system' (discussed below). This is because unprofitable enterprises are more difficult to sell and restructuring, which usually involves labour shedding to reduce 'disguised unemployment' and raise productivity, becomes politically more difficult when the level of unemployment is high and rising. In the event, however, the budget deficit was lower than anticipated and was financed by the sale of government bills to the National Bank of Poland and other banks.

Following the elections in October 1991 a seemingly unstable coalition government was eventually formed and Balcerowicz was replaced as finance minister.

2) 1992: A NEW PHASE

In February 1992, a policy watershed appeared to have been reached. The new government lowered the priority of reducing inflation. It aimed to achieve single digit inflation in 1994 rather than 1991, which had been Balcerowicz's target, and to reduce inflation from 60% to 40% during 1992. A higher priority was given to combatting recession and raising investment and exports. This change of direction provoked the Mr Lutowski, who had replaced Mr Balcerowicz as finance minister, to resign after about six weeks in office. To achieve these goals: the zloty was devalued by 12% and was to remain on the 'crawling peg' against a basket of currencies introduced in October 1991; privatisation was to be accelerated; tough wage controls were to be re-imposed, with a view to reducing real wages by 5%; and a turnover tax was to be introduced, to raise government revenues and reduce consumption and, therefore, imports.

The mass privatisation programme was to be given top priority in the restructuring programme and the aim was to transfer half of Polish industry to the private sector in two years. In 1991, 12% of a total of approximately 8,500 state-owned companies were privatised, the larger ones by stock exchange flotation (conventional public share offers as pioneered in the UK). In 1992, it was hoped that a mass privatisation of at least 200 companies would be executed and a further ten companies would be sold through stock-exchange flotation, leading to a doubling of companies quoted on the Warsaw stock exchange. In addition 30 to 40 factories would be sold to foreign investors, compared to eight in 1991. It was hoped that revenues from disposals would be more than double those for 1991 and the privatisation minister wanted to retain half the proceeds to create a fund for restructuring companies remaining on the state sector prior to privatisation. In the event, however the new privatisation minister, Gruszecki (who replaced Lewandovski who had served as privatisation minister in the previous two governments) called a halt to the privatisation programme. This was because of fears that people who had benefited under the communist regime were using their wealth to gain control of privatised firms and would thereby maintain their dominant position in society. The Olszewski government, which was based on an unstable coallition, collapsed in June 1992 and was replaced by the Suchocka government, in which Lewandowski again served as privatisation minister. The preparations for the mass privatisation programme were soon underway again. Evidence was accumalating that suggested that the transition recession was nearing its end in the first half of 1992. If this is so, and if the Suchocka government maintains its initial popularity, the economic (including the privatisation) programme seems to have a better chance of being successfully completed.

Under the Polish mass privatisation programme, the ownership of the 200 companies are to be transferred to investment agencies (funds) which will be run by Western fund management experts. Shares in the funds will be 'sold' to the public in exchange for vouchers, which have been distributed to the general public (with management and employees receiving additional allocations), at a nominal charge. S.G. Warburg, the London based merchant bank, is advising the privatisation ministry and the fund managers will be chosen by June 1991. The scheme is being financed with the help of a World Bank loan. Partial compensation is to be offered to former owners of nationalised property. A commercially run privatisation agency, which would handle the sale of state property, is also planned and funding is being sought for the World Bank (IBRD) and the European Bank (EBRD); which began operations in 1991 with a view to facilitating development in Central and Eastern European (CEE) countries. Its activities include the promotion of capital markets in these countries. The development of domestic government bond markets is particularly important if the government is to be cease to rely on the central bank, and the wider banking sector, for deficit funding. As far as the privatised sector is concerned, banks are likely to remain the most important source of finance in the medium term.

3) THE WAY AHEAD

The Suchocka government's plans rest on accelerated privatisation, crawling devaluation, wage control and a new turnover tax. With regard to wage control, an attempt is being made to replace the unpopular tax-based incomes policy (Popiwek) with a wage compact built on consensus. Further, part of the privatisation 'proceeds' are to be retained for the restructuring (and refinancing) of state enterprises and thereby facilitating further privatisation. Devaluation was an integral part of the Balcerowicz Plan but seemingly failed to have the desired effect. This could have been because the zloty appreciated in 1991, at least relative to the dollar, prompting the government to introduce a crawling-peg devaluation that October. The restricted access to the EC markets in 1990 and 1991, combined with the collapse of trade with the former COMECON countries and the move to dollar pricing of oil imports from the former USSR, also explains at least some of the deterioration in the balance of trade in 1991. An alternative view is that the undervaluation of the zloty failed to stimulate the state sector but did help the emerging private sector, which accounted for 20% of total exports and 46% of total imports in 1991. Seabright (1991) postulates that state firms used their, often considerable, monopoly power to pass costs on to consumers and were, therefore, able to make comfortable profits at home and postpone restructuring. The state sector also seems to have built up large interfirm credits to reduce reliance banks. This increases inefficiency, by allowing stronger 'enterprises' to keep weaker ones afloat, and slows down restructuring.

This raises the question of whether the behaviour of the state sector might have been different if instead the zloty had been overvalued. Seabright contrasts the Polish experience with that of the former German Democratic Republic (GDR). The latter joined the Federal Republic of Germany as five New Federal States (NFS) in 1990 and Ost Marks were converted into Deutsche marks at a much more generous exchange rate than the Bundesbank had advocated. The NFS, therefore, effectively for irrevocable overvaluation. Not surprisingly the populous acquiesced in this monetary reform because it was exchanging Ost marks of uncertain value for Deutsche marks, whose value was protected by the Bundesbank, at a generous exchange rate. Seabright notes that the state sector in the NFS failed to respond to the blast of Western competition and the erosion of their monopoly power. He argues that this may have been because the overvaluation was so great that the management of state firms were effectively demoralised and responded by colluding with their employees by paying higher wages so that they could make the best of things prior to the inevitable shut down. An alternative view is that a credible threat of closure, or 'a hard budget constraint' (Kornai, 1980), was not present because the Treuhandanstalt ('Treuhand'), the German privatisation agency, was pursuing a policy of maintaining, as far as possible, employment and promoting investment.

The new Polish plan remains to use an undervalued zloty to promote an export led growth. With greater access to EC markets, a positive response from the state sector might now be forthcoming if its behaviour has been conditioned by the experiences of the last two years. Seabright's view is that the authorities cannot afford to wait for privatisation because in the medium term a considerable part of the economy will remain in the state sector. Commercialisation and restructuring must take place prior to privatisation and hard budget constraints must be imposed on state firms, which should be forced to seek funding from the financial sector and not from the state budget. In other words, 'corporate governance' and 'monitoring' should be made the responsibility primarily of banks (at least until 'deeper' capital markets develop), and less reliance should be placed on overvaluation or undervaluation of exchange rates to condition state firms' behaviour. Action should also be taken to stimulate small and medium sized enterprises (SMEs); to create jobs to replace the inevitable losses resulting from the restructuring of state firms. The SMEs cannot, however, be expected to become significant employers in the short term. Further, it should be noted that successive UK governments found it difficult to instill a commercial ethos into nationalised industries and that this is one of the reasons why the Thatcher administration embarked on its renowned privatisation programme in the early 1980s.

It is clear that the banks will be expected to play a key role in financing SMEs as well as recently privatised large enterprises and, if hard(er) budget constraints are to be imposed, the remaining state sector firms too. Unfortunately, they are in no fit state to perform these tasks. It is estimated that approximately 40% of bank loans are non-performing and they desperately need to be recapitalised. Banks are also understaffed, and the staff they do have lack training and experience. The large commercial banks are state-owned and were created as part of a 'two-tier' banking system introduced in 1989, when the state bank began to concentrate on central banking functions and hived off its commercial banking activities to nine regionally organised commercial banks of roughly equal size. The authorities have been advised to privatise these banks, but cannot do so until their debt problem has been resolved and they have been recapitalised. This would be expensive and appears virtually impossible, given the rapid deterioration of the state budgetary position, without financial assistance from outside. By mid 1992, only one state bank, the export development bank (Bank Rozwoyu Eksportu, BRE), had been privatised. This was done in the summer of 1992 when the large private bank (BIG) was also floated on the Warsaw stock exchange. The EC (through its PHARE programme) and the World Bank, by sponsoring 'twinning' arrangements with Western European banks, are, however, trying to help to raise the level of banking expertise.

There are still considerable shortcomings in the financial infrastructure, however. The reliability of the clearing and giro based payments system, which is particularly crucial if SMEs are to avoid cash-flow problems, must be enhanced, and an efficient interbank market urgently needs to be developed to promote efficient credit allocation. Prior to the creation of the 'two-tier' banking system, the state savings bank collected most of the deposits and the state bank did the lending. In most OECD countries, the savings and cooperative banking sectors commonly have a surplus of funds which is lent to the commercial banking sector via the interbank market. A similar arrangement is required in

Poland, where there is a danger that the savings banks will accumulate funds. A large portion of these funds will be lent to their traditional household customers; to purchase houses and consumable durables, at relatively cheap rates. The remainder may well remain underutilised. In contrast, the commercial banks will be starved of funds for lending to the commercial sector. The clearing house could be an independent institution holding the accounts of banks and clearing their net end of day balances. It could also act as a broker between banks with surplus funds and banks that are short of funds, and thereby serve as an interbank market (See Chapter 8). There are plans to open a clearing house at the end of March 1993. It will be owned by the big banks and there are consequently fears amongst smaller banks that they will be disadvantaged. Also, a money broker has been established but it is expensive to use and banks usually prefer to make bilateral arrangements to exchange funds. There are, therefore, doubts about the efficiency of the proposed reforms to the clearing system.

As well as needing an efficient clearing and payments system, SMEs need to be able to raise working and investment capital in order to thrive. In most OECD countries, banks have to be induced, via loan guarantees, to lend to SMEs that cannot provide adequate security and collateral to back their borrowing. Given the relatively low risk thresholds of banks, the high level of uncertainty in a transition economy, and the relative lack of privately owned financial and physical assets to serve as capital, such guarantees appear to be essential in Poland if the SME sector is to grow rapidly. In the OECD countries in the 1980s, venture capital funds began to make equity-like investments in SMEs. These funds increasingly become interested in financing management buy-outs (MBOs), rather than providing 'seed-corn' capital, however. Some funds have recently begun to operate with a view to channelling Western capital into CEE countries. They are more likely to be involved in sponsoring privatisations through MBOs than providing seed-corn and development capital for SMEs, however. The SMEs can, therefore, be expected to have to rely on the banking sector for fiance, as they do in most OECD countries.

The German banking system is one of the most heavily geared towards SME finance (See Chapter 7). The development banks (particularly the KfW) extend subsidised loans to the SME sector and provide loan guarantees to commercial banks, as does a system of specialised guarantee banks. These arrangements have been supplemented, post German unification, by liquidity loans and guarantees to commercial but loans in the NFS, by the 'Treuhand'. The German authorities are, therefore, aggressively promoting the SME sector to try and absorb some of the unemployment created by restructuring. The major German banks made handsome profits in the process in 1991, despite having to make substantial outlays on equipping their new branch networks in the NFS and on staff training. Not only did they enjoy generous loan guarantees, keeping their bad debt provisions down in the NFS, but they were also able to collect retail deposits relatively cheaply. This was because the 'monetary overhang' was not eliminated as a result of German Economic and Monetary Unification (GEMU) on 1 July 1990 and real wealth was probably increased in the NFS (relative to the CEE countries) by the generous conversion rate and the subsequent (again relative to the CEE countries) price stability.

The provision of subsidised loans and loan guarantees to sponsor the SMEs should be actively pursued by Poland too and could be provided via the Polish development bank. In Germany, the funds to sponsor such a programme have been raised by increasing taxes in the Western German states. In Poland, the cost would ultimately fall on the state budget.

It might be better, however, to encourage the privatisation ministry to view its task more broadly as one of restructuring the economy, as the new government seems to be implicitly wanting it to do. In which case, the proceeds for privatisation should be retained and used for restructuring the remaining state sector firms, as the government's new plan indicates will be done. The agency should, however, perhaps take a yet broader view, as the Treuhand seems to have done: by providing loan guarantees and liquidity loans to sponsor SMEs and ameliorate the rapid rise in unemployment; and by not selling firms to the highest bidder or those with restitution claims, but selling to bidders with the business plans that guarantee reasonable levels of employment and promise the most new investment.

The Treuhand, therefore, implicitly takes into account of the 'social costs' of the restructuring programme. Further, the provision of a 'safety net' for people who loose their jobs should also be regarded as part of the cost of restructuring should perhaps and bet met out of the privatisation revenue. This is not the case in Germany, but nevertheless the Treuhand runs at a sizeable loss (See Chapter 7). The Treuhand has been urged, particularly by representatives of for the major opposition party, to develop a more coherent industrial and regional policy (which has been dubbed a rehabilitation policy) and to provide support for 'structurally' and 'regionally' essential industries and employers. In contrast, many influential economists are urging the government to force the Treuhand to concentrate more on revenue maximising privatisation, leaving the restructuring and 'safety net' costs to fall on the budget, to which it would make a positive revenue contribution.

The new government in Poland seems to be leaning towards a more active industrial policy. The goal of the Polish privatisation ministry is not revenue maximisation. The voucher system seems to be designed to achieve rapid and equitable privatisation and yet, apart from the small privatisations (via MBOs and auctions) which started in 1990; the privatisation programme was tentatively pursued in 1991 and mass privatisation was postponed until 1992. As with the UK in the 1980s, one objective is to popularise capitalism by promoting wider share ownership and giving employees and management vested interests in the performance of their companies. Privatisation via sales and stock exchange flotation, aimed at raising substantial revenue, will clearly be slower than distribution by voucher; which is also to be undertaken in the CSFR. The speed of privatisation by sales depends on pricing and financial constraints. Given that the 'monetary overhang' has probably been eliminated, and wealth eroded, by price liberalisation the subsequent inflation, speed depends largely on ability and willingness to attract foreign capital; either for outright purchases of firms or plants; or to participate in 'joint ventures' with the state. The latter are often more politically tractable given sensitivity to widespread foreign ownership, and are related to the 'partial privatisation' programmes being developed in Italy and France.

If 'voucher distribution' were quickly executed and 'popular capitalism' was equitably engendered, then there might be considerable advantages to the 'voucher' approach. The disadvantage is that it does not raise as much revenue as sales and lack of revenue is a serious brake on the restructuring process. The Hungarian authorities have long argued that a peaceful, equitable and self-financing transition cannot be hurried. Hungary began to liberalise the service and SME sector two decades ago, and created a 'two-tier' banking system and began to attract foreign banks in 1987. A financial infrastructure to support SMEs and service foreign investments was already in place at the beginning of the 1990s, therefore. However, because inflation has eliminated the monetary overhang and reduced household sector wealth, the supply of domestic credit is limited and expensive.

Hungary has hitherto opted for privatisation through sales and made a deliberate effort to attract foreign investment. The net result is that the privatisation programme is further advanced than in Poland and the CSFR and that in 1991 it attracted considerably more foreign capital per capita than the other CEE countries in 1991. In January 1992, the Hungarian authorities announced measures designed to build on the successes of the privatisation programme. These will entail ploughing back some of the proceeds of privatisation into three funds to be administered by the state privatisation agency. One fund is to finance the restructuring of state enterprises; another is designed to temper unemployment; and the third is to provide guarantees against environmental liabilities. The latter, incidently, are also provided by the Treuhand to accelerate privatisation. At this stage it seems to be a race between the Hungarian tortoise and the Polish hare. The Hungarian authorities have, however, faced growing public resentment at the increasing foreign control of major companies and declining interest from prospective foreign investors. In October 1992 it was decided that voucher-type mass privatisation scheme would be launched in 1993 in an attempt to accelerate the privatisation programme and win back popular support for it.

4) BANKS AND RESTRUCTURING - WHAT NEED TO BE DONE

In Hungary, banking reform was started two years earlier than in Poland and considerable technical assistance has been provided by the Austrian monetary authorities. Successful banking reform is crucial if a thriving SME sector is to develop, as noted above and discussed further in Chapter 7 and 8. The newly privatised medium to large scale companies also need access to working and investment capital if they are to thrive, and the state enterprises being restructured also require finance. In Germany, the Treuhand has encouraged banks to supply funds for the latter purpose by providing generous guarantees.

Banks also need to be able to perform 'monitoring' and 'corporate governance' functions. Overvalued exchange rates cannot be relied upon to condition the behaviour of state monopolies. Excessive overvaluation, as in Germany, is likely to demoralise management and encourage inefficient and counter productive practices, as noted above. In Fry and Nuti (Chapter 3) make a strong case, based on the experience of East and South-East Asian countries, for a slight undervaluation. Because Poland, like most other CEEs, needs to service its outstanding international debt in hard currencies, a balance of trade surplus is clearly required. Consequently overvaluation cannot be used to provide a corporate governance stick. As the key financial institutions, banks should therefore perform this function instead.

One way of imposing discipline is via hard(er) budget constraints on state and private sector firms. This would require the central bank to refuse to bail out banks in difficulties, forcing them in turn to push unprofitable firms into liquidation. A prerequisite for this is that the state must itself stop funding state sector firms and be willing to sanction the consequential mass unemployment. It would take time for this brutal approach, which may well be accompanied by bank failures, a credit crunch and probably a financial crisis (Chapter 2) to work. This is because the authorities would have to earn credibility by sticking to the policy in the face of, probably considerable, political unrest. Given the outcome of the October elections in Poland, a political consensus behind such an approach does not exist and the current fragile coalition could not hope to execute it. Such a policy may well be inconsistent with democratic government.

If the stick of overvaluation and strict hard (as opposed to harder) budget constraints on state enterprises are to be eschewed, is there an alternative? In Germany, the banks are closely involved in corporate governance by virtue of being both providers of debt to and shareholders in firms. It commonly argued (see Chapter 7) that this engenders 'long-termism', in the sense that investment and other decisions can be made with a view to maximising long term probability, and that this has contributed to the postwar economic success of Germany. Similar arguments are often advanced to help explain Japan's spectacular postwar growth too. In contrast, the 'Anglo-Saxon' economies, particularly the US and the UK, are often criticised for 'short-termism' (Chapter 7). The major shareholders in these countries, are non-bank financial institutions such as insurance and pension funds. These institutions have not been actively involved in 'corporate governance', hitherto, preferring to leave it to the capital market. The mergers and acquisition booms in the late 1980s in the US and the UK, which encouraged a substantial rise in corporate indebtedness with adverse subsequent consequences, seem to have persuaded 'Anglo-Saxon' institutional investors to become more actively involved in corporate governance. It is to early to gauge whether this is a temporary phenomena, or whether it will have any significant effects on economic performance.

Poland can choose between, and possibly combine, these approaches to corporate governance. It cannot rely on the stock market, because this will remain underdeveloped, certainly relative to those of the US and the UK, for the foreseeable future. Potentially, it can rely on the banks or the Western managed investment funds; which will own the privatised stock, and shares in which will be bought by voucher holders. The general public will, therefore, not develop their own narrow portfolios of shares, but will buy into Western managed, and state regulated, funds, thus diversifying their portfolio risk. In the CSFR, in contrast, unregulated (to date) privately run investment funds are being rapidly introduced with potentially disastrous consequences (Chapter 7). To the extent that the management of the Polish investment funds can exert an influence on the behaviour of the managements of the firms in which they hold shares, corporate governance will be enhanced. Drawing on the Germany experience, it might also be sensible to encourage banks to take an active interest in monitoring the behaviour of their clients through share ownership of non-financial firms. The new banking law in fact allows banks to hold bonds and equity up to 25% of their own capital. This is not particularly restrictive and is broadly in line with current German banking practices and the Second EC Banking Directive (Mullineux, 1992); which Poland will have to abide by if it continues to pursue EC membership.

The problem is that the commercial banks' activities are severely constrained by their bad debts, which are accumulating during the restructuring recession. They appear to be in no position to advance much more credit, let alone start taking equity participations in their clients, and are effectively insolvent. The new small banks are also struggling in the recession and cannot be expected to grow fast enough to serve the needs of the whole commercial sector. Further, the credibility of the state banks, including the central bank, was damaged by a series of scandals in 1991, along with a new one in early 1992, involving fraud perpetrated by bank officers. The authorities have since tightened banking regulations by introducing minimum own capital requirements, which must be met by the end of 1992, and imposing strict requirements on banks wishing to undertake foreign trade related business, for example. There remains a pressing need is for the banks to be recapitalised. It is hard to see how the privatisation and restructuring process can succeed without the support of a viable banking system. This, of course, is a crucial difference between the former GDR and Poland and other CEE countries. The debt of the state bank of the former GDR was taken over by the Treuhand. Its branches were sold to the major West German commercial banks, which then rapidly set up operations in the NFS. Furthermore, its central banking functions were taken over by the Bundesbank.

It should be noted that the German universal banks, like the Swiss universal banks (Mullineux, 1987), often built up their share holdings in the process of participating in the financial restructuring of clients in financial difficulties. In modern parlance, they swapped debt for equity and, in so doing helped firms out of short term difficulties whilst buying into future profits. Given the size of the debt problem in the state sector in Poland (and most other CEE countries), the banks could be encouraged to engage in debt for equity swaps. These are likely to be resisted by banks, however, because of the fear that they will be left with unsaleable (at least without substantial capital loss) shares in companies whose value is currently difficult to guage. For such swaps ever to become attractive, however, the banks' own debt problems need to be resolved and they need to be recapitalised. Comprehensive bank recapitalisation would impose an immense burden on the already deteriorating budget and would probably mop-up the proceeds of the proposed 1992 mass privatisation. If a successful transition is to be made in the short to medium term, and a return to hyper-inflation (which would help solve the debt problem), to be avoided, however, there seems to be no alternative. It is hard to see how it can be done without substantial external financial assistance.

REFERENCES

Kornai (1980) '*Economics of Shortage*', 2 volumes, Amsterdam: North Holland.

Mullineux, A.W. (1987), '*International Banking and Financial Systems*', London: Graham & Trotman.

Mullineux, A.W. (1992d) '*European Banking*', Oxford: Basil Blackwell.

Seabright, P.B. (1991), 'Exchange Rate Management when there are Failures of Corporate Control: Dilemmas in Eastern Europe', pp 68-79 in O'Brien, R. (ed.), '*Finance and the International Economy*': 5, Oxford: Oxford University Press.

CHAPTER 11

SOME MICROECONOMIC ASPECTS OF THE MONETARY POLICY IN THE POLISH TRANSITION, 1990-1991

Marek Belka

INTRODUCTION

Restrictive monetary policy was a key element in the economic strategy of stabilization pursued by the government after January 1990. A positive real rate of interest supported by credit rationing was to help stem the inflationary pressures and increase allocative efficiency. Bearing in mind the tradition of soft budgets and the price of capital approaching zero, this was a revolutionary change for both state-owned enterprises and the banks.

The policy of economic stabilization, or to be more precise, of economic transformation received rather mixed reviews two years after its inception. There had been: an elimination of shortages, a successful introduction of internal convertibility of the zloty, relative stability of foreign exchange rates, an opening of the economy, and a reduction of inflation to the (still far from tolerable) rate of 60-70% per annum in 1991. This has been accompanied by a dramatic drop of rate of industrial output and GNP, and an equally striking increase in employment.

Most disturbing for the policy makers is the slow pace of the restructuring process. Privatisation is proceeding with much more difficulty than expected and the state-owned enterprises (SOEs) in some respects still do not behave like profit maximizers. The poor performance of these firms, although much improved after mid-1992, is of utmost importance as they remain the source of most budgetary revenue. After a very good 1990, the profitability of the SOEs dropped precipitously in 1991 and many became insolvent. Instead of going out of business, the vast majority of them survive at a cost of accumulating tax arrears, obligations to their suppliers and bank debts. As a result, the process of liquidation and possibly restructuring, has become very complicated and costly.

A closer look at the behaviour of the SOEs with respect to bank credit and inter-firm credit can facilitate a more comprehensive evaluation of economic policy.

A. THE JANUARY 1990 EPISODE

One of the puzzling phenomena concerning the developments in the Polish economy was a sharp, immediate and generally uniform drop in production and sales that occurred in January-February 1990; just after the stabilization programme had been introduced. Another puzzle concerned the behaviour of wages which barely rose in January despite monthly inflation close to 80%.

Most of the hypotheses advanced link these developments. Some of them are summarized below.

(1) Monopoly behaviour: Firms decided to exploit their monopoly position, preferring to raise profits by restricting output and raising prices attempting to raise productivity and lower costs.
(2) Demand Barrier: The sharp decline in real wages in January combined with a strong real balance effect led to a reduction in spending that reduced sales and production. Further, restrictive wage policy deepened the decline in real wages.
(3) Credit Crunch - Volume: The tight monetary policy, combined with much higher inflation and input costs increases, led to a situation where enterprises did not have enough cash to buy inputs, having reduced production and cut real wages in response to their sharply reduced liquidity.
(4) Credit Crunch - Interest rates: Uncertainty combined with high nominal interest rates on working capital credit in January (National Bank of Poland (NBP) refinancing rate was 36% for the month; average rates on working capital for the best credit rated firms ranged from 38% to 55%) deterred firms from borrowing and paying wages, so real wages fell and a demand barrier resulted.

There may be some truth in all of these stories, although some appear to be less plausible in the light of the firm-level data collected on the largest SOEs. Firstly, the monopoly power hypothesis is not supported by the fact that metallurgical firms, which belong to a heavily centralized industry, actually maintained output in January despite falling profit margins. On the contrary, output in the textile industry - much less concentrated in Poland -fell immediately. More broadly, monopoly price power should not be an issue in a small open economy such, as Poland in the 1990s. The well-known experience of the FSO car company illustrated the truth that import competition will eventually put a lid on price increases. Therefore the output drop has to be explained by other factors. As a matter of fact, the monopoly power hypothesis which was popular with some Polish economists in late 1989 and early 1990, seems to have been rejected almost completely.

The evidence also raises some doubts about the credit crunch-volume story[1]. It cannot be dismissed, since the interest rate increased significantly in January 1990 and this applied to all past credits, not just to new ones. Many firms rushed to repay some of the credit outstanding using whatever liquid assets they had. The economy-wide turnover credit (working capital financed by bank credit) was zloty 19.9 trillion at the end of December 1989. It felt to zloty 19.4 trillion at the end of January. This suggests that there was a serious liquidity problem. Many enterprises had large amounts of foreign currency, however. These so-called retention accounts were earned from the past exports. They could, and were, used to help cushion the liquidity squeeze. For the sample of 75 SOEs examined[2], dollar deposits fell from $ 110 million at the end of December 1989 to $ 54 million at the end of January 1990, while zloty loans (working capital plus investment) rose in nominal terms only by 18% despite PPI inflation of 110% for the month. Moreover, anecdotal evidence suggests that not a single enterprise manager complained about lack of credit or insufficient liquidity. There were, however complaints about the cost of credit.

The piling up of inventories of finished goods after the introduction of the new policy points to a demand barrier, rather than to the shortage of cash, as being the immediate reason of the initial drop in output and sales. The developments in the late 1989 strengthened support for the demand barrier hypothesis. Households rushed to spend their zlotys, either on dollars or on goods, in anticipation of huge price increases at the beginning of 1990. There was also a speculative build-up of inventories in the enterprises. Consequently, the level of purchases that could be maintained after the "big bang" was artificially low.

A recurring theme during the interviews held with the managers to identify the reasons for and the mechanics of the January collapse turned out to be interest rates. They stressed their exceptionally high nominal level, which prevented them from operating the firm in a normal way. At first glance this opinion looks suspicious. After all, the real interest rate in January was negative by all measures, rising steeply only in the two subsequent months and coming close to zero in the mid-year (see Table 1).

Standard reasoning would compare the rate of PPI inflation with the interest rate, and conclude that real interest rates were significantly negative. Hence, firms should have wanted to borrow and the credit ceiling must have been the binding constraint. This did not square with firm behaviour. There was

---

[1] See for example: G.Calvo and F.Coricelli, (1990) Stagflationary Effects of Stabilization Programs in Reforming Socialist Countries: Supply-side versus Demand-side, IMF/WB mimeo.

[2] Most results of the empirical research quoted here are from a study carried out in 1991-1992 and summarized in: B.Pinto, M.Belka and S.Krajewski, Microeconomics of Transformation in Poland. A Survey of State Enterprise Responses. The World Bank Policy Research Working Paper, The World Bank, September 1992, WPS 982.

a rapid repayment of zloty credits, indicating that firms did not want to borrow and were responding to nominal interest rates.

Another view is that firms compare the nominal interest rate with their own margins and not with the inflation in a general price index such as PPI. If output prices rise faster than input prices, so that margins are increasing in line with inflation, it may pay firms to "invest" in working capital and to borrow more. In other words, it is the inflation of value added that needs to be compared with the interest rate, not so much price inflation. In a steady state, with all prices growing at the same rate, it is correct to relate the nominal interest rate to the general inflation; but, in a transition from a centrally planned to a market economy, such comparisons can be misleading.

Specifically, in the case of Poland, much of the increase in the general level of prices was (and still is) due to administrative changes linked to elimination of subsidies and gradual adjustment of the domestic prices to the world level. As a result, the structure of prices undergoes substantial change, with industrial prices usually growing less than prices of services.

Table 1 ([3])
Nominal and real interest rates in 1990
(in % monthly)

Month	refinancing credit	max.working capit.credit	real CPI	measured by CPI
I	36.00	62.00	-9.80	-22.78
II	20.00	23.00	-0.65	12.33
III	10.00	12.00	7.38	12.22
IV	8.00	9.50	1.86	7.25
V	5.50	8.00	3.25	7.46
VI	4.00	5.50	2.03	3.94
VII	2.47	2.60	-0.97	-0.68
VIII	2.47	2.60	0.78	-0.30
IX	2.47	2.60	-1.92	-0.10
X	3.03	3.20	-2.36	-1.62
XI	3.26	3.63	-1.21	0.03
XII	3.72	4.42	-1.40	1.48

[3] G.Kolodko et al. Polityka finansowa, stabilizacja, transformacja. Instytut Finansow Warszawa 1991 p.20

If this is true, the enterprises which can more easily mark-up price over costs are less likely to reduce output. This view was tested by running the following regression based on 55 firms in the sample for which a complete data set was available:

$$\text{SALRATIO} = f(\underset{(+)}{\text{MRATIO}}, \underset{(-)}{\text{INRATIO}})$$

where SALRATIO stands for the ratio of a firm's sales in January 1990 to its sales in December 1989; MRATIO is the ratio of January's mark-up to its value in the preceding month; and INRATIO is the ratio of the share of interest costs in the total cost over the two months in question. Mark-up was calculated as (pre-tax profit - net extraordinary gains)/total costs, in order to eliminate the effect of inflationary gains on dollar deposits in December 1989 and to capture the mark-up over costs on the basic business of the firm. The expected signs are shown in parentheses below. The explanatory variables: ability to mark up and pass through costs (inelastic demand, low demand resistance) would encourage firms to produce more, while an increase in the share of interest in costs (low dollar deposits, greater dependence on bank loans) would discourage firms from borrowing and producing. Based on the log specification, the results were (t-statistics shown in parentheses):

$$\text{SALRATIO} = \underset{(-0.18)}{-0.0177} + \underset{(+4.10)}{0.2089}\ \text{MRATIO} - \underset{(-3.71)}{0.1465}\ \text{INRATIO}$$

Rsqd.=0.28, S.E. of regression=0.32, F-stat.=11.31

Both elasticity of demand and interest burden were important in explaining the January output decline. Since, on average, the interest share in costs grew by only 23% (compared to an average reduction in mark-up of 90%) demand constraints were much more significant in explaining the drop in output.

The analysis of the microeconomic data suggests both that demand considerations were very important in explaining the output and sales behaviour in the beginning (and crucial) stage of the stabilization policy, and that interest rate played a fundamental role in limiting the credit expansion in early 1990. As a matter of fact, the interest rate policy emerges as the most effective instrument of restriction in the new macroeconomic policy. After the vagaries of the first quarter of 1990, the interest rate dropped temporarily to the level of 0% and climbed again in late 1990 to a not trifle 1.5% monthly. For the whole of 1991 real interest rates on working capital credit approached zero. This could easily be interpreted as a dramatic relaxation of the monetary policy. If we remember the considerations mentioned above, the true meaning of this can be seen quite differently. However, the initial reaction of the enterprises to the hardening of the credit policy does not preclude different long term behaviour in this respect.

B. BANK DEBT DYNAMICS

In a system of labour-managed SOEs, in relation to which there is little or no oversight function performed by the founding organs (ministries, local authorities), the role of banks in resource allocation becomes crucial. One of the aims of the restrictive monetary policy was to introduce a hard-budget environment in which the scarce capital would be allocated to its best uses.

The bank credit burden of the firms in the sample (measured both by the ratio of bank debt divided by pre-tax profit plus interest and by the ratio of bank debt to cost of sales) fluctuated greatly in the period between the third quarter of 1989 and the first quarter of 1991. Four phases can be distinguished: (a) debt erosion as a result of quasi-hyperinflation of late 1989; (b) stabilization of debt at a low level as a result of the cushioning effect of dollar deposits in first quarter of 1990; (c) sharp increase of the debt burden in the rest of 1990 due to new credits, interest capitalization and stabilization or a drop of total sales or profits, respectively; (d) stabilization of the debt burden at a relatively high level in early 1991. During 1991, the total volume of working capital credit in the whole Polish manufacturing industry rose by 118%, with output falling by 20% and prices growing by 70%. In sum, the debt burden, however measured, must have risen significantly.

Important question to be answered are what made the firms borrow money from the banks; and which of them were more eager to incur this kind of debt. To examine this, a time series-cross section regression was run for 50 firms on which complete data was available, for the seven quarters 1989:III-1991:I. It was assumed that the bank debt burden (debt to total costs ratio or DCOST) is a function of: (1) inter-firm credit (specified as payables minus receivables divided by total costs) denoted NPCOST; (2) profitability of the enterprise (measured as pre-tax profit plus interest cost to sales) denoted PROFSALES; and (3) difficulty to sell output (measured by the ratio of finished goods inventories to sales) denoted FGSALES. In short the specification was:

$$DCOST = f(NPCOST, PROFSALES, FGSALES).$$

The following results were obtained (t-statistics in parentheses):

$$DCOST = -0.0533\ NPCOST \underset{(-0.78)}{} - 0.3414\ PROFSALES \underset{(-3.77)}{} + 0.3274\ FGSALES \underset{(+3.59)}{}$$

DCOST =-0.0533 NPCOST -0.3414 PROFSALES +0.3274 FGSALES
(-0.78) (-3.77) (+3.59)

R sqd.=0.48, S.E.of regression=0.27, Autocorr. of error=0.15

While the inter-firm credit has the right sign (enterprise substitute inter-firm for bank credit), it is statistically insignificant. However, profitability and finished goods inventories are significant, with signs indicating a soft budget constraint. One may conclude that: (a) either banks did not lend to profitable firms, or, more likely, that such firms were reluctant to borrow, preferring to rely on their own resources; and (b) debt is rising fastest where firms are unable to sell, as captured by rising finished goods inventories.

These disturbing results imply a serious adverse selection problem in the banking system which undermined the whole hard budget oriented policy of monetary restrictions. Good firms avoid taking credit, whilst weaker units, in order to continue operating, are forced to incur bank debt at existing high interest rates, which they will probably never be able to repay.

Much deeper insight into bank behaviour would be needed to understand the mechanics of the process whereby banks acquired portfolios of bad loans. Recent estimates set the share of uncollectible loans at 40%. The banks were presumably unable or unwilling to select good customers (perhaps because of lack of knowledge and incentives). Their unwillingness to do so may be linked to the special conditions in 1990 when banks enjoyed a virtually monopolistic position and the current profitability of most SOEs was quite high.

The interviews with the managers carried out in the course of this study support the above results. Banks were perceived: as inflexible; unwilling to take risk; and preferring old customers to the ones. This is also reflected in the sluggish uptake of lines of credit offered by foreign financial institutions (World Bank, European Investment Bank), where procedures and risks may differ from the usual business and require innovativeness and exposure to international banking standards.

Additionally, the banks might have been unwilling to force liquidations when it became evident that enterprises were insolvent because this would have confirmed that their balance sheets contained substantial bad debts and encouraged a fundamental reappraisal of bank managements' performance. In any case, any effort to reclassify the bank assets was blurred by poor accounting in the SOEs and the high level of uncertainty characteristic of transition economies.

There is also some truth in the argument that both banks and enterprises know that some state-owned enterprises, although entirely self-financing and working in a supposedly hard budget regime, can, in a very difficult situation, count on some sort of special treatment from the state. The immediate result of this presumption is that non-bank enterprises treat their tax liabilities amongst their least urgent obligations, without hesitation accumulating tax arrears and only exceptionally incurring overdue bank credits. This privileged treatment of the bank creditors by enterprises was reciprocated in 1990-1991 by the aforementioned reluctance of banks to classify the loans of their troubled enterprise properly. Whether this was solidarity or well calculated interest remains an open question. The main point is that the fortunes and misfortunes of the banks and non-banks are closely linked. The widely discussed problem of rescheduling and cancellation of bad debts of the SOEs will in fact most benefit banks.

To make the matter more complicated, according to some unofficial estimates of the Central Planning Office (CUP), the vast majority of the banks' bad assets was not accumulated in the transition period i.e. in 1990-1992, but was inherited from the 1980s as the former central investment credits. These were credits used to finance major investment projects, determined by the central investment plan and ascribed only to the separate enterprises after the elimination of the system in the late 1980s. Obviously, these credits turned out to be a huge burden on the enterprises and were either not serviced properly or became the reason for enterprise bankruptcies, liquidation or insolvencies. If this is confirmed by harder data, the whole discussion of the inefficiency of the post-socialist banking system must be redirected.

INTER-FIRM CREDIT (IC)

The unregulated obligations of enterprises to other enterprises within the state sector are not a completely new phenomenon. In the CPEs, due to the inefficiency of their banking systems and lack of proper legal structure, IC usually played a role of additional liquidity created by firms themselves. IC exceeded the total volume of working capital credit in the economy by about 50% by the end of 1989.

Payments by enterprises in Poland are normally due two weeks after delivery. Thereafter, interest is calculated on the basis of a penalty rate which is officially determined and which far exceeds the bank rate on working capital. However, firms are permitted to make side deals on payment terms. Further, payment enforcement is more difficult than for banks' arrears, for which the account can be frozen. For suppliers to get their dues, a court decision is needed. This is costly and time-consuming. On the other hand, penalty interest is tax-deductible, making the extraordinary losses thus incurred less painful.

It should be stressed that the accumulation of payables and receivables, while possibly being a result of conscious decisions in the hyperinflationary environment of 1989, is largely due to a liquidity crisis suffered by most enterprises in the subsequent 1990-1991 period. Firms' customers were forced to delay payment because of lack of cash, while their suppliers were forced to tolerate this, knowing that a delayed payment may be better than no sales. Only as a last resort would suppliers stop deliveries, in the process totally disrupting, the shaky position of their partners.

The accumulation of overdue obligations between enterprises became an important factor crippling the economy. Good firms have their profit on paper, while bad firms incur debt that they will never repay, making the liquidation and restructuring process even more complicated and costly.

IC of such character has both macroeconomic and microeconomic implications. It can be treated as: additional liquidity capable of diluting the restrictive monetary policy of the government (macro) and as an element of microeconomic distortion, if certain types of enterprises use the credit at the expense of others. More precisely, there is a presumption that the volume of IC is negatively correlated with the changes of overall monetary policy and that the structure of payables and receivables among the firms varies with their economic situation in that the units in better economic condition are financing the weaker ones.

The macroeconomic data available in Poland are highly incomplete and not comparable over the period 1989-1991. The information collected from the sample do not give the full picture of the problem either. Nevertheless, the data we have sheds some light on the problem, generally confirming the afore-mentioned hypotheses.

Firstly, the ratio of both payables and receivables to monthly sales grew in the period between January and June 1990, which is usually associated with the "big bang" policies, fell in VI-XI 1990, when the monetary squeeze was relaxed, and it resumed an upward trend afterwards. A similar pattern is shown by the data on the ratio of payables to bank credit+cash+dollar deposits. However tentative and inexact these results are, they suggest that IC growth is a natural reaction of SOEs to a liquidity crunch. The official statistical data for the whole manufacturing industry in 1991 tell a similar story. The ratio of payables to the total bank credit of enterprises between IQ1991 to IVQ1991 by 12 percentage points, i.e. from 106% to 118%. Payables related to monthly sales grew much faster in this period (from 100% to about 160%) reflecting both stagnation in the economy and increasing problems with liquidity.

There are also some suggestions stemming from the sample concerning the second question. An observation picked up during the interviews in the enterprises was that firms in weaker financial condition tend to be financed by better, more liquid and more profitable, units. This finds some support in the regression of receivables to payables on the gross rate of profit (profit to total costs) for three periods: 1st half of 1990, 2nd half of 1990 and 1st quarter of 1991. For the whole sample the correlation turned out to be statistically stronger, significant and growing over time, but rather weak (t-stat. well over 2, R sqd. rising from 0.05 to 0.13).

This tendency was not well reflected in the sectoral analysis of the sample (we examined SOEs from 5 important sectors: the metallurgical, chemical, electromechanical, light and food-processing industries) but we tried to compare the situation of the firms using other criteria: investment goods producers and consumer goods producers, quasi competitive firms and monopolistic/oligopolistic firms. The gross profitability of investment goods producers was consistently higher for the whole of 1990, but in 1991 the proportions were reversed. We found that the first group allowed receivables to accumulate more freely than the latter (consumer goods producers) since the macroeconomic policy was relaxed in mid-1990, whereas the ratio converged in 1991.

The gross profitability of monopolists/oligopolists and quasi competitive firms was similar up to February 1990. After that the competitive firms show consistently lower rates of profit and consistently lower ratios of receivables to payables.

The data seems to confirm the following pattern: better firms accept that their customers delay payment and just go on producing as long as there is any hope of getting the money back in the future. As liquidity becomes scarce, firms become more cautions and start refusing supplies without immediate payment and/or attempt to extract the due receivables more actively.

Inter firm credit, as it developed in Poland, softened the hard budget constraint to some extent and distorted the picture of the economy by providing some breathing space to the weaker firms at a cost to the better ones. One cannot help noticing characteristic analogies to the lending behaviour of the banks, which seems to have a similarly perverse influence. In conclusion, a restrictive monetary and credit policy was tried in Poland in a basically unchanged microeconomic environment, i.e. with labour-controlled state-owned enterprises and state-owned banks not used to active credit-risk appraisal policy. The result seems to be ambiguous. Shortage was eliminated, the currency was made convertible, inflation was subdued and a hard budget was imposed on the economy as a whole, but much less so on individual enterprises. As a result, both potentially viable and export competitive firms and their weaker brothers were in almost equal difficulty. The hands-off policy of the government turned out to be untenable. Massive intervention by the government in the functioning of individual enterprises, although costly and politically dangerous, is still better than waiting for the market to do the job: restructure the potentially viable firms, liquidate the rest. Both the Pact on SOEs and the Law on Financial Restructuring of Banks and Enterprises passed in early 1993 are meant to deal with what the restrictive macroeconomic policy alone could not. Besides, economic growth, which resumed after mid-1992, helped to soften some of the problems that appeared in the early stages of the transition in Poland.

CHAPTER 12

A STATISTICAL ANALYSIS OF CHANGES IN THE POLISH BANKING SYSTEM

Jaroslaw Bauc, Boguslaw Grabowski and Andrzej Raczko

INTRODUCTION

The analysis presented in this paper aims to provide a statistical description and an assessment of economic agents behaviour on the Polish credit market during the first stage of the Polish stabilization programme. Three main kinds of agents will be considered: banks, public sector firms and private sector firms. The period covered by the study is 1990-1991 and it will enable us to evaluate the adjustment behaviour of the agents during the process of transition of the Polish economy to market economy.

The estimates were made using monthly data. This can cause some distortion to the final results because the monthly periods are not sufficient for the adjustment processes on the credit market to be accomplished. However, the time which has passed since the Balcerowicz Plan was introduced (1st January 1990) is too short for quarterly data to be used. Anyway econometric forecasting is not a purpose of our analysis. The process of Polish financial sector reform was initiated at the beginning of 1989 and then advanced with the broad range of economic reforms introduced by the "Solidarity" government. Among the most important changes to the banking system were the following.

- Creation of nine state-owned commercial banks on the basis of regional branches of Narodowy Bank Polski (NBP). According to the new banking bill these banks were granted independence in their credit and deposit policy and the right to decide about their profits allocation.
- Setting a liberal law for the establishment new banks (including private and foreign banks).
- Liberalization of banking regulations to enable banks to undertake a full range of financial, activity including foreign exchange operations.
- Introduction of the right of state-owned firms to choose their own banks.

All these elements of the new financial sector regulations were introduced in the new economic environment consisting of: free prices; internal convertibility of the Polish zloty; strict budget constraints on the stateowned enterprises. They should therefore bring the examined agent behaviour closer to that observed in more market-oriented economies.

The hypothesis of market responsive behaviour by all major agents acting on the Polish credit market will be examined by means of the simple model of the banking system.

1. THEORETICAL MODEL

The starting point is the balance sheet of the consolidated banking system which gives rise to the following identity:

1. M0 + M1P + M1S + MFP + MFS = CP + CS + CB + RES + E1

where:
M0 - is cash in circulation (excluding cash in banks vaults);
M1P - is zloty savings deposits of the private sector (individual and firms);
M1S - is state-owned enterprises' zloty funds;
MFP - is the foreign exchange deposits of the private sector;
MFS - is the foreign exchange deposits of the state-owned firms;
CP - is credit extended to the private sector;
CS - is credit extended to the state-owned firms;
CB - is credit to finance the budget (net);
RES - is foreign exchange reserves;
E1 - is other items of the balance (net).

Also important is the balance of the Central Bank. This constitutes the basis for the identity:

2. CBS + CR + RESC = M0C + OR + VR + BCR + E2

where:
CBS - is Central Bank's credit to finance state budget (net);
CR - is credit extended to others banks;
RESC - is the foreign exchange reserves of the central bank;
M0C - is cash;
OR - is the obligatory reserves of commercial banks;
VR - is the voluntary reserves of commercial banks;
BCR - are the aggregate current account balances of the commercial banks;
E2 - is other items of the balance (net).

Examining the items of the balance sheet of the consolidated banking system and the balance sheet of the Central Bank enables one to describe the expected behaviour of the main agents participating in the credit market. Assuming that the real value of credit is determined by the demand side of the market, the credit equations can be written as follows:

3. $\Delta(CP/p) = f_1 (r_c - \pi, u)$
4. $\Delta(CS/p) = f_2 (r_c - \pi, u)$

where:
r_c - is the interest rate charge on credits;
π - is the expected rate of inflation;
p - is the price index (CPI);
u - is an indicator of economic activity.

We assume that an increase in the real value of the total credit granted by the banking sector is the proper measure of the increase in the demand for credit. Next we assume that the most important factors of credit decisions (on the demand side) can be best represented by the following explanatory variables: current interest rate, expected rate of inflation, and some measure of economic activity.

To assess inflationary expectations, we apply the adaptative expectations model. This seems to be the most suitable for the Polish economy, with its inflationary experience and its lack of market tradition, during the period of restrictive, anti inflationary policy. The estimates are based on the simplest assumption that $\pi_t = \pi_{t-1}$. There is no reason to differentiate between private and state-owned firms in this respect.

To analyze the depositor behaviour of state-owned firms and private sector agents it's necessary to separate the markets for deposits denominated in zlotys and in foreign exchange deposits. We assume the following behaviourial relations for the home currency (zloty) market:

5. $\Delta(M1P/p) = f_3 (r_d - \pi, YY)$
6. $\Delta(M1S/p) = f_4 (r_d - \pi, Y)$

Therefore we assume that the real increase in deposits depends on the real interest rate on deposits ($r_d - \pi$) and the rate of increase in income adequate for each sector (Y,YY).

Foreign exchange deposits have always played a special role in Poland. During the centrally planned period, foreign exchange deposits (when permitted) or foreign currencies (when deposits did not exist legally) served as a means of wealth holding by private agents. This was because of the permanently negative real interest rate on the zloty deposits and the black market real exchange rate deterioration. In other words, there was always much higher rate of return on the foreign exchange assets. The situation changed at the beginning of 1990 when the Solidarity government introduced internal convertibility of the zloty, based on a fixed exchange rate. Along with the high rate of inflation and the policy of positive real interest rates, it made the foreign exchange deposits less attractive. For the above mentioned reasons, we postulate the following functional form for the currency structure of the private sector deposits:

7. $MFP/(MFP+M1P) = f_5 (r_d - r_r, E)$

where:
r_r - is the interest rate on foreign exchange deposits;
E - is the real exchange rate.

For state-owned enterprises, foreign exchange deposits played a different role. When allowed, they were a source of import financing. Under central planning, when foreign exchange was strictly controlled, the possibility of keeping a foreign exchange account was a significant privilege for state firms. Nowadays, with a convertible currency and a stable exchange rate, most economic agents in the public sector are not allowed to open deposit accounts denominated in a foreign currency. For this reason, the foreign exchange deposits of state-owned enterprises is excluded from our analysis.

Having described the behaviour of the private sector and the state-owned firms, we turn to the behaviour of the banking system. The commercial banks' demand for refinancing credit (NBP's credit extended to the commercial banks) will be regressed on the difference between the interest rate on credit provided to firms and the interest rate on refinancing credit. The basis for such an estimation is provided by the following functional relation:

8. $\Delta(CR/p) = f_6 (r_c - r_f)$

where r_f represents the refinancing credit interest rate. Deposits, in addition to refinancing credit, stand for the other source of credit supply. So far we have assumed that the total value of deposits is mainly dependent upon the interest rate on deposits. To make the interest rate endogenous, we assume that its level can be explained by banks' behaviour. The banks are supposed to set their interest rates to obtain the funds necessary to cover a credit demand. One has to mention that the demand for refinancing credit cannot be fully satisfied due to the limits imposed by the central bank. Thus a reasonable function determining the interest rate on deposits can be presented as follows:

9. $r_d = f_7 [(CF+CP) - (M1P+M1C-CR), r_{res}]$

where r_{res} is the rate of mandatory reserve.

The model just described was estimated using data published in the Monthly Information Bulletin of NBP for the period January 1990 to November 1991. January 1990 was the first month of Balcerowicz's shock therapy. Because the data from this period could distort the results of the estimations we ignored it.

2. THE RESULTS OF THE ESTIMATIONS AND THEIR IMPLICATIONS

In this section, the results of the estimations are presented. The functions of the demand for credit were estimated using equations (3) and (4). The indicator of economic activity is represented by the ratio of the current to maximum volume of sold production. The expected rate of inflation in each period was assumed to be equal to the observed rate of inflation in the earlier period. The results of our estimates are as follows[1]:

$$3.1\Delta(CP/p) = \alpha_0 - \alpha_1 (r_c - \_) + \alpha_2 (Y/MAX\,Y)$$

	-149.4	0.85	1773.2
t	-0.2	1.54	1.6
0.092		D-W 1.58	

$$4.1\Delta(CS/p) = \alpha_0 - \alpha_1 (r_c - \_) + \alpha (Y/MAX\,Y)$$

	-2683.4	-1.64	7595.1
t	-0.64	-0.63	1.47
α		0.52	0.16
R^2 0.054		D-W 1.50	

[1]Where:

t - a value of t-statistic

a_ - a level of a statistical significance of a variable

R^2- a value of coefficient of determination

D-W a value of Durbin-Watson statistic.

The value of coefficient of determination (R^2) is very low for both equations. None of the independent variables turned out to be significant. Moreover, the level of the real interest rate parameter in the equation of the demand for credit by the private sector is positive (rather than negative, as one would expect). Although the values of all other independent variables have the expected signs, we can conclude that an increase in the credit demand is determined by other factors.

Estimation of the deposit supply functions yielded the following results:

$$5.1\ \Delta(M1P/p) = \alpha_0 + \alpha_1 (r_d - \pi)$$

	2340	-1.13	
t	8.95	-0.94	
α		-0.30	
R^2	0.000		D-W 0.56

$$6.1\Delta(M1S/p) = \alpha_0 + \alpha_1 (r_d - \pi)$$

	1432	8.41	
t	3.47	1.69	
α		0.11	
R^2	0.085		D-W 0.62

The values of R^2 and t-statistic show distinctly that the deposit supply (represented by an increase in the total value of deposit accounts) does not depend on the real interest rate.

To explain this one should mention that, in the Polish economy, which lacks capital and even real estate markets, banking deposits play a different role than in more developed market economies. They are practically the only temporary abode of purchasing power with a reasonable degree of liquidity. To support such a statement we regressed the real value of deposit accounts of state-owned firms on the volume of their sales (eq. 6.2) and the real value of private sector deposits on its real income (eq. 5.2). The results we have obtained support the proposition that in the absence of a developed capital market, the value of banking deposits were determined by the level of real income and sales, but not by the interest rate.

5.2.M1P/p $= \alpha$ YY

	0.68
t	46.3
α	0.00
R^2	0.990

6.2M1S/p $= \alpha$ Y

	0.51
t	28.2
α	0.00
R^2	0.97

As mentioned above, foreign exchange deposits were the alternative financial asset available, at least for the private sector. To examine the currency structure of the private sector deposits, the following equation was estimated:

7.1 $MFP/(MFP+M1P)= \alpha_1 (r_d - r_r) + \alpha_2 E$

	-0.029	0.009
t	-1.69	35.97
α	0.11	0.00
R^2 0.924		D-W 0.35

The results show that, in this case too, the interest rates do not explain the level of deposits. The share of foreign currency deposits in the total value of deposits can be explained by the change in the real exchange rate. Perhaps the policy of fixing the nominal exchange rate during the period of high inflation is the main reason for such a result.

Next to be examined is the way in which the refinancing credit interest rate was determined. The first step is to describe changes in the supply of refinancing credit. We regressed this variable on the difference between the interest rate on banks' credit, the refinancing credit interest rate and the rate of obligatory reserves. The results of this estimation are presented below and show that the refinancing credit was not granted according to commercial decisions.

8.1 $\Delta(CR/p) = \alpha_0 + \alpha_1 (r_c - r_f) + \alpha_2 r_{res}$.

	11334	-33.1	6980
t		-0.88	1.08
α		0.39	0.29
R^2 0.053		D-W 0.70	

As far as commercial banks' behaviour is concerned, the results of the estimation shows that banks tried to adjust their interest rates on deposits so as to guarantee the necessary level of their liabilities:

9.1 $r_d = \alpha\ (CF+CP)-(M1P+M1C+CR-OR)$

	0.00047
t	4.23
α	0.00
R^2	0.46 D-W 0.21

On the other hand, the low level of the coefficient of determination means that there were other important explanatory factors which were not included in the set of independent variables in our model. Perhaps most significant is the fact that, according to the long run plan of the Polish banking system reform, the refinancing credit of the central bank should be gradually replaced by other items of commercial banks' liabilities (i.e. deposits or own capital).

3. CENTRAL CONTROL OF THE POLISH BANKING SYSTEM: EMPIRICAL EVIDENCE

The estimates of the supply of credit and savings equation show that neither variable was determined by the independent variables that market economic theory would suggest should influence then (such as the interest rate and income). On the other hand, such instruments of credit control as the interest rate on the refinancing credit, the obligatory reserve rate and exchange rate hardly influenced credit expansion. This, however, does not mean that all participants of the credit market behaved irrationally. The more likely explanation is that the value of credit and deposits of were influenced by other factors. In that sense, our estimates support the opinion that the banking sector in Poland was controlled in a way characteristic of centrally planned economies.

In accordance with this hypothesis, we assumed that the volume of credit supply and the level of interest rate were subject to administrative control. As the data on the total credit supply "planned" by the central bank for each period are impossible to get hold of, we assumed that the central bank spread the planned increase in the credit supply evenly over the period. According to this assumption the following estimation was derived:

10. $CP + CS = \alpha_0 + \alpha_1 \, TIME$

	α_0	α_1
	41722	6680
t	23.9	50.3
α	0.00	0.00
R^2 0.992		D-W 0.42

In equation (10), the value of parameter α is of special importance since it characterizes the average monthly increase in the credit expansion "planned" by the central bank. The 95% confidence interval estimated for this coefficient is presented below:

Estimate α_1	St. error	Lower limit	Upper Limit
6680	132	6403	6957

Following our line of reasoning, let us call the upper limit of the confidence interval the credit limit for the banking system. Since the interval is a very narrow one, we can conclude that the credit control in the period under analysis was very restrictive and the credit limits were binding most of the time.

Applying the same procedure to both sectors of the economy, we obtained the following results:

10.1 $CP = \alpha_0 + \alpha_1 \, TIME$

	α_0	α_1
	-3875	2061
t	-5.3	37.2
α	0.00	0.00
R^2 0.985	D-W 0.44	

10.2 $CS = \alpha_0 + \alpha_1 \, TIME$

	α_0	α_1
	45597	4619
t	23.1	30.6
α	0.00	0.00
R^2 0.978	D-W 0.35	

The confidence intervals (shown in the tables below) for the "planned" increase in the credit supply (i.e. for the credit limits) also support the hypothesis of the strict control of credit expansion.

Private sector

Estimate α_1	St. error	Lower limit	Upper Limit
2061	55	1946	2177

State sector

Estimate α_1	St. error	Lower limit	Upper Limit
4619	151	4304	4934

The credit control efficiency can be measured by the ratio of the standard error of the estimate to the value of the _ parameter. The smaller the value of this ratio the more effective was the central bank's control over the banking system's credit supply. The lowest estimated value of the "efficiency ratio" for the total supply of credit (2%) implies that the central bank was much more interested in the level of total supply of credit than in its structure.

If the value of the total supply of credit was determined by the credit limit set by the central bank and did not depend on the interest rate, the question arises: what were the factors that determined the interest rate? We hypothesised that interest rate setting was based on a mark-up procedure (an interest rate always equals interest rate on refinancing plus a constant mark-up). The following model was then estimated:

11. $\Delta r_c = \alpha \, \Delta r_f$

	1.12	
t	38.08	
α	0.00	
R^2	0.987	D-W 2.193

The high explanatory power of this model (R^2 =0.987) strongly supports this hypothesis.

Finally, we considered what determined the interest rate on refinancing credit. We assumed that the central bank used it as an anti-inflationary tool. First, the examined interest rate was regressed on the rate of inflation and the foreign exchange reserves, as follows:

12. $\Delta r_f = \alpha_0 + \alpha_1 \Delta\pi - \alpha_2 \Delta(BCRES/p)$

	α_0	α_1	α_2
	-5.11	0.09	-0.006
t		7.29	2.10
α		0.00	0.05
R^2	0.75	D-W 1.76	

The result of this estimation justifies the proposition that the interest rate on refinancing credit was adjusted to the rate of inflation. Under the conditions of: credits limits; direct control of the refinancing credit supply; and give the strict correlation of the interest rate on banks credit with the interest rate on the central bank credit; the adjustment process in commercial banks should focus on deposits policy.

CONCLUSIONS

The Polish banking system was still subject to administrative control in the 1990-1991 period. The market conditions hardly affect the behaviour of the credit market agents.

Both the volume of credit and interest rates were strictly controlled by the monetary authority. The former was restricted by credit limits, the latter was determined by the refinancing credit interest rate.

CHAPTER 13

SOME ASPECTS OF BANKING RISK DURING ECONOMIC TRANSFORMATION: The Case of Poland

David G. Dickinson

INTRODUCTION

This paper is concerned with analysing certain key factors which impinge upon bank behaviour during the economic transition taking place in the former Socialist Economies of Eastern and Central Europe. Particular attention is paid to bank loan risk and the implications of the transition process for the development of a sound portfolio of loans.

The paper is divided into three parts. In the first section, some basic theoretical analysis of the role of financial intermediaries, of their lending process, and of the risks that they face, is conducted. This draws heavily upon the recent work viewing banks as liquidity insurers and/or delegated monitors. The second section contains an analysis of the impact of the key features of the transformation process on the financial system paying specific attention to bank lending and finance for investment. The third section outlines the policy implications of the preceding analysis, as well as drawing together the main strands of the discussion.

In identifying important issues, reference will be made to the specific case of Poland but the analysis is generally applicable to all the reforming countries of Central and Eastern Europe.

SECTION ONE: THEORY

The role of the financial system in the development of emerging market economies (EME's) of Central and Eastern Europe (CEE) has been discussed extensively. Alongside the key policies of price reform, macroeconomic stabilisation and privatisation of enterprises it has been argued that financial reform is essential to support the free market system which is being developed (e.g. Lipton and Sachs (1989)). This is not just in relation to the development of a well-functioning stock market but also recognises the importance of the banking system; indeed it has been argued that the banks should play a more important role in this process such that the financial system develops more along the lines of Germany and Japan than the US and UK (e.g. Lipton and Sachs (1990), Corbett and Mayer (1991)). However, as we shall discuss, the development of the financial system has been slow and threatens to retard the economic reform process.

Informational deficiency arguments have been at the forefront in explaining the current position of financial markets in CEE. Thus, for example, Calvo and Frenkel (1991) suggest that the financial markets in CEE economies will not have enough information to separate good and bad companies. The policy prescriptions of Fischer and Gelb (1991), which include the need to introduce appropriate accounting and legal frameworks, with standard valuation principles and bankruptcy laws, can also be seen to evolve from the recognition that the first step to creating efficient financial markets is to correct the major deficiencies in information which are endemic in CEE.

Recent advances in understanding about why financial institutions (banks) exist will inform our discussion of what are the fundamental determinants of bank risk. Specifically, we are interested in three issues; (a) the role of financial institutions as delegated monitors in the presence of asymmetric information about the intentions of borrowers; (b) the importance of long-term relationships in lending; (c) the distinction between macro and micro sources of risk in lending decisions. Note the emphasis in the analysis on bank lending decisions, which are crucial for the development of the EME's.

The remainder of this section will outline the main features of these three areas which will then be used to guide the discussion of the development of the banking system in the early stages of the Polish economic transformation.

(a) Asymmetric Information and the Role of Financial Institutions

The nature of financial contracts in a world with asymmetric information and moral hazard has been used extensively in recent years to explain the existence of financial institutions and particularly banks. The basic premise of this literature is as follows. If individuals choose one type of institutional arrangement over another it must be because it is optimal for them to do so. At first sight, banks appear to be costly methods of achieving the type of lending contracts which are observed. However, as Diamond (1984) argued, in the presence of asymmetric information and the need to monitor the performance of borrowers, banks can very effectively exploit the economies of scale which are exhibited by monitoring cost functions. In addition because they are able to invest across a wide range of different projects, they are able to pool the risks involved and consequently offer their own investors the type of liquid debt (deposit contracts) which they desire.

These arguments can be used to explain why there are different types of financial arrangements across economies. In comparing the German/Japan and UK/US models of the financial system, we have the arguments of

Gerschenkron (1962) that it rests upon the size of the need for capital in the early stages of development, where the larger the requirements the more likely that banks will provide the main source of funds. Hellwig (1991) uses the Diamond arguments to suggest that delegated monitoring is important when enterprises are bidding for large sums of money and consequently uses this in support of the Gerschenkron hypothesis. Hellwig also argues that the financial conditions which banks face have a major effect on the likely development of the financial system. Hence, in circumstances where short term liquidity is relatively plentiful, it is more likely that the banking system will be the main source of credit, since they are particularly good at utilising this sort of funds.

There are two specific problems with the delegated monitoring function if the financial contract is drawn up after the monitoring has taken place. In particular, there is the 'free rider' problem, where a bank which does not participate in any form of monitoring can offer favourable terms to borrowers who have been offered contracts by banks which are monitoring. In addition, we have the 'winners curse' affliction (see Greenbaum, Kanatas and Venezia (1989)), where banks will be naturally cautious with new borrowers because they will not know if they have been rejected by other banks. In an environment of significant structural change, these two problems are likely to be particularly acute. The importance of inside finance also cannot be overestimated. It can be regarded as the least cost form of funding because of the lack of monitoring required, and the protection it affords the firm against volatile macroeconomic conditions.

(b) Information, Reputation and the Lending Process

In discussing the role of imperfect and asymmetric information, we have identified the problem of assessing the credit-worthiness of loan applicants, and in particular the cost of such monitoring as being important to explaining why banks exist. If banks have had dealings with potential customers in the past, this may reduce their monitoring costs and also increase the average probability of loans being repaid, since they will be able to assess more accurately the credit rating of past customers. This idea leads us naturally into discussing the concept of reputation which has become an increasingly popular tool to use in economic analysis and has recently been applied to the case of bank loans, from the borrowers perspective by Diamond (1989,1991) and from the lender's viewpoint by Armendianz de Aghion (1990)).

Diamond (1989) is specifically concerned with analysing how long-term relationships can avoid the moral hazard problem implicit in lending, when the borrower's actions cannot be observed. Essentially, the successful completion of a loan signals to the bank that the borrower should be regarded as a better risk and hence more favourable loan terms can be offered in the future. The continued completion of loans will enhance the borrower's reputation for being sound and the benefits from retaining this reputation. Thus, only in the early stages of the bank-customer relationship will it pay for the borrower to gamble with projects that have a high probability of failure. The moral hazard problem exists only whilst a borrower is building a reputation.

Diamond (1991) extends these ideas to consider how to explain the choice that firms can take between bank loans and directly-placed debt. Banks will act in their monitoring role and hence borrowers with no or little reputation for being sound will need to use banks as the source of funds. Over time, in line with the earlier argument, the borrowers acquire a reputation and this results in greater access to the cheaper funds available via directly-placed debt. This argument is consistent with the proposal that banks will be the major source of finance for investment during the early stages of the economic transformation process (see also Gerschenkron (1962) for discussion of the role of banks in Germany during industrialisation).

The long-term nature of the relationship between bank and customer has been considered by other authors. Wood (1975) argued that banks may find it worthwhile to engage in less profitable loans now so as to secure business in the future. Broecker (1990) suggests that the existence of long-term lending relationships may imply some type of natural monopoly will exist in the credit market. Hellwig(1991) introduces the possibility of an incentive for borrowers to look to long-term relationships with banks via the possibility of rescue should projects fail to provide the expected profits. Haubrich (1989) argues that banks will enter into long term relationships because this is the most cost effective way of monitoring.

These arguments for borrowers and lenders to develop commitments to each other suggest that financial contracts should be of a one-to-one type. However there are advantages to both parties for the borrower to have a number of different sources of finance. This reduces the moral hazard problem that the lender may put pressure on the borrower to pay a larger share of profits in the event of success. Alternatively, if the project is a failure, there is advantage to the lender in having that risk shared around in that individual bank losses are reduced and consequently there is less pressure to rescue an ailing enterprise. Bizer and DeMarzo (1992) argue that new lenders will be able to offer better terms to borrowers than their existing lender since their exposure will be less. Consequently, multi-bank relationships will be the norm, even if they tend to be of a longer-term variety. This assumes that reputation is portable, which may only be true for mature enterprises.

To this point we have only considered the incentives for borrowers to acquire a reputation. However there may also be incentives for the banks to acquire a reputation for being a 'tough' lender. Armendiariz de Aghion (1990) has considered this aspect in the context of bank lending to heavily indebted countries. The key insight is that negotiation and renegotiation of a loan is a sequential process, with the potential for reputational effects. Thus a bank may be tough in its negotiation with a borrower now, with the possible cost of debt repudiation, on the grounds that this may improve future profits by creating a sounder loan portfolio. The reverse action will reduce the possible costs of default now, at the expense of increasing the probability of future default. The size of the debt is a key factor in this, and it could be argued that such an analysis is really only applicable to sovereign borrowers since they are the only ones large enough to effect the bank if default occurs. However, for example, if the regulatory regime is dependent upon the perceived behaviour of the bank to its customers, or if there is a cost to monitoring which can be reduced by signalling to borrowers that the bank will act toughly in debt negotiations, then the major aspects of the analysis will apply. An extension to these ideas is that large banks tend to lead in debt renegotiations and then must persuade smaller banks to agree to the course of actions upon which they have settled. In this framework Fernandez and Kaaret (1992) have shown that banks tend to act more toughly and hence terms are less favourable to the defaulters.

One of the implications of the reputational forces in the lending process is that information sharing may or may not be a good thing. Some analysis of information exchange in markets with asymmetric information has been conducted in the context of the insurance market (Jaynes (1978) and Hellwig (1988)). In his paper, Hellwig identifies the information sharing problem as one where firms must identify two things; how much information to send to their competitors and how to use the information they receive from them. Clearly this is a question of strategies and this is exactly the point Hellwig makes by pointing out that the timing of information communication relative to the setting of (in this case) insurance rates determines what the market equilibrium looks like.

Pagano and Japelli (1991) have developed ideas of information exchange specifically for the credit market which will provide some insights for this study. They are interested in identifying the conditions when it is profitable for banks to share information on the credit-worthiness of their customers. They set up a model where each bank has an effective local monopoly on lending by assuming that although there is the possibility of entry into other banks' markets, it is at a higher cost than the local bank. Their model has a number of implications which are interesting to us. Firstly, the more that borrowers can move around (i.e. go to different banks) the greater the advantage to information sharing. The reason for this is that there are less borrowers that the bank knows about and consequently it can reduce its expected costs by sharing information with others. Secondly, the larger the market, the greater the benefits of information sharing. Thirdly, any agency which is set up to share information will tend to be a natural monopoly - once it has reached a certain size there is an incentive for all banks to join. Fourthly, additional competition between banks may discourage information sharing. This is because banks will worry that providing information for competitors will put them at a competitive disadvantage. These implications have a certain appeal to the particular case that we are considering and we will return to them later.

(c) Sources of Banking Risk

The last section has concentrated on aspects of the lending process and how the risks inherent in making loans are affected by the acquisition of information, either over time or by the use of resources in information gathering efforts. In this section, we will consider to what extent the risks a bank faces are under its control. This leads us into a discussion of the source of risks and whether they are generated at the individual or aggregate level. This study will not consider in detail how banks should react to the various disturbances to which it is subject. It is interested in classifying, in a rather general way, what are the core causes of these random disturbances, with a view to analysing the financial environment which banking systems face. Of course, we shall naturally refer to risk management strategies appropriate to the cases analysed, but will not describe them in great detail.

Stochastic changes in the environment, in which banks find themselves, result from both macro- and micro-economic forces. Microeconomic risk results from the non-performance of loans as a result of lender-specific financial difficulties. An obvious example of this is an enterprise which, through poor management, incurs losses. From the point of view of lenders, this risk is dealt with through a well-diversified loan portfolio. However there may be external constraints which prevent the achievement of this, for example because of past lending decisions which have not been subject to normal bank evaluation. This is a particular issue which we shall discuss later for the case of Poland and is a common theme among financial institutions of the EME's of CEE.

Macroeconomic risk relates to the impact of unexpected variation in the aggregate economy. As far as macroeconomic risk is concerned, this may be, at least partly, dealt with through spreading wealth across a wide range of different assets which fortunes vary according to the state of the economy (for financial assets this means we have different beta coefficients). However from the point of view of assessing the behaviour of banks, we need to recognise that such macroeconomic uncertainty can impinge greatly upon bank management and hence upon the role that they play in the economy. Thus, for example, government monetary and fiscal policy has a key (if short-run) role to play in determining the pattern of and changes in the interest rate structure and hence is a major factor in determining the interest rate risk which the banking system faces. Portfolio selection models of bank behaviour (e.g. Parkin, Gray and Barrett (1972)) provide an immediate analytical hold on how uncertain monetary policy can impinge on the banking market. Alternatively, Cosimano (1988) has considered the way in which banks' loan policy is a function of monetary policy and argues that the future course of interest rates is a key determinant of current credit allocation. Aharony, Saunders and Swary (1986) have empirically analysed whether changes in the Federal Reserves' operating system for monetary policy in 1979 affected the profitability and risk of commercial banks and found a negative relationship between the price of bank stocks and interest rate variability.

If we are looking at macro sources of risk we can use simple aggregate demand and supply analysis to provide a hold on how aggregate shocks impinge on the banking industry. The analysis of policy above is, of course, one role of macroeconomic analysis. More generally, we can identify both demand and supply shocks. For example, a negative aggregate demand shock will imply a fall in output which starts a deflationary process in the economy. The profitability of enterprises would be hit. The government would also run into increasing budget deficits. Unemployment would also hit the household sector. The implication for the banking sector is fairly clear-cut. They would come under pressure from their commercial customers to provide short term working capital to ease financial pressures resulting from the shock. In addition, the loan portfolio would also deteriorate, particularly if the fall in aggregate economic activity is large enough to generate significant financial distress for households and firms.

The analysis can also be extended to consider how the reaction of the banking system to these shocks has further repercussions. There is increasing attention being paid to the role of banking at the level of the aggregate economy, emanating from the general dissatisfaction of macroeconomists with the conventional explanation of monetary policy channels (see for example Bernanke (1983), Bernanke and Blinder (1988), Duca and VanHoose (1990)). As a result of a down-turn in the economy, the reaction of banks to unexpected events can either alleviate (by providing additional loans to healthy enterprises) or worsen (by calling in loans from firms experiencing financial distress) the financial environment for economic agents and hence generate either positive or negative feedback on the economy. The key point here is that the optimal action of banks to the economic difficulties resulting from the macroeconomic shock may actually make the situation worse.

In analysing any developments of the banking system during a major economic restructuring we need to be careful to distinguish between macro- and micro- risk since they have quite different policy implications. In particular, risks which are micro-based are best left to the prudential management of the banks themselves. There should be no presumption that a bank will be rescued from its own bad management, which should imply a poor but not catastrophic financial result. Of course, bad management or the underdevelopment of the financial system generally, could possibly imply bank failure as a result of micro-risk and in this case there is a policy decision to be made concerning the protection of depositors and also of the integrity of the financial system as a whole. Policy choices also arise with regard to macro-risk, since here the government has a number of tools at its disposal. What is important is for it to recognise that decisions at the macro level have implications for the operation of the financial system.

In addition, the distinction between micro and macro sources of risk can play a role in the acquisition of reputation which was discussed in the last section. Financial problems arising from temporary cash flow problems for customers may very well reflect short term macroeconomic constraints, while the collapse of the firm's market at the micro level is much more likely to signal catastrophic failure. In analysing a loan market equilibrium which has reputational effects, along the lines of Diamond (1989,1991), we should note that the process of reputation building is affected by the additional noise created by macro-risk. The argument here relates to the conventional problem of moral hazard/adverse selection in the presence of imperfect information. An enterprise will always argue that it is unable to meet its commitments because of unexpected events outside of its control and it may be impossible for the lender to determine exactly which are telling the truth. Hence the process of reputation building is delayed and banks may well foreclose on a larger number of loans in an attempt to build a tough reputation. This strengthens the argument for trying to get a hold on the relationship between the financial performance of enterprises and the overall macroeconomic environment. It is also an argument for the borrower to acquire a reputation for soundness as quickly as possible and should also improve the incentives for banks to share information about the credit-worthiness of their customers. From the policy point of view, it suggests that the monetary authorities should try and create as stable a financial environment as possible in order not to contaminate signals which the banks use to judge the credit-worthiness of their customers.

SECTION TWO: RISKS IN POLISH BANKING - CURRENT DEVELOPMENTS AND FUTURE PROSPECTS

The current structure of the Polish banking system has evolved from the break-up of the old State Bank into nine separate commercial banks, mainly regionally based, and a Central Bank. This type of two tier structure created from the old monobanking system is characteristic of EME's. In addition, there are a few, but significant, specialist state banks still in existence, although they are intended for future privatisation and a large number of small private banks which have been set up. These have little capital but can play a potentially important role in the future, as I shall outline (for full details of the changes which have taken place see Bauc, Grabowski and Raczko (1992) and Belka, Pruski and Raczko (1992)).

The way in which the commercial banking system was created has led to particular problems in the context of efficient bank lending. Prior to the break-up of the monobanking system, the banks were required to provide the finance necessary to fulfill production plans consistent with central management decisions. Hence credit allocation was not determined with reference to normal market signals, and, as a result, banks inherited a loan portfolio which was likely to be unsustainable in a market environment. This situation prevailed not only in Poland but also in the other EME's of CEE. More information on the particular case of Poland can be found in Belka, Pruski and Raczko (1992). Clearly banks created out of the old monobanking system will have a significant inherited debt problem which will affect their lending behaviour and lead to the problem of "creditor passivity" where banks have not called in non-performing loans because the cost of doing so outweighs the benefits (which may not all be economic).

The growth in inter-firm credit worsens the problems created by bad debts (note that Begg and Portes(1991) argue that 'creditor passivity' affects inter-firm credit). A normal feature of a developed financial system are significant financial interrelationships caused by enterprises being creditors to their suppliers and debtors to their customers, but in a fragile financial and economic environment, this can generate significant multiplication of financial distress, with healthy, as well as sick firms suffering from a credit squeeze. Part of this has arisen from the failure of enterprises to recognise the effects of the imposition of hard budget constraints, at least until recently, when it appears more and more firms are operating within a cash economy. The layering of extra-bank debts does however distort the operation of normal lending arrangements, with banks clearly faced with additional uncertainties when evaluating the credit-worthiness of their customers now and in the future.

One of the problems of the current banking structure is that there is considerable geographical and industry-specific character to their loan portfolio. Hence they is insufficient diversification to prevent micro-risk having implications for the financial health of individual banks and hence of the financial system as a whole. This creates particular difficulties with assessing the performance of the banking system, since the decline of traditional industries located predominantly in certain areas will cloud the issue. In addition, there has been and will continue to be political pressure put upon banks to support ailing enterprises, particularly if they are major employers.

The stance of Polish macroeconomic policy since the beginning of the economic reform process has been one of stringent stabilisation. This is characteristic of the early stages of reform in the other EME's of CEE (see, for example Blejer and Sagari (1992)). To consider the specific case of Poland, the inception of the policies designed to move the economy to a free market structure saw a major increase in the rate of price inflation, negative real interest rates, a large fall in industrial output generating a significant increase in unemployment which was a part cause of a rising real budget deficit. After this initial shock, there has been a more stable macroeconomic picture emerging, with stabilisation of output followed by a gradual rise supported by growth in the new private sector enterprise sector (failure to properly account for production of private sector enterprises may have led to an overstatement of the initial output decline), control of inflation at admittedly high levels (40% per annum), the establishment of small but positive real interest rates; the main disappointment has been a failure to control the burgeoning real budget deficit. This latter feature is, in part, a reflection of political instability which has been a particular problem in Poland, as well as the continued increase in unemployment allied to the need to provide a basic social security system.

The extent to which the output collapse is a result of macroeconomic factors is of considerable interest to this study. As outlined in the last section, the non-performance of loans may result from normal enterprise wastage or because of general adverse macroeconomic circumstances. Recent studies have tackled this issue. Borenstein et al (1993) have considered the cases of Rumania, Bulgaria and the Czech and Slovak Federal republics; they argue that the evidence strongly supports the view that the output decline is a reflection of macroeconomic factors rather than of the major structural changes which accompany the transition process. They test whether these aggregate causes are demand (resulting from the stabilisation policy and world recession) or supply (energy price shocks and credit constraints) based. The evidence is rather mixed but attributes importance to both types of disturbance. The importance of the credit crunch on the supply side of the economy is supported by a multi-country study by Calvo and Coricelli (1993). In addition they argue that the shocks generated by large relative price changes creates additional problems for banks when determining the credit-worthiness of customers.

The macroeconomic environment and the problems of the Polish economy have not been conducive to the development of a soundly based banking system. Macroeconomic volatility has added to the risks inherent in lending and made the process of separating good and bad customers more difficult. In addition, the bad debt problem will impinge upon the process of building a sound customer base, for two reasons. Firstly, enterprises will find it a slower process to build a reputation because of the natural caution of banks with significant nonperforming loans. Secondly, banks may have little incentive to acquire a reputation themselves, since they have an expectation that their balance sheet will at some stage in the future be cleaned. Hence the natural development of a sound banking system is being delayed by failure to announce a policy on bad debts. This is compounded by the lower incentives to obtain and share accurate information on the financial state of borrowers, resulting from the smaller benefits from this process in an environment where banks will expect to be rescued from their own bad management.

The development of the banking sector from now on will depend upon exploiting the information that the banks have on good customers and for policy to be developed with regard to the bad ones. The concept of reputation, and the incentive for enterprises to acquire it, provides a market-led method for this to occur and as the economic environment becomes significantly more stable and there must be good prospects for the banking system to build up a solid base of good customers who will form the foundation for building a profitable future. However, for the case of EME's at present, information on loan quality is sketchy, to say the least.

The need for precise and up-to-date financial information is, of course, paramount to the speedy development of a sound banking system. The major commercial banks in Poland have developed some form of credit-sharing arrangement. It is interesting to note that the sort of bank structure which has been created seems to be conducive to the sharing of information, in that the individual commercial banking networks are geographically discrete, which will reduce the perceived dangers of information sharing, namely assisting your competitors. In this regard, it is interesting to note that the small private banks appear not to have access to this information. It seems that the large commercial banks regard the small private banks as their main competitors and consequently do not seem prepared to let them join their information networks since they would regard them as free riding. This raises serious issues with regard to the operation of the private banking sector. In particular, these banks are concerned with lenders using the same collateral against multiple loans at different banks. However borrowers may find it optimal to go to a number of different banks. Hence, the presence of inadequate information exchange may lead to the forestalling of perfectly appropriate borrower activity. In addition we have the winners' curse problem which could be alleviated by more formal information-sharing arrangements.

The development of a banking system has preceded other types of financial institution, and in particular the stock market, where the privatisation process has been beset by problems. However this is not necessarily a bad thing because of the need for enterprises to acquire reputation before finding placement of debt or equity to be a lower cost source of finance. As a result the financial sector as a whole has been and will continue to be relatively underdeveloped into the immediate future. Whilst the banking sector may be the main source of funding until borrowers become endowed with credibility the lack of properly developed short term money markets has delayed the efficient allocation of banking sector resources in response to short term unexpected developments. The creation of the interbank market has helped but trading is still very thin and there is very limited access to these funds.

Whilst the commercial banks will provide the main source of investment finance for large firms in the foreseeable future, there has been considerable growth in the private banking sector. The problem of finance for small and medium sized enterprises (SME's) is a particular concern for EME's, since the private sector plays an increasingly important role in the industrial base (e.g. estimates suggest that, by 1993, over 50% of Polish industrial production comes from private sector enterprise). The private banks are playing a role in providing finance to this sector of the economy, effectively taking on the role of venture capitalists. However their growth is being stifled by the closed nature of the inter-bank market. Although such banks engage in highly risky lending it should be noted that all bank lending is very risky in the current economic environment.

SECTION THREE : BANKING RISKS AND ECONOMIES IN TRANSITION - SOME POLICY ISSUES AND CONCLUSIONS

The second section has identified a number of key areas which have hindered the development of the banking system in Poland. Particular attention has been paid to factors which have influenced the risks in the lending process:

(i) The formation of the commercial banking system created out of the monobanking system implied that all the problems of the monobanking system were handed on to the new system. Specifically, the 'new' banks had to cope with the debts inherited from the past, which created confused signals and perverse incentives in the credit allocation process. This problem was compounded by the way in which the commercial banks networks were structured, with industrial and geographical concentration in the customer base.

(ii) The process of macroeconomic stabilisation was a further obstacle to the development of an efficient banking system. It implied not only high rates of inflation and negative real rates of interest but also a collapse in output of the traditional industries which prevented proper servicing of the inherited debts. This is a particular problem if inherited debts are not a good indicator of the health of an enterprise in a market economy. More generally, macroeconomic instability contaminates signals about the reasons for poor loan performance, and hence generates inefficiencies in the allocation of credit.

(iii) The creation of information sharing arrangements between banks is an important development which can aid the efficiency of credit allocation. However there will be obstacles to this, in the sense that individual banks may not have an incentive to engage in this type of activity, which may require policy intervention. In the case of Poland this has been evidenced by a very slow move to sharing information and the complete exclusion from this process of the small private banks.

(iv) The small private banks have a role to play as providers of finance to private sector enterprises. This is a rapidly expanding sector of the economy and is likely to provide the main source of growth to the economy as a whole. Hence the provision of finance is an important issue but it should be recognised that the small private banks take on the role of venture capitalists rather than banks in this activity.

Given these basic arguments we can consider the policy implications of our analysis of the lending process in the early stages of the transition process.

(a) The inherited debt problem

The first issue which has attracted a significant amount of interest is the problem of the inherited debts from the central planning regime. This is a major obstacle to the economic reform process and to the banking system playing its full role in the transition to a market economy. The existence of debts carried forward from the centrally planned system, which are passed onto the newly created commercial banks, creates a situation where the banks will provide additional credit and roll-over of existing loans to those large former state-owned enterprises who are their main creditors. Otherwise there is the prospect of the bank failing (the 'creditor passivity' problem). The banks cannot impose hard budget constraints onto enterprises because they themselves could not cope with this policy. Yet, the problem of imposing hard budget constraints on enterprises is, of course, a crucial feature of the reform process and the banking system should play a crucial role in imposing hard budget constraints. McKinnon (1991) argues that it can only play that role if liberalised enterprises are excluded from using banks as a source of investment finance and hence, effectively, can use only internally generated funds. However this solution to the problem will surely slow the process whereby the banking system develops into a fully-functioning, market-led, system, for example, by preventing the formation of the long-term relationships which have been identified as being important. The experience of Poland during the early stages of the reform process suggests that it is crucial to deal with the inherited debt problem, otherwise the situation deteriorates and the costs of correcting the problem become greater.

A consensus appears to be emerging about the appropriate policy to undertake to deal with the bad debt problem. This is to develop a scheme to convert the debt to another form so as to "clean up" the balance sheets of the commercial banking system and the enterprises. Arguments for this action are: that only will it then be possible for the proper assessment of credit risks and hence a sensible allocation of funds to investment projects (Calvo and Frenkel 1991); that it is a necessary step for the privatisation process (Caprio and Levine, 1991); that it frees up management resources to the important task of lending to new investment (Caprio and Levine(1991); that there will be less bankruptcy and hence a reduction in social costs of privatisation (Levine and Scott, 1992); that there is an increase in retained earnings which will aid investment (Levine and Scott, 1992).

That the debt conversion proposal is preferred to the 'flow' solution where banks are given temporary relief from bad debts on the understanding that this gives them time to make provisions against the bad debts, arises because of the scale and permanent nature of the problem. However, in making proposals for a 'loans for debt' conversion, it is important to recognise the implications for future macroeconomic policy decisions (Sheng(1991)). The cleaning-up of balance sheets now may be creating implications for future fiscal and monetary policy which will add to aggregate economic volatility. It has been suggested that additional growth of GDP in the region of 1% a year might be required in order to correct fiscal imbalances arising from the assumption of bad debts by the government (Levine and Scott , 1991).

Information on the extent of the bad debt problem, and its implications, is required as soon as possible, so that policy decisions can be made. In the same way as there is a general recommendation to alleviate the problem of bad debts for the banking system, it is also important to assist profitable enterprises which have been forced into adverse financial circumstances by the failure of their creditors (the inter-firm credit problem). However, this problem is more appropriately dealt with through a temporary flow solution than via a wholesale writing off of the debts. The reason for this is that once the bad debt problem is overcome, all enterprises will have financial circumstances which are representative of their overall health, and sensible financial planning should encompass the implications of management of these enterprises since the transition process began. Otherwise there is the danger that the credibility of the whole economic strategy will be lost. Note that this argument also implies that the bad debt problem needs to be resolved quickly. Otherwise the banks will continue to lend perversely in the knowledge that the government will, at some stage have to clean their balance sheets of the mistakes they have made.

To summarise, inherited debts are preventing the normal operations of a market-led banking system. Until this obstacle is removed, efficient allocation of credit cannot be expected. Furthermore the problem can only become worse until bank balance sheets are cleaned and hence the implications of current loan policy becomes transparent. In hindsight, the bad debts should have been cleared near the start of the reform process (not at its inception as explained below). This may have been impossible from a domestic budgetary viewpoint, but could have been facilitated by international credits. It should be noted that such assistance is now starting to appear, but clearly the costs of the scheme will be greater than if it had been introduced at the outset. The lessons of the delay is that any proposed solution should be enough to completely solve the problem, with a clear indication that further assistance for future mistakes will not be forthcoming. If the balance sheets are cleaned, and, as a result, banks start behaving in an efficient manner they will quickly become profitable and will grow along with the economy. The costs of implementing any debt write-off will, to some extent, be offset by future taxes which the banks will pay; it would certainly be feasible to impose such taxes in the future.

(b) Macroeconomic Instability

A further factor which we have emphasised is the impact of aggregate level uncertainty, relative to microeconomic risk, which will impinge upon the loan risks a bank faces. As has been pointed out, the EME's of CEE have undergone major macroeconomic stabilisation as a key area of the first stage of their reform process. Hence not only have enterprises experienced a major structural shock as prices move to world levels, but also a collapse in aggregate demand. These two shocks together have plunged many enterprises into financial distress, evidenced by failure to service loans. From the banks' viewpoint, the key problem is disentangling the signals about the future financial health of the enterprise. Additionally, but over a longer time span, the process of reputation building and of information dissemination will also be harmed by general macroeconomic volatility. Essentially, the presence of additional noise in signals received about the financial health of customers, would create a slowing down of the process of reputation acquisition by borrowers, while, at the same time, giving banks a reason to establish themselves as 'tough', since the benefits of avoiding bad loans would be greater in times of general instability - in the short term this effect will be overwhelmed by the bad debt problem and its effect on the loan decision. Consequently, we would expect to see higher interest rates and fewer loans being granted. The implication is that swift and sharp macroeconomic stabilisation measures are preferable to a more gradualist approach, to prevent delay in the process of developing a sound banking system.

The recognition of the impact of macroeconomic volatility will place a constraint on how quickly can policy on bad debts be implemented. It would be foolish to clean balance sheets at the same time as imposing macroeconomic policies which make it necessary to go through the same process at a later stage. If the banks are to experience their own 'big bang' it should only occur once. The experience of Poland is that within about 12 months the economy is starting to stabilise, at admittedly low levels of output, and hence this might indicate a suitable time frame.

It has been common among EME's to impose, within an appropriate interval, the regulatory requirements consistent with developed economies, as institutionalised in the Basle Accord. During the period of transition these are not standards which have any meaning. Accounting standards are not in place to properly evaluate bank balance sheets (as, for example, in determining the volume of bad debts). The central bank does not have specialised staff trained to carry out this function. In addition, the importance of macroeconomic risk in determining loan risk means the imposition of these requirements adds significant costs to bank activities at a time when any obstacle to bank lending is detrimental to the economy as a whole. The time perspective for introducing the Basle convention should be long enough not only to permit the solution to the inherited debt problem but also to allow for the macroeconomic stabilisation process to be fully seen through.

(c) Information Sharing

The creation of credit rating agencies is a necessary development for the banking system, and more generally for the financial system to flourish. Whilst this would be a problem best left to the market for a developed financial system, some form of policy intervention seems to be appropriate in the case of the EME's of CEE. Encouragement needs to be provided to the large banks to set up a formal credit-rating network, as part of the overall development of information gathering and dissemination services. One way of doing this would be to impose capital requirements on the banking system which weighted the loan portfolio according to the credit-rating given to it by the bank. This would provide an incentive for the bank to bring information on its customers into the public domain. Alternatively, the authorities might wish to play an active role in the creation of a credit-rating service. A number of financial scandals, in Poland have highlighted the importance of ensuring that banks do share information and do it quickly so there is a regulatory issue here which would provide grounds for central bank intervention if necessary. This would also allow opportunity to solve the problem of exclusion of the small private banks from the existing information sharing arrangements.

(d) The Role of Small Private Banks

One early manifestation of the development of the commercial banking system in Poland was the creation of a large number of very small private banks. There may have been initial expectations that these institutions would provide some sort of competitive fringe within the system, but experience has suggested that this has not been the case. These banks are just too small to properly compete with the commercial banks created out of the old monobanking structure. Development of the banking system in the future will rest upon solving the problems of these large banks. The question then arises of the role for these small private banks. They could indeed take on the mantle of commercial banks, but as they become successful it is clear that they will be taken over by one of the large banks. Alternatively, they could become a focus of finance for small and medium-sized enterprises, taking on the role of venture capitalists. This is a vital area for the EME's to tackle and should be a cause of policy discussion. In order to achieve this, it would be necessary to create a category of institution (Venture Banks ?), which could be called a bank, but which are of a different character, and, most importantly, not subject to the normal regulatory requirements. Investors would need to recognise that deposits with such institutions were not protected in the same way as for the 'normal' banks but that, correspondingly, the potential rewards were higher. This category of institution might itself be transitory. A situation can be envisaged where they play a role as the initial source of finance for enterprises which have no credit history and which are hence too speculative for the large banks. At present this is characteristic of most of the private sector. Over time, these enterprises would build a reputation which would then be used to buy lower cost finance from the main banks. It would be expected that a successful small bank would, at some stage, become a subsidiary of one of the large banks.

The suggested policy measures above are elements of a process which can be described as the financial sector's 'big bang'. The experience of the early stages of transition in Poland, which is reasonably characteristic of other EME's is that, of its own, enterprise reform is not sufficient to impose hard budget constraints on the former state-owned enterprises. The role of the banking system has been recognised, but the conditions which were imposed on the banks meant that there was no incentive for managers to carry out the intended policy. This issue needs to be resolved as soon as possible, particularly now that the EME's appear to be emerging from the initial shock which liberalisation imposed and entering the second stage of the process where finance for investment is a crucial requirement for economies which have the potential to grow rapidly.

BIBLIOGRAPHY

Aharony, J., Saunders, A. and I. Swary (1986), "The Effects of a Shift in Monetary Policy regime on the Profitability and Risk of Commercial Banks", *Journal of Monetary Economics*, 17, 363-77.

Armendiariz de Aghion, B. (1990), "International Debt: An Explanation of Commercial Banks' Lending Behaviour after 1982", *Journal of International Economics*, 28, 17386.

Baltensperger, E. (1980), "Alternative Approaches to the Theory of the Banking Firm, *Journal of Monetary Economics*, 6, 1-37.

Bauc, J., Grabowski, B. and A. Raczko (1993), "The Transition Programme of the Polish Banking System", *This Volume*

Begg, D. and R. Portes (1991), "Enterprise Debt and Economic Transformation", *CEPR Discussion Paper*, No. 695.

Belka, M., Pruski, J. and A. Raczko (1993), "The Evolution of the Polish Banking System and EC Regulatory Standards", *This Volume.*

Bernanke, B.S. (1983), "Non-Monetary Effects of the Financial Crisis in the Propagation of the Great Depression", *American Economic Review*, 73, 257-76.

Bernanke, B.S. and A.S. Blinder (1988), "Credit, Money and Aggregate Demand", *American Economic Review*, 78, 435-39.

Bizer,D.S. and P.M. DeMarzo (1992), "Sequential Banking", *Journal of Political Economy*, 100, 41-61.

Blackwell, N.R. and A.M. Santomero (1982): "Bank Credit Rationing and the Customer Relation", *Journal of Monetary Economics*, 9, 121-129.

Blejer, M.I. and S.B. Sagari (1992), "Hungary: The Initial Stages in the Financial Sector Reform of a Socialist Economy in Transition", *Applied Financial Economics*, 2, 33-42.

Borenstein, E., Demekas, D. and J.D. Ostry (1993), "An Empirical Analysis of the Output Declines in Three East European Countries", *IMF Staff Papers*, Vol. 40, 1-31.

Broecker, T. (1990), "Credit-Worthiness Tests and Inter-Bank Competition", *Econometrica*, 58, 429-52.

Calvo, G.A. and F. Coricelli (1992), "Stagflationary Effects of Stabilisation Programmes in Reforming Socialist Countries: Enterprise-Side and Household-Side Effects", *World Bank Economic Review*, 6, 71-90.

Calvo, G. and F. Coricelli (1993), "Output Collapse in Eastern Europe: The Role of Credit", *IMF Staff Papers*, Vol. 40, 32-52.

Calvo, G.A. and J.A. Frenkel (1991), "Credit Markets, Credibility and Economic Transformation, *Journal of Economic Perspectives*, 5, 139-48.

Caprio, G. Jr. and R. Levine (1991), "Reforming Socialist Economies: Issues for the Financial Sector", *World Bank Working Paper*, Washington DC,

Chan, Y-S, Greenbaum, S.I, and A.V. Thakor, "Information Reusability, Competition and Bank Asset Quality", *Journal of Banking and Finance*, 10, 243-53.

Corbett, J. and C. Mayer (1991), "Financial Reform in Eastern Europe: Progress with the Wrong Model", *Oxford Review of Economic Policy*, 7, 57-75.

Cosimano, T.F. (1988), "The Banking Industry under Uncertain Monetary Policy", *Journal of Monetary Economics*, 12, 117-39.

Diamond, D.W. (1984), "Financial Intermediation and Delegated Monitoring", *Review of Economic Studies*, 51, 393-414.

Diamond, D.W. (1989): "Reputation Acquisition in Debt Markets", *Journal of Political Economy*, 97, 828-62.

Diamond, D.W. (1991), "Monitoring and Reputation: The Choice between Bank Loans and Directly Placed Debt", *Journal of Political Economy*, 99, 680-21.

Duca, J.V. and D.D VanHoose (1990), "Loan Commitments and Monetary Policy", *Journal of Money, Credit and Banking*, 22, 178-94.

Fernandez, R. and D. Kaaret (1992), "Bank Heterogeneity, Reputation and Debt Renegotiation", *International Economic Review*, 33, 61-78.

Gerschenkron, A. (1962), *Economic Backwardness in Historical Perspective*, Harvard University Press, Cambridge, MA.

Greenbaum,S.I., Kanatas,G. and I.Venezia (1989), "Equilibrium Loan Pricing under the Bank-Client relationship", *Journal of Banking and Finance*, 13, 221-35.

Hardy, D.C and A.K. Lahiri (1992), "Bank Insolvency and Stabilisation in Eastern Europe", *International Monetary Fund*, Working Paper 92/9, I.M.F.,Washington DC.

Haubrich, J.G. (1989), "Financial Intermediation: Delegated Monitoring and Long-Term Relationships", *Journal of Banking and Finance*, 13, 9-20.

Fischer, S. and A. Gelb (1991), "The Process of Socialist Economic Transformation", *Journal of Economic Transformation*, 5.

Hellwig, M. (1988), "A Note on the Specification of Interfirm Communication in Insurance Markets with Adverse Selection", *Journal of Economic Theory*, 46, 154-63.

Hellwig, M. (1990), "Banking, Financial Intermediation and Corporate Finance", in *European Financial Integration*, A. Giovannini and C. Mayer (ed.), Cambridge University Press, Cambridge.

Ho, T.S.Y. and A. Saunders (1981), "The Determinants of Bank Interest Margins: Theory and Empirical Evidence", *Journal of Financial and Quantitative Analysis*, 16, 581-602.

Jaynes, G.D. (1978), "Equilibria in Monopolistically Competitive Insurance Markets", *Journal of Economic Theory*, 19, 394-422.

Levine, R. and D. Scott (1992), "Old Debts and New Beginnings: A Policy Choice with Dynamic Implications for Transitional Socialist Economies", *World Bank Working Paper*, World Bank, Washington DC.

Lipton, D. and J. Sachs (1990), "Creating a Market Economy in Eastern Europe: The Case of Poland", *Brookings Papers on Economic Activity*, No.l, 75-133.

Lipton, D. and J. Sachs (1990), "Privatisation in Eastern Europe: The Case of Poland", *Brookings Papers on Economic Activity*, No.2, 293-333.

McKinnon, R.I. (1973), *Money and Capital in Economic Development*, Brookings Institution, Washington D.C.

McKinnon, R.I, "Financial Control in the Transition from Classical Socialism to a Market Economy", *Journal of Economic Perspectives*, 5, 107-22.

Pagano, M. and T. Japelli (1991), "Information Sharing in Credit Markets", CEPR *Discussion Paper*, No. 579, CEPR, London.

Parkin, J.M, Gray, M.R. and R.J. Barrett (1970), "The Portfolio Behaviour of Commercial Banks", in *The Econometric Study of the UK*, K.Hilton and D.Heathfield (ed.), Macmillan, Edinburgh.

Santomero, A.M. (1984), "Modelling the Banking Firm", *Journal of Money, Credit and Banking*, 16, 576-602.

Shaw, E.S. (1973), *Financial Deepening in Economic Development*, Oxford University Press, New York, NY.

Sheng, A. (1991), "Bad Debts in Transitional Socialist Economies", *World Bank Working Paper*, World Bank, Washington DC.

Stiglitz, J.E. (1989), "Financial Markets and Development", *Oxford Review of Economic Policy*, 5, 55-68.

Sundararajan, V. (1990), "Financial Sector Reform and Central Banking in Centrally Planned Economies", *I.M.F. Working Paper*, International Monetary Fund, Washington, D.C.

Wood, J. (1975), *Commercial Bank Loan and Investment Behaviour*, John Wiley and Sons, London.

Zarruck, E.R. and J. Madura (1992), "Optimal Bank Interest Margin under Capital Regulation and Deposit Insurance", *Journal of Financial and Quantitative Analysis*, 27, 141-49.

Zarruck, E.R. (1989), "Bank Spread with Uncertain Deposit Level and Risk Aversion", *Journal of Banking and Finance*, 13, 797-810.

CHAPTER 14

THE EVOLUTION OF THE BANKING SYSTEM IN POLAND AND EC REGULATORY STANDARDS

Marek Belka, Jerzy Pruski and Andrzej Raczko

INTRODUCTION

Allocation of productive factors determined by an obligatory central plan formulated in physical terms is probably the characteristic feature of CPEs. The fulfilment of a central plan in such a system is achieved through a network of obligatory plans of individual enterprises. Money seems to be redundant in so defined CPEs, and hence so is a banking system. In reality, however, a banking system of special sort turned out to be necessary. First, even under central planning, economic calculation (on the central level) is indispensable; hence the existence of "accounting" money. Second, the Polish economy has never been purely centrally-planned. Wages have never been paid out in kind (or in coupons) but in money. Consequently, institutions servicing money circulation had to be built. There was also a private sector in the economy, particularly in agriculture, where market mechanisms survived. Last but not least, an institution for settlement of international payments had to be preserved.

STRUCTURE OF THE BANKING SYSTEM

The structure and functions of the banking system resulted from its economic and political environment. Narodowy Bank Polski (NBP - Polish National Bank), through the intermediation of its regional offices controlled the behaviour of enterprises, Powszechna Kasa Oszczednosci (PKO - Universal Savings Bank) serviced the money circulation of the households cooperative banks handled the monetary transactions of private sector. It is worth noting, that in agriculture there was a "division of labour" between a bank serving the state-owned farms, so-called PGRs (Bank Rolny - Bank of Agriculture, later BGZ - Bank Gospodarki Zywnosciowej) and many smaller cooperative banks serving private farms. International settlements were carried out by Bank Handlowy SA, dollar accounts for the population were handled by Bank Polska Kasa Opieki (see table).

FUNCTIONS OF THE BANKING SYSTEM

The main function of the banking system under central planning was to control the fulfilment of the central bank. Plans of enterprises constituted the main element of the central plan. A central plan consisted of two parts: target formulation determining the production structure to be achieved; and the operational part - defining inter-enterprise cooperation links securing the fulfilment of the plan. The banks played a significant role in the second part of the plan. Financial flows with fixed prices (set according to cost plus rule) made it possible to control the flow of goods between firms. Thus the financial plan became an instrument of control to ensure plan fulfilment.

Control of financial flows was easier, as cash circulation has been consciously limited. Enterprises could realize their revenues in cash only to a very small extent; all cash received had to be deposited in the bank immediately. The analysis of firms' accounts and non-cash flows made it possible for the banks to control whether firms did not fulfil central directives.

Structure and network of banks in Poland 1946-1982
(Number of regional offices)

Bank	1946	1953	1971	1982
Narodowy Bank Polski	79	445	443	437
Bank of Agriculture (1946) (from 1975) BGZ	18	18	49	49
Cooperative Banks	1180	1356	1578	1651
Universal Savings Bank (from 1953) before 1953 Postal Savings Bank	18	18	241	251
Bank Polska Kasa Opieki (1946)	9	10	13	13
Bank Handlowy SA (1946)	45	1	5	5

Source: Orabowski, E., Jaworski, W. and Krzyzkiewicz, Z. "Bankowosc w godspodarce socjalistycznej", PWE, Warsawa 1975,. p.36, 42. Krzyzkiewicz, Z. "System kredytowy w Latach 1982-1988", IF, Warszawa, 1990, p. 20.

Another means of control that banks had at their disposal was a system of "target" credits. Banks granted credits not on commercial terms but according to the plan. Thus the whole investment process could be controlled.

Banks servicing the private sector (for example the cooperative banks) had analogous functions: to make the private sector's behaviour conform to the assumptions of the central plan. It was done by credit rationing operated through by a detailed, centrally determined system of preferences.

The Universal Savings Bank (PKO) and Bank Polska Kasa Opieki acted in a different way although their main role was the same: to serve the fulfilment of the central plan. A notorious feature of the CPEs has always been that the flow of incomes exceeded the value of the flow of consumer goods (remember administrative controls of prices). A monetary overhang, resulting from this, stimulated black markets and drove up the unofficial exchange rate of foreign currencies.

The role of PKO was to absorb the excess money balances of the population by offering attractive savings alternatives. In this sense its functioning was similar to the same institutions in a market economy. The Bank Polska Kasa Opieki was to absorb the dollar holdings of the people.

3. MONEY CIRCULATION

Two kinds of money were in use: cash and "accounting" money. All incomes of the population were paid out in cash; as a result its circulation was rather specific (fig. 1). Initially the whole supply of cash was held by the bank, afterwards it was transferred to enterprises, which paid out wages. The people spent the money to buy goods, thus it returned to the enterprises, that were obliged to deposit cash in banks immediately. Cash didn't circulate freely among economic agents but made a characteristic shuttle movement between the bank and the population.

Accounting money, contrary to the first impression was not cheque-money used by enterprises. Cheque-money can be used like cash, whereas accounting money was given in a predetermined amount for predetermined purposes (according to the central plan). To put it in a different way, many kinds of accounting money were in existence serving different purposes (for example, one kind of money could be used to buy raw materials, another one to buy investment goods or services of labour). The principle was, that accounting money couldn't be transferred from one usage to another (if you received money to buy foreign machinery, you had to do it and not replace it with domestic raw materials or tools). Figure 2 presents circulation of the accounting money.

Figure 1. Cash flows in CPE

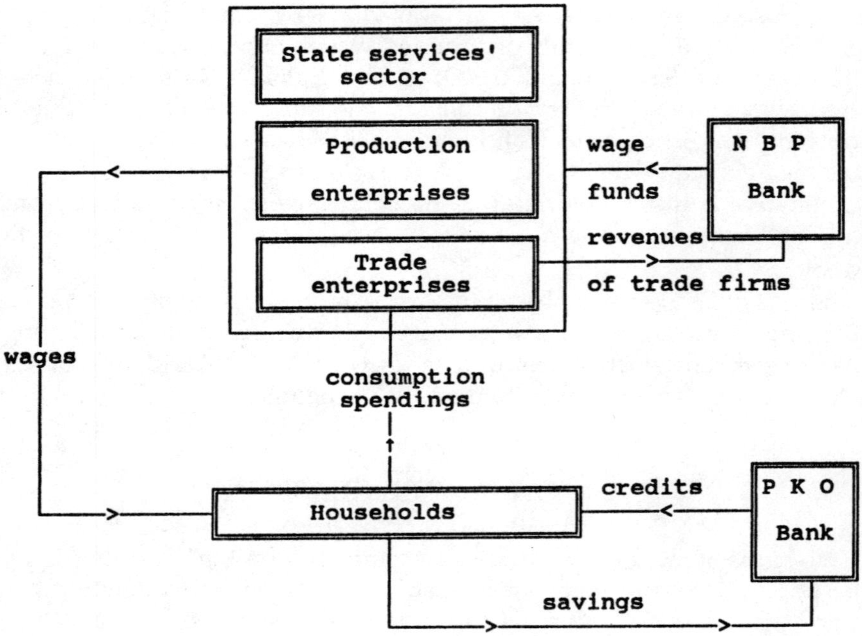

Figure 2. Flows of "accounting" money

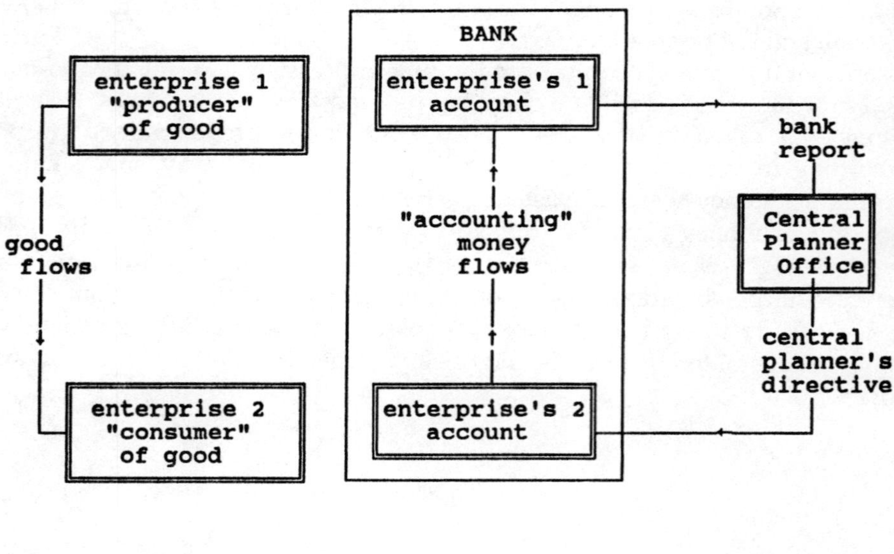

Let us now compare a system of commercial banks in the market economies (ME) with the NBP-type system present in a CPE:

- in MEs banks are intermediaries between savers and investors, in CPEs banks are controlling organs in the hands of a central planner,
- in MEs banks are profit maximizers, in CPEs banks are evaluated according to their efficiency in controlling enterprises,
- in MEs banks make economic decisions, i.e. are active players in the market game, in CPEs banks are controlling institution, whose officers act upon detailed instructions coming from outside the bank (central planner),
- in MEs the volume of credit depends on money supply, interest rate etc., in CPEs it depends on the central plan,
- in CPEs the banking structure is very limited (mainly transfers between banks and enterprises according to the financial plan), which results from the very primitive money market: with only cash and accounting money in use, without such instruments as bills of exchange, bonds, treasury bills and with the capital market non-existent.

BANKING REFORM IN THE 1980S

The main assumption of the economic reform of the 1980s was that it was possible to reconcile central planning with the market mechanism. Economic agents, mainly enterprises were to have full freedom to make economic decisions (the system of obligatory plans for enterprises was abolished). They were supposed to sell their products on the market and maximize profits. The principal difference between the proposed system and a market economy was that prices were not to be freely determined by forces of demand and supply but were to be set and controlled from the centre. Changes in the price structure brought about by changes of interest rates, tax rates and, of course, prices of goods were designed to make the enterprises behaviour conform to the plan. The role of banks in the new system was to be essentially the same, i.e. to control the fulfilment of the plan, but the methods used were to be more refined. Banks analyzed the financial flows between enterprises, but, as a result, orders could not be issued any more (enterprises were legally autonomous); instead, prices or interest rates could be changed.

A different kind of bank behaviour was required in system so reformed. Banks ceased to be passive institutions financing enterprises' activities according to the central plan. In the new situation they were supposed to pursue a policy towards enterprises (with a limited set of instruments) inducing them to act according to the central plan. The first step in this direction was made in 1982, when the system of "target" credits was abolished, a system within which firms were granted credits for purposes that were strictly determined by the bank and had to conform with the their production plan. Instead, a system emulating a market system was introduced. Credit begun to be granted conditional on a firms' application. An application had to include description of how it would be used and a forecast of profitability of the undertaken project (some sort of a feasibility study). Credit was granted on the basis of the estimated "credit ability" of the firm, i.e. whether it was able to service and repay the debt. Bank could reject the application if the credit didn't meet the priorities of the central plan and suspend the credit, if it was used for purposes different from these indicated in the credit application.

Three kinds of credit existed in the bank-enterprise relations:

- credit for permanent (normal) needs, or normal working capital credit,
- additional credit for current needs,
- investment credit.

The first kind, used to finance the bulk of current needs of the enterprise was (also) called converted credit. It was granted when a firm was classified as having the so-called permanent credit ability. It was repaid in annual instalments from the "enterprise fund" (essentially profit). A fixed interest rate of 9% was used. Additional credit for current needs was granted when the first kind of credit turned out to be insufficient. In firms with seasonal type of output (food-processing) it was used to finance purchases of inventories. It was repaid from the firm's current account. When difficulties appeared the enterprise could obtain a short-term "capital" loan.

Investment activity was financed in two ways: by "development" credit used to finance increasing volumes of inventories due to expanding level of output (repaid in 5 years from the enterprise fund) and by investment credits granted according to the assumptions of the central investment plan.

The structure of banks has not been changed significantly. The domination of NBP is illustrated by the fact that its share in the total volume of credits extended in the economy was 81% in 1970, 78% in 1975, 77% in 1980 and 76% both in 1985 and 1987. Its regional branches were administratively subordinate to the central office in Warsaw. Banks were obliged to a pursue credit policy conforming to the central plan. In this sense they were not profit maximizers. Banks were local monopolists, at least in their field of activity. (This iron rule was first broken in 1987, when PKO was allowed to expand its activity beyond its traditional domain financial services for the population and compete with NBP.) New banks were founded only to serve new functions, for example a Bank of Export Development (Bank Rozwoju Eksportu SA) was created specially for the purposes indicated in its name.

To sum up, in the proposed (partly reformed) system most enterprises were to behave in a way similar to their counterparts in the market economies (profit maximization). Banks were to stay as non-commercial units serving the central planner. The role of banks, compared to the previous, classical CPE grew, nevertheless. In the old system banks were only "informers" for the central authorities which managed the economy with direct commands. In the new system, the Central Bank monetary policy (among others) was to replace direct commands. To put it differently, banks, using the tools at their disposal, were to persuade enterprises to behave according to the central plan.

It turned out that such a system was unstable, in the sense that it quickly evolved towards a traditional command CPE. Banks couldn't also perform their above mentioned functions.

The instability of the economic system resulted from two factors. Most important, the main idea of the system was based on a faulty assumption that it was possible to pursue central planing by means of the market. The production structure that the central planner purports to impose on the economy is different from the production structure that would ensue from the operation of the market forces. When such an "artificial" production structure is being forced on the economy, shortages emerge or/and the resulting price structure makes some of the economic agents (producers, traders) necessarily unprofitable. Another important reason of the failure of this system was an utopian assumption that the central planning authorities are able to control prices successfully. Because of the number of prices in the economy they couldn't be controlled directly from the centre. Hence a system of "regulated" prices was introduced, which meant that prices had to be determined according to a fixed formula: costs plus certain mark-up. Under excessive global demand and omnipresence of monopolistic structure this policy stimulated inflation.

Economic chaos resulted. On the one hand shortages emerged that couldn't be eliminated by gradual price increases. On the other hand some of the enterprises turned out to be loss-making (although their output was necessary from the point of view of central planner's preferences) and had to be subsidized (e.g. mining). Attempts to master the economic process made the central authorities abandon the practice of managing the economy with the "parameters", i.e. prices and other indirect tools, and more frequently resume the infamous practices of "manual steering" with direct commands.

Banks were among the first "victims" of this tendency. Let us recall, their role was to encourage enterprises to act according to the central plan and, by means of credit policy, to enforce economic efficiency. In practice both functions could not be performed. An active, market oriented credit policy was impossible, because the level of interest rates, determined by the central authorities was lower than the rate of inflation. The rate on "converted" credit was 9% (from 1988 18%), and on the other credits granted to enterprises -12% (from 1988 30%), while the rate of inflation was significantly higher.

Years	1981	1982	1983	1984	1985	1986	1987	1988	1989
inflation rate	21	105	21	15	16	18	26	61	244

Source: Polish Statistical Yearbook

The price of credit was not able to limit the demand for credit. An excess demand, characteristic for a CPE appeared. This can be illustrated by the fact that bank frequently reduced the value of credit granted. According to a questionnaire in 1983 90 enterprises out of 107 reported such practices, in 1984 75 out of 85 firms. Demand for credit was stimulated additionally by the price formula used in the system of regulated prices. The cost of repayment and servicing the loan was included in the overall production cost and pushed on forward to the consumer. The volume of credit was limited by means of certain kinds of rationing. The main criterion that had to be met to obtain credit was the acceptance by the central authorities, or conformity to the central plan. As we see, it was a rather arbitrary solution. An exception was made for converted credit, that was granted in proportion to own means of enterprises used to finance inventories. The command management of credit policy had disastrous effects on the economic efficiency of enterprises. Remember, that banks were supposed, according to the assumptions of the reformed system, to monitor firms' efficiency through credit policy. Only firms having the so-called credit ability were eligible to obtain credit. In reality the decision to grant credit to enterprises had little to do with their economic conditions. Instead it was subject to bargaining between different institutions and branches of government, with banks playing only a minor role. A telling example of politicisation of the credit decisions is a paragraph 17 of NBP President's guidelines on credit policy making it obligatory for the banks to inform the local party committees on the financial standing of the enterprises, including information on the list of units losing bank credibility.

In the sphere of investment the centralised control of investment credit meant, for all intent and purposes, that there was a return to the old system of central investment rationing. Not surprisingly, the share of credits to finance central investment projects (usually continuation of projects started in the 1970s) in the total amount of investment credit was substantial. The table below contains data on the size of extended credits for central investment projects and for enterprises' own investment projects.

billion zl	Years						
Credit for:	1982	1983	1984	1985	1986	1987	1988
Central investments	488	535	698	881	1118	1352	1776
Firms' investments	925	1019	989	978	1102	1270	1687

Source: Data are taken from materials of Narodowy Bank Polski

An additional factor destroying the banking system was connected with state budget deficit financing. NBP was obliged to finance the growing budget deficit, losing control over the money supply and stimulating inflation even more. The next table contains information about the percentage of total credit extended in the economy used to finance the state budget deficit.

Years	1982	1983	1984	1985	1986	1987	1988
% of credit	4.8	6.2	7.8	8.3	7.0	7.9	8.7

Source: Polish Statistical Yearbook

The conclusion to draw from the experiences of the 1980s is following: the creation of a normal banking system should be connected with the introduction of fully functioning market economy.

However the fundamental changes in the institutional and functional framework of the Polish banks had only occurred in 1989, one year before the Balcerowicz stabilization programme was introduced. As the result of the new banking bill, and the bill on Narodowy Bank Polski becoming law[1] , nine state-owned commercial banks were formed on the basis of regional NBP branches. New legislation provided the basis for the radical reform of the financial sector in Poland. The reform was initiated with the aim of creating, a vigorous, market-oriented system which was capable of responding in a competitive fashion to the financing needs of a rapidly changing economy.

POLISH BANKING SYSTEM AND THE STANDARDS OF MARKET ECONOMY

The aim stated above suggests no essential inconsistency between the postulate to build a competitive, market oriented, system of financial institutions and the necessity to finance rapidly changing economy. It is implicitly assumed that the market oriented banking system is capable of financing and supporting the transition from centrally planned economy to market economy. More specifically, the founding of a market oriented banking system is consistent with introducing a stabilization program as well as the privatisation program.

It must be underlined that the desire to form a market oriented banking system is not the same as the willingness to design a "free banking" system. A market oriented banking sector means a system of banks which, apart from state-owned banks, consists of a relatively strong (not necessary dominant) segment of private banks which is competitive enough to introduce new

[1] The Act on Narodowy Bank Polski of January 31, 1989 (Dziennik Ustaw No.4/89 item 22) and the Banking Act of January 31, 1989 (Dziennik Ustaw No.4/89 item 21).

banking services, lower costs and engage to some extent in risky activities (such as restructuring of the economy). Market oriented banks operate also under the objective of profit maximization so as to force them to think in terms of hard budget constraints, careful evaluation of credit opportunities and so on. Therefore even before the process of privatization starts the banks might force state-owned firms to engage in restructuring and impose on them hard budget constraints. Such a banking system must be protected from degenerating to an unstable one and therefore some dose of regulation and supervision on the part of central bank is urgently needed. And D. Lacoue-Labarthe is right that "this could result in a fairly important and durable discrepancy between the financial system of EMU and CEE ".[2]

Before dealing with this problem let us analyze the distance of the Polish banking (or broadly speaking financial) system from the European standards. In order to answer this question it is useful to adopt some measure able to evaluate the maturity of the financial system in the well developed market economy. Raymond Goldsmith proposed the ratio of financial and tangible assets as a suitable indicator of financial maturity. He found this ratio to reach the level of unity in most developed countries by the end of the 19th century or the eve of the World War I.[3] Since that time he ratio in most of the developed countries has shown no upward trend. However considerable changes have occured during shorter periods, for instance sharp decreases were observed during inflation as well as significant changes taking place in the relative importance of the various types of financial instruments.

From this point of view the Polish financial system is still before World War I. Up to 1989 there were only a few financial institutions. Except banks they were only state-owned insurance companies dominated by Panstwowy Zaklad Ubezpieczen and Zaklad Ubezpieczen Spolecznych. Therefore it is not surprising that were few if any signs of financial intermediation in the centrally planned economy. In this respect, since 1989 the situation has been changed dramatically. At the end of 1990 there were more than 75 banks including 30 dominated by private capital; 20 new banks were formed in Warsaw, 7 in Poznan, 4 in Katowice, 4 in Gdansk, 3 in Bydgoszcz and 2 in Szczecin, Lodz, Wroclaw and Lublin.

The share of private capital in the total capital of banks reached the highest level in the following banks:

- Private Commercial Bank LEONARD" SA in Zielonka near Warsaw;
- Poznan Bank AG" SA in Poznan;
- Private Bank EL-GAZ" SA in Gdynia;

---

[2]See Chapter 6

[3]R.W. Goldsmith, Financial Structure and Development: A Study of Twenty Countries, 1688-1978, Chicago: University of Chicago Press, 1985.

- Commercial Bank PRIVAT" SA in Poznan;
- Land Bank SA in Warsaw;
- Bank PROSPER-BANK" SA in Cracow;
- First Commercial Bank SA in Lublin;
- Commercial Bank GECOBANK" SA in Warsaw.

In order to obtain the consent of the NBP president to the establishment of a bank, one has to fulfil a few simple conditions:

- to provide the bank with suitable equity (the minimum requirement is 20 billion zloty or 2 million U.S. dollars with regard to a Polish bank and $6m in the case of a bank with foreign capital involvement). This condition is very close to the European standard of 5 million ECU;
- to have premises suitable for the pursuit of banking operations;
- to entrust senior positions in the bank to people with suitable education and professional experience.

This liberal regulation has encouraged rapid growth of independent banks has been growing rapidly. However as compared to the average numbers of inhabitants per bank branch in the separate EEC countries the Polish banking system is still far below Western European standards.

Numbers of inhabitants per bank branch in the EEC countries in 1989

Belgium	-	2747
Denmark	-	2645
France	-	5080
Greece	-	5377
Spain	-	2330
Holland	-	3712
Ireland	-	5050
Luxembourg	-	1260
Germany	-	9382
Portugal	-	5937
Great Britain	-	3920
Italy	-	5832

Source: Financial Times, 23 May 1991

Actually in Poland only the state-owned PKO-bp has the nation-wide network of branches. This is the reason why PKO-bp occupies a dominant position with regard to private saving deposits.

The numbers from the table show also that the banking sector in Poland is completely dominated by the large state-owned banks. Many incentives directed to promote fast development of private banks have been effective in promoting emergence of a relatively large number of private banks. They are, however, very small as compared to state-owned banks. The comparison of balance sheets in private and state-owned banks makes it evident.

Saving deposits in Polish banking system
(in million zloty)

Bank	Amount of saving deposits		Structure (in%)	
	31.12.90	30.06.91	31.12.90	30.06.91
PKO-bp	23 554,9	32 689,4	58,1	48,3
Cooperative banks	7 024,8	10 310,4	17,3	15,2
Bank Gospodarki Zywnosciowej	799,6	3 382,6	2,0	5,0
Bank PeKao SA	1 334,5	2 400,5	3,3	3,6
Bank Handlowy in Warsaw SA	420,6	567,4	1,1	0,8
9 commercial banks formed on NBP basis	6 367,8	16 110,6	15,7	23,8
Other banks	1 027,7	2 218,5	12,5	3,3
Total	40 529,9	67 679,4	100,0	100,0

Source: Bank i Kredyt, 7-8/1991, p.35; 12/1991, p.25.

The above comparison makes clear that private and cooperative banks in Poland can play only very limited role in the process of restructuring and transmission from centrally planned economy to market economy. They are too weak to the absorb high risks related to investment decisions needed during restructuring economy. It seems hardly possible for private banks to develop on their own to compete effectively with state-owned large banks. Quite to the contrary, facing the deep recession, and unanticipated shocks resulting from transition, they face the great challenge of surviving in such unfavourable circumstances.

In general, the structure of ownership of the Polish banking system is significantly different from the standards appropriate to the market standard economy. The Polish banks, especially private ones, are very small as compared to their counterparts in the EC. The size of banks in Spain, which became the

Private and cooperative banks by total liabilities and own-funds capital
(in billion zloty)

Name of Bank	Total liabilities		Own Funds	
	1991 06.30.	1991 05.31.	1991 06.30.	1991 05.31
BIG SA in Warsaw	3940	3319	55	55
Bydgowski Bank Komunalny SA	1405	1309	53	49
Bydgowski BankBudownictwa SA	194	171	44	44
Bank Spoldzielczy in Zielona Gora	144	145	5	5
Lubuski Spoldzielczy Bank Gospodarczy in Slawa	100	-	10	-
Bank Ziemi Radomskiej SA	95	94	13	1

Source: Gazeta Bankowa, 33/1991, p2

State-owned banks by total liabilities and own funds-capital
(in billion zloty)

Name of Bank	Total liabilities		own funds
	1991 09.30.	1991 01.31.	1991 09.30.
PKO-bp	58557	58499	
Bank Handlowy	40898	119093	5362
BGZ	92679	91717	527
PeKaO SA	61804	56120	
Bank Zachodni	51153	27072	1100
Pomorski Bank Kredytowy	51034	34518	700
Powszechny Bank Kredytowy	37583	25641	1311
Bank Slaski	36589	22302	1938
Bank Gdanski	36228	22003	1971
Powszechny Bank Gospodarczy	31217	11315	685
Wielkopolski Bank Kredytowy	21178	14041	1399
Bank Przemyslowo -Handlowy	19865	28638	1366
Bank Depozytowo -Kredytowy	19700	12117	731
Bank Rozwoju Eksportu	7017	6978	864

Source: Gazeta Bankowa 14/1991,p.2

member of EC in 1986 and succeeded in adopting its banking system to the EC requirements, provides a good reference point. After the process of mergers within the banking sector the largest Spanish banks are as follows:

Spanish banks in 1991
(in billion peseta)

Name of bank	Assets	Capital stock	Deposits	Number of branch
Central Hispanamericano	8.800	490	5.769	4.612
Corporation Bancaria de Espana	8.300	485	3.345	1.303
Banco Bilbao Vicaya	7.700	530	5.372	2.765
La Caixa	5.200	266	3.612	2.296
Banco Sontonder	3.100	408	3.482	1.365
Caja Madrit	2.500	185	1.838	937
Banco Popular	1.400	150	1.829	1.657

Source: Financial Times, 28 May 1991

Therefore the only way to meet standards of the market economy is to privatize large state-owned banks and initiate the process of mergers among private banks. The necessity of privatisation seems indisputable in the light of long experience of centrally planned economy. There is, however, additional argument in favour of privatisation. The banking sector in Greece is dominated by two state-owned banks, which possess 70 per cent of savings deposits. And according to Greek economists, this ownership structure is responsible for the failure of adjustment of the banking sector in Greece to the unified European market.[4]

There are, however, at least two obstacles preventing immediate privatisation in Poland. In 1991, the share of bad loans appeared to be considerably above previous expectations. According to estimates[5] the share of bad loans in the best banks is above 20 per cent, while in the worst banks it exceeds 40 per cent. Furthermore, the collateral for many loans is not sufficient to cover debt in the short-run. Even worse - large portion of money seem to be completely lost. This is the case of large state-owned banks, which have financed large, inefficient state-owned firms. Many of these funds have lost creditworthiness.

---

4 Jan K.Solarz, Harmonizacja polskiego systemu bankowego ze wspolnota europejska, Materialy i studia, Zeszyt nr 20, p.9.

5 Slawomir Lipinski, Pierwszy zastrzyk", Gazeta Bankowa, 47/1991, p.6.

Number of firms which lost creditworthiness
(30th September 1991)

Industry

Total	PKO bp	BGZ	Bank Slas	PBK	BPH	Bank Slas	WBK	BDK	Bank Zach	PBG	PBK	BBK SA	BIG SA
943	134	179	69	107	87	102	33	75	51	55	44	3	4

Building

Total	PKO bp	BGZ	Bank Slas	PBK	BPH	Bank Slas	WBK	BDK	Bank Slas	PBG	PBK	BBK SA	BIG SA
156	27	54	7	6	8	23	1	4	3	10	8	-	-

Agriculture

Total	PKO bp	BGZ	Bank Slas	PBK	BPH	Bank Slas	WBK	BDK	Bank Slas	PBG	PBK	BBK SA	BIG SA
753	6	674	2	24	-	38	4	2	2	-	-	1	-

Service

Total	PKO bp	BGZ	Bank Slas	PBK	BPH	Bank Slas	WBK	BDK	Bank Slas	PBG	PBK	BBK SA	BIG SA
132	-	-	-	1	-	77	20	-	-	34	-	-	-

Trade

Total	PKO bp	BGZ	Bank Slas	PBK	BPH	Bank Slas	WBK	BDK	Bank Slas	PBG	PBK	BBK SA	BIG SA
401	137	15	14	20	19	117	8	18	16	19	16	2	-

Transportation

Total	PKO bp	BGZ	Bank Slas	PBK	BPH	Bank Slas	WBK	BDK	Bank Slas	PBG	PBK	BBK SA	BIG SA
27	18	4	2	-	-	-	2	1	-	-	-	-	-

Others

Total	PKO bp	BGZ	Bank Slas	PBK	BPH	Bank Slas	WBK	BDK	Bank Slas	PBG	PBK	BBK SA	BIG SA
133	12	54	4	22	1	24	6	5	3	-	-	-	-

Total

Total	PKO bp	BGZ	Bank Slas	PBK	BPH	Bank Slas	WBK	BDK	Bank Slas	PBG	PBK	BBK SA	BIG SA
2545	334	980	98	180	115	386	74	105	75	118	68	8	4

Source: Gazeta Bankowa, 48/1991, p.2

The problem of bad loans has to be resolved if privatisation of the banking sector is to proceed successfully. Otherwise it would be difficult to find people willing to invest in the banking sector in Poland. One way to deal with this problem is to provide state-owned banks with additional funds from the government budget. Unfortunately, growing government budget deficit prevents decision-makers adopting of such a solution. Therefore the resolution of the bad loans problem has to be supported by external financial assistance.

Additionally, the profitability of the banking sector has been decreasing rapidly. The drop in profitability has been caused mainly by bad investments, growing competitiness within the banking sector and a lower rate of inflation. During one year the rate of return dropped from 80.7 per cent to 23.3 per cent. In such an unfavourable situation it is hardly possible for the banking sector in Poland to meet the EC standards in the sense of creating large, effective private banks able to copy with restructuring at the same time as competition from abroad. The above numbers confirm the observation that private banks are much more market oriented compared to the state-owned banks.

It is generally assumed that the activity of private firms are dominated by the condition of profit maximization to a much greater extent than the activity of their state-owned counterparts. From that perspective the behaviour of privately-owned institutions, including banks, is more efficient and hence they among others diversify and evaluate risk better than state-owned banks.

However the government aim in the form of restructuring of the Polish economy might diverge seriously from the optimization rule which dominates the activity of private banks. The risk is inseparable from restructuring activity and might be significantly higher than the maximum risk tolerable by bank from their microeconomic perspective. Therefore private banks and especially small ones are unlikely to lend without state guarantees. To absorb high risk, related to the restructuring process, special venture capital institutions are urgently needed. Alternatively the process of restructuring might be supported to some extent from sources of external assistance and to some extent by large state-owned banks which very often can be strongly persuaded by central authorities to undertake such investment.

To create a strong, private banking sector still remains one of the most important task facing the Polish economy. This is the precondition of being close to the European standards. There is an urgent need to follow very closely the behaviour of the European banks which by merging and creating large units have been preparing to meet the challenge of the unified Europe.

Therefore the change in the ownership structure in favour of private banks has to be supported by formation of large private units able to compete on the European market while financing the restructuring of the Polish economy. Small private bank would create an obsolete structure unwilling and incapable of financing investment decisions connected with the task of restructuring the Polish economy.

ACTIVITY OF COMMERCIAL BANKS IN POLAND

In order to increase the level of financial intermediation the increase in the supply and scope of banking services is as important as increases in the number of commercial banks one of commercial banking's primary concerns is with the receipt, creation, and transfer of demand deposits for the private sector. It provides services using the most sophisticated technology. From this point of view commercial banks in Poland are hardly comparable with their Western counterparts. Therefore there is the urgent need to equip banks with modern computer systems and install telecommunication network. Otherwise it is impossible to provide people with a service quality which is to be comparable to the EC standards. Perhaps in that respect the discrepancy from the EC standards is the most spectacular.

FINANCIAL INTERMEDIATION

In the face of the underdevelopment of equity market and more generally, financial markets in Poland, banks must involve themselves more deeply in the financing high-risk task of restructuring economy. This task requires high-quality services to be supplied by the banking sector to economic agents and especially savers. Traditionally these services are supplied within a very complete process of financial intermediation. During this process outside privately owned wealth of the economy is converted into quite different forms in which ultimate owners hold their accumulated savings.[6] There are several reasons explaining why ultimate savers and lenders, creditors prefer the liabilities of financial intermediaries. Generally speaking the intermediation of financial institutions enables convenience of denomination; efficient allocation of risk maturity; transforming illiquid assets into liquid liabilities.

---

[6] James Tobin, "Financial Intermediaries", Cowles Foundation Discussion Papers No.817, New Haven, January 1987, p.10.

Revenues, costs and income of credit banks
(in billion zloty)

Item	1990 01.01-06.30	1991 01.01-06.3
1.Revenues	39778	48937
included:		
a) interests	136786	142379
share in %	92.5	86.6
b) commissions	1933	2106
share in %	14.9	14.3
2.Costs	22009	39682
included:		
a) interests	12284	25894
share in %	55.8	65.3
b)salaries and taxes	1803	11856
share in %	3.6	4.7
3.Gross income	17769	9255
4.Ratio (2a:1a)	33.4	61.1
5.Profitability (3 : 2)	80.7	23.3
6.Cost ratio (2 : 1)	55.3	81.1

Source: Gazeta Bankowa, 47/1991, p.6.

All of these activities are of crucial transformation for the process of restructuring economy and all of them seem to be indispensable for successful reform in Poland. Let us mention only about the importance of transformation of illiquid assets into liquid liabilities or risk diversification. It is hardly possible to exaggerate the importance of the firms facing payments problems or for people wanting to invest their money with relatively low risk of failure. Everything should be done to reach that standard as soon as possible. The positive feedback between financial intermediation and the progress in restructuring the economy clearly exists. Therefore it is not surprising that the deviation from this European standard could be the most harmful.

New approaches to financial intermediation concentrates on the question of the costs of information and monitoring.[7] For ultimate savers it is much more costly to obtain information about the issue of new bonds in the securities market as compared to cost of passing that task on to a financial intermediary. Owing to it is also more costly for individual to check and monitor the activity of ultimate borrowers with respects to service of their debt and efficient utilization of borrowed funds.

The existence of financial intermediaries is not only beneficial for savers but for ultimate lenders (firms) as well. For firms such cooperation with financial intermediaries can lead to lower cost of borrowing, and access to the credit market produces very important information about their creditworthiness and willingness to accept financial intermediaries' monitoring.

DEVELOPMENT OF FINANCIAL MARKETS IN POLAND

Three mutually related elements are needed for efficient intermediation: financial intermediaries, inside assets and money, financial and capital markets. None of these requirements is met in Poland today.

There are only two types of financial intermediary: commercial banks and insurance companies. The task of creating financial institutions for savers (mutual funds, mutual savings banks, investment funds, trust funds, private pensions funds), and for the consumer (sales finance companies, consumer finance companies, industrial banks) is still to be fulfilled.

A wide range of financial assets are the prerequisite of the existence of financial markets. Commercial banks operate mainly on the money markets. Therefore they are the agents able and willing to operate on this market. Unfortunately they face problems which effectively prevent them from doing their job. The lack of special institutions and sufficient telecommunication

[7]See Chapter 6

Turnover of the NBP bills (bln zl)

Time	Amount of sold bills		Average weighted discount rate p.a	Additional sale and purchases before maturity	Amount of outside bills
	in nominal prices	in purchase prices			
31.07 1990	500,0	490,1	23,76	0,0	490,1
31.08 1990	1645,2	1608,3	26,92	0,0	1608,3
30.09 1990	3400,0	3327,3	25,66	0,0	3327,3
31.10 1990	4612,9	4491,7	31,53	684,6	3807,1
30.11 1990	2898,5	2803,6	39,28	160,1	2643,5
31.12 1990	1083,6	1040,8	47,42	540,6	500,2
31.01 1991	2778.2	2667,9	47,66	84,0	2583,9
28.02 1991	2598,8	2503,9	43,84	4,3	2499,6
31.03 1991	2207,6	2107,8	47,80	(12,5)	2120,3
30.04 1991	4394,2	4103,1	44,42	118,4	3984,7
31.05 1991	2053,4	1831,3	42,78	(25,0)	1856,3
30.06 1991	1938,2	1736,2	41,24	0,0	1736,2
31.07 1991	1844,1	1676,4	31,27	2,1	1674,3
31.08 1991	2324,4	2121,9	29,64	(17,9)	2139,8
30.09 1991	2237,8	2050,2	28,14	(17,9)	2068,1
31.10 1991	2269,4	2103,0	24,07	(17,9)	2120,9

Source: Data are taken from materials of Narodowy Bank Polski

system is responsible for underdevelopment of inter bank loans market. The establishment of the Polish Brokers Company which hopes to play a role of a middleman on this market changed the situation a little at the end of 1991. Undoubtedly by lowering the amount of excess liquid reserves this institutional change positively effects the market.

The main task, however is to organize an open money market and the central bank has to play the major role in this process. In other words, the central bank has to organize a market the for the following money market instruments: treasury bills, bank acceptance, commercial paper, certificate of deposit, warehouse warrant, deposit receipt, trust receipt.

Government budget surpluses have made it difficult for treasury bills to appear as the instruments on the money market. In these circumstances in order to promote the development of money market and to absorb the excess of liquid reserves in PKO-bp, Bank Handlowy in Warsaw and Bank Gospodarki Zywnosciowej (BGZ) following the recommendation of the IMF, Narodowy Bank Polski decided to issue its own securities in the form of one-month bills of a face value of 10 billion, 1 billion and 100 million zloty. These bills, sold at a discount, are offered to domestic banks and economic agents ant at weekly auctions. The buyer may sell the NBP bills back to the issuer before they mature, at a price announced by NBP at weekly intervals.

Besides playing the role of a monetary policy instrument serving the purpose of absorbing excess reserve money of the banks NBP bills became the only instrument in the money market. In that way the Narodowy Bank Polski became a rival of commercial banks departing from its duties of a central bank.[8]

It was clear that efficient behaviour of money market depends on the issue of treasury bills. These instruments are especially important at the initial stage of money market. At the beginning they are bought by commercial banks and firms. The money market in Poland has already reached that stage of development. Later on treasury bills should become one of the assets in the households portfolio. As any other instrument in money market the treasury bills should be easily sold before their maturity. Unfortunately secondary market in Poland is still to be built. The most important information related to the treasury bills are mentioned below.

This basic information about the money market in Poland shows very clearly how much must be done in order to reach the European standards with respect to variety of instruments and amount of turnover. Moreover, there are only primary markets with respect to NBP bills and treasury bills. Therefore the Polish economy has to still wait for the money market to play a full role in economic restructuring.

[8]Pawel Wyczanski and Krzysztof Nowinski "Poland's Banking System: Current Developments and Prospects",Economic and Social Policy, Warsaw, March 1991, p.23

The scope of activity of commercial banks on the capital market is very negligible. Banking Law adopted in Poland allows commercial banks to purchase shares and bonds issued by other financial and non financial institutions up to 25% of their own capital. In Great Britain, for example there are no formal limits on commercial banks investments in equities but they are strongly urged by central bank not to undertake it. In Germany, while there are no formal limits, all portfolio investments are very closely monitored and supervised. In France banks are not allowed to buy more than 20 per cent shares of other institution. Additionally these investments should not exceed the amount of their own capital. As compared to these regulations the banking Law in Poland is not vastly different. Such regulation may enhance the security of the banking sector. On the other hand more liberal regulations could improve the financial situation of non banking institutions. The observed reluctance of banks to invest in shares of other firms should be mentioned. (One of exceptions is purchasing the shares of Prochnik by Bank Slaski). Generally speaking, the main explanation of this behaviour is low profitability of these investments and negligible turnover at the Warsaw stock exchange.

Though the engagement of commercial banks in capital market operations is below standards achieved in the European Community some activities are worth mentioning. First of all, the scale of involvement is relatively large in the case of issuing their own shares. Some banks issued bonds (Lodzki Bank Rozwoju) and bonds convertible for shares (Bank Ziemi Radomskiej).

Banks have engaged in much lower activity with respect to organizing the share issue of other economic agents. Up till now only Bank Inicjatyw Gospodarczych (BIG) SA provided that kind of service for Universal SA. This activity of commercial banks should increase considerably in the near future.

The distribution of shares appears to be the main field of interest for banks in Poland. Low risk and relatively high returns provide explanation for such behaviour. PKO-bp engaged as the first bank in the distribution of shares issued by Drewbud. Then PeKaO SA, Bank Gdanski, Bank Slaski and Wielkopolski Bank Kredytowy joined this activity during the public issue of the first privatized Polish firms.

A relatively popular activity is brokerage by banks themselves or their subsidiaries. The lack of highly qualified specialists and nonexistence of a secondary market with regard to many financial instruments prevents banks from extending this field of activity. Quite to the contrary, banks behave in the role of dealers on the financial markets. The unstable macroeconomic situation and, in some sense unpredictable positions of firms during the transition to a market economy induces caution behaviour.

Turnover of the treasury bills
(in billion zloty)

Time	Amount of sold bills		Average weighted discount rate p.a.	Additional sale and purchases before maturity	Amount of outside bills
	in nominal prices	in purchase prices			
10.05 1991	185,6	180,1	37,93	0,0	180,1
20.05 1991	885,6	853,7	38,22	0,0	853,7
31.05 1991	2053,6	1975,9	38,78	0,0	1975,9
10.06 1991	2400,0	2310,4	39,04	0,0	2310,4
30.06 1991	3245,2	3108,8	38,94	0,0	3108,8
10.07 1991	3695,5	3533,3	37,52	0,9	3532,4
20.07 1991	3940,9	3766,3	36,00	0,9	3765,4
31.07 1991	5259,0	4996,5	33,75	0,0	4996,5
31.08 1991	5774,7	5500,1	29,01	0,0	5500,1
30.09 1991	6822,2	6528,1	26,05	0,0	6528,1
31.10 1991	9210,1	8810,3	22,21	9,8	8800,5

Source: Data are taken from materials of Narodowy Bank Polski

CONCLUDING REMARKS

In this paper we have discussed some essential aspects of the commercial banks activity in Poland. Simultaneously the paper presents an attempt to compare this activity with the standards reached by the banking sector in the European Community. The interesting question is as follows: how approaching the EC standards might influence the ability and willingness to finance high-risk tasks during restructuring the economy. Commercial banks are the most important financial intermediaries and therefore we could reformulate our question as follows: how coming closer and closer to the EC standards of financial intermediation might influence the financing of the high-risk task of restructuring the economy or more broadly, how such complex intermediation might influence the process of restructuring itself.

There are at least three reasons explaining why the correlation between financial intermediation and restructuring of the economy is highly positive:

- financial intermediaries transfer risk from those who are risk averse to those who are willing to expose themselves to increased risk. Consequently financial intermediaries promote savings and investment;
- financial intermediaries change illiquid assets of economic agents into liquid liabilities. The positive influence exerted by such transformation is hardly controversial and it might have special importance nowadays in Poland;
- and more generally, financial intermediation unproved effectiveness of the allocation of scarce resources in the economy.

Could we find some arguments against the existence of positive correlation between convergence to European standards and financing of the restructuring in Poland. One question is disputable. The domain criteria of a market economy is to establish a strong privately-owned banking sector in the economy. It seems difficult for the Polish economy to duplicate such a sector in the near future. According to more realistic expectations the banking sector in Poland can be characterized by great number of private banks each with small amount of own funds. Such banks might evaluate the risk attached to financing the restructuring of the economy at a very high level. Consequently without strong support from the government they might not engage in restoring the Polish economy.

Therefore from the point of view of the ownership structure in the EC the structure of the Polish banking system should be mixed. The monetary authority should elaborate a plan to establish the banking system so as to compete on the European market and finance restructuring of the economy as well. Currently the banking sector is based mainly on state-owned large banks and they will preserve their important position in the near future. That structure has to be supplemented by strong, large private banks able to create a market environment in the banking sector. Such strong, large private units can emerge during the complex process of privatisation and merging among small private banks.

The paper presented above concerns the development of the Polish banking up to the last months of 1991. Since then banking sector has experienced considerable changes. Two of them seem to the most important. The first one is related to the rapid development of money and capital markets. This trend should to be continued. On the other hand the total profitability of banks established after 1989 decreased significantly to about minus 2 per cent in 1992. This fact provides bad prospects for creation strong private banking sector in Poland in the near future.

BIBLIOGRAPHY

The Act on Narodowy Bank Polski of January 31, 1989, Dziennik Ustaw No. 4/89 item 22.

The Banking Act of January 31, 1989, Dziennik Ustaw No. 4/89 item 21

Goldsmith R.W., 1985, Financial Structure and Development: A Study of Twenty Countries, 1688-1978, Chicago: Univ. of Chicago Press

Lipinski S., 1991, Pierwszy zastrzyk, Gazeta Bankowa No 47

Solarz J.K., 1990, Harmonizacja polskiego systemu bankowego ze wspolnota europejska, Materialy i studia, Zeszyt No 20.

Tobin J., 1987, Financial Intermediaries, Cowels Foundation Discussion Papers No 817

Wyczanski P., Nowinski K., 1991, Poland's Banking system: Current Developments and Prospects, Economic and Social Policy, Warszawa

SUBJECT INDEX